ENDORSEMENTS

At a time when many people are on a crazed quest to fundamentally change America and shape the world, no doubt inspired by unseen spiritual forces, skilled spiritual warriors are desperately needed. In his 1910 classic *Power Through Prayer*, E.M. Bounds said, "The Church is looking for better methods; God is looking for better men." Indeed, people are God's methods. Never has that been more clearly demonstrated than through Jon and Jolene Hamill. The assignments Holy Spirit has engaged them in have been both numerous and very strategic. Frankly, while reading this book, you may find yourself wondering, *Did these things really occur?* This actually happened. And now, not only do you get to enjoy the stories, but you can learn the lessons gleaned from their high-level assignments.

DUTCH SHEETS
Dutch Sheets Ministries, Leesville, SC

Jon and Jolene Hamill of Lamplighter Ministries believe that this new era is being defined by a great drama that will shape the course of the future of America, Israel, and the nations. This is not a "one act play" with only one main character. Through the pages, you'll discover that you are being offered a major role! Want to make history before the throne of God? Then read this inspirational and highly intriguing drama titled, *White House Watchmen*. You were born to stand in the gap and to seize this divine moment where every voice counts and every sacrifice matters.

JAMES W. GOLL
Founder of God Encounters Ministries and GOLL Ideation LLC /
Author, Consultant, Communications Coach, and Recording Artist

White House Watchmen takes you behind the scenes and beyond the veil to see the real "influencers" in Washington, DC, special ops prayer teams. Their mission? To battle an invisible enemy and wrestle in prayer to help bring about Heaven's foreign policy and restore America's covenant with God. Jon and Jolene weave one of the major policies on Heaven's heart— America's relationship with Israel—throughout the book. It's a policy that stands on His promise that *"whoever blesses Israel will be blessed."* This prophetic and inspirational work asks the penetrating question of us all: *"Watchman, what of the night?"* This book will help answer that question and equip you to define history during this generation's prayer watch *"for such a time as this."*

CHRIS MITCHELL
CBN News Middle East Bureau Chief, Jerusalem, Israel

The Lord Himself declared that a generation would arise who would repair the historic breaches of covenant and restore His ancient pathways. As Jacob discovered when He encountered the Lord in Genesis 28, restoration of covenant opens the gates and sets the path for the King of Glory to make entrance. Original intent is restored, and the blessing of the covenant is released upon both the people and the land. I personally do not know of anyone who embodies these truths more than Jon and Jolene Hamill. *White House Watchmen* is the latest testament to this, covering more than a decade of repairing the altars of our fathers and securing breakthrough for the nation. Be warned, this book is not a casual read. This is a call to action as within its pages are the seeds of revolution, and a call to arms for every Naboth who refuses to give up the inheritance of their forefathers.

CHRIS MITCHELL JR.
Founder, King's Gate International Church, Virginia Beach, VA

As proven watchmen in Washington, DC, Jon and Jolene Hamill have great insight into the godly and ungodly workings in and through our nation's capital that have influenced our country and the world. In *White House Watchmen*, they have developed a book of facts and strategies to help us see the history and God's future strategy to continue in advancing the Kingdom of God. This book is a great read and instruction for all of us as we are all called to be watchmen. Thank you so much, Jon and Jolene, for your wonderful and exciting insights. Thank you for blessing our nation!

DR. JOHN M. BENEFIEL
Heartland Apostolic Prayer Network—Presiding Apostle
Church on the Rock, Oklahoma City—Founder and Senior Pastor

White House Watchmen is a must read! Jon and Jolene's prophetic gifting to connect the spiritual dots within today's events will provide you with supernatural insight. You have wondered why things are happening and what God's intended purposes are, well wonder no more! Jon and Jolene take you on a journey step by step to see current events through Scripture and give us all much-needed hope for the future of our nation.

DAVID KUBAL
President and CEO, Intercessors for America, Purcellville, VA

"If the trumpet does not sound a clear call, who will get ready for battle?" (1 Cor. 14:8). I believe we are in one of the most strategic battle seasons in history, with the USA and the nations definitely in the "valley of decision." I thank the Lord for my good friends Jon and Jolene Hamill, and this book which sounds a clear trumpet call as to the true nature of this warfare. I have seen firsthand that Jon and Jolene do not pray their political opinion but wait on the Lord in worship and listening until they know what He is doing, resulting in story after story of great turnarounds. I have carefully read this book and can assure you that it will renew hope and faith in your heart to see the shifts you long for in your family, your city, your state, and your nation.

RICK & PATRICIA RIDINGS
Founders, Succat Hallel, a 24/7 House of Worship in Jerusalem
Authors, *Shifting Nations Through Houses of Prayer*

My friends Jon and Jolene Hamill have written a book that is very much in season and important for those who are called to governmental intercession. They speak with revelation and authority from their assignment to Washington, DC, and our government. This book will help to develop your understanding and right alignment with this call!

ANNE TATE
Prayer Director, Glory of Zion, Corinth, TX

My friends Jon and Jolene Hamill are two of the strongest and clearest voices in the global prayer movement. The Lord has fashioned them into two silver trumpets to awaken a watchman movement in this crucial hour of history. In Numbers 10, God commanded Moses to fashion two silver trumpets. They were used for various means as described in Numbers 10, but both were blown in unison with a long blast to summon the Lord's covenant people to war. *White House Watchmen* releases that sound, a strong prophetic unction, that will awaken the watchman anointing in you and the covenant people of God. I know you will be greatly inspired by their testimonies of turnaround demonstrated through faithful intercession as well as challenged to believe for great exploits in your relationship with the Lord.

ED WATTS
Apostolic Overseer, Gateway Hope Center, Flint, MI

This book is for those who wish to learn to move in a high level of spiritual engagement—and win. Through constant practice, they have learned to discern the nuances of the spiritual battles at hand and, more importantly, to perceive how God is moving in ways that transcend the everyday clatter of events and headlines. Jon and Jolene reveal how being led by God enables you to receive the strategies needed to expose and resist the constant encroachment of ungodly agendas in places of power, and to declare God's heart and light into those realms. The book is packed with scriptural insights on what it means to be a "watchman" over your sphere. Jon and Jolene's experience on the wall, holding the ground, gives them a unique authority to teach and mentor the next generation of watchers.

MARTIN FRANKENA
President, Rushing Streams Ministries, Hagerstown, MD

When Moses spoke to a generation at a crossroads, about to come into the Promised Land, he encouraged them to *"remember the Lord your God, and all He has done!"* The pages of *White House Watchmen* resound with a similar message from a couple who have walked out a watchman calling for a nation at a most critical crossroads. They share insights from personal encounters in moments of national and even international turnarounds that not only mark our present, but define our future. As I have had the privilege to walk with Jon and Jolene over the years, I have come to deeply honor and respect the "Moses" voice of freedom that they are in our day. You will be equipped to take your place as a watchman on the wall to see deliverance come to your sphere and nation.

JAMIE FITT
Director, Philadelphia Tabernacle of David

Some authors seem to be graced beyond measure in their ability to place elements together and help us all to connect the dots. Jon Hamill is one of those gifted ones. He and Jolene are tenacious warriors. I believe that, as you read this wonderful piece of prophetic art, you will also be mantled with understanding and insight that will fan the warrior's flame deep within your own heart.

If you are reading this book, it is because Father is giving you an invitation to move ahead, to step into the depths of the promptings and unctions that have been living as whispering songs in your own heart. But fair warning—you must be prepared for a journey far beyond what you may intend!

For instance, I never intended to become a long-term White House watchman when, in 2016, I joined countless intercessors in praying for our president during his first hundred days in office. On day one hundred, Father asked me a question: "What are you going to do now?" As I have the great honor of endorsing this historic book, I am also in the 1,192nd consecutive day of penning a prayer for our president and the leaders of our nation. You just never know where following a heavenly unction will lead you.

Wherever Father's promptings lead you, you will find the adventure to be exciting beyond imagination, at least I always have. Thank you, Jon and Jolene Hamill, for your labor in giving watchmen this wonderful insightful tool!

JAMES NESBIT
Prophetic Artist, Prepare the Way Ministries, Florence, AL

As governmental watchmen over America, Jon and Jolene Hamill have seen incredible supernatural breakthroughs and turnarounds for our nation. As strategic apostolic leaders, they are ushering in God's end-time shift for America. Readers will be instructed and activated to make a difference as modern-day Daniels, Josephs, and Esthers. *White House Watchmen* is an essential read for anyone involved in governmental intercession.

APOSTLE MARIO BRAMNICK
Latino Coalition for Israel, President

I'm a firm believer in the truth that history belongs to the intercessor. In *White House Watchmen*, Jon and Jolene Hamill will take you on a spiritual and historic journey. They lay out clearly the calling of a watchman on the wall as one who contends for spheres of influence, governments, cities and nations. As you read, the watchman anointing will be awakened in you and you will be fully equipped and inspired to become the history maker God has called you to be. We are in a now time of the greatest awakening of Christianity in the history of the world. And it is the watchman who will "shamar" to usher in awakening, transformation, aligning of governments and nations. Thank you, Jon and Jolene, for this now word of the Lord for our nation and releasing the clarion call to arms to the prophetic watchmen and empowering us to cross over to possess the Promised Land.

REBECCA GREENWOOD
Christian Harvest International
Strategic Prayer Apostolic Network
Author of *Glory Warfare, Authority to Tread,
Your Kingdom Come, Defeating Strongholds of the Mind*

WHITE HOUSE
HOUSE
WATCHMEN

NEW ERA PRAYER STRATEGIES TO
SHAPE THE FUTURE OF OUR NATION

JON & JOLENE HAMILL

ACKNOWLEDGMENTS

The pages ahead convey perhaps the most important message Jolene and I have ever attempted to convey. First, thank you Jesus for inspiring the content and walking us through the process—may Your heart and countenance shine through every page. And may all who read be infused with hope for the future that can only come from You.

In addition to Heaven's prevailing influence, this book would have been impossible without the prayer, clarity and competence of these incredible teams.

First, thank you Lamplighter family for responding with such strength and consistency in prayer. And especially for taking this journey together.

Second, thank you Tom and Lynnie and everyone in our ever-dynamic home group. Your prophetic coaching preserved God's best intentions for this book!

Third, thank you Gideon Group for your fierce resolve to see our nation turned back to God—and for paying the price.

Finally, Jolene and I extend our highest gratitude to Larry Sparks and the Destiny Image publishing team. From the conception of White House Watchmen to its publication and promotion you have brought the project to a level of excellence I had only dreamed of achieving. Thank you, Tina Pugh, for your inspiring guidance and awesome promotional work. Thank you to the designers who captured the essence of this message through powerful graphics and pagination. Having sputtered through this process myself, your contribution is very much appreciated. Thank you, John Martin and Edie Mourey, for your diligence in editing, your creativity, and especially your persistence on encouraging documentation for sources cited. The readers will gain so much more thanks to your efforts.

DESTINY IMAGE® PUBLISHERS, INC.

P.O. Box 310, Shippensburg, PA 17257-0310
Promoting Inspired Lives.

This book and all other Destiny Image and Destiny Image Fiction books are available at Christian bookstores and distributors worldwide.

Cover design by Eileen Rockwell

For more information on foreign distributors, call 717-532-3040.
Reach us on the Internet: www.destinyimage.com.

ISBN 13 TP: 978-0-7684-5706-3
ISBN 13 eBook: 978-0-7684-5707-0
ISBN 13 HC: 978-0-7684-5709-4
ISBN 13 LP: 978-0-7684-5708-7

For Worldwide Distribution, Printed in the U.S.A.
2 3 4 5 6 7 8 / 24 23 22 21 20

CONTENTS

FOREWORD

by Cindy Jacobs

YOU are about to read a book filled with supernatural adventures and spiritual intelligence. *White House Watchmen* is an extraordinary manual for both beginning pray-ers and experienced intercessors.

Many Christians know that we are commanded to pray for those in authority over us so *"that we may lead a quiet and peaceful life"* (1 Tim. 2:2 ESV). However, not many really know how to pray in an informed way for government leaders. Jon and Jolene Hamill don't just read the Bible in this regard; they do the stuff! They fast, and they pray! They live their lives interceding for the White House, as well as Israel, Italy, and many other nations; so, don't think that this book is not for you, wherever you may live.

The Bible is clear that humankind was called to *"guard"* the garden (Gen. 2:15 ISV). In fact, when you read Genesis, you see there was a snake in Adam and Eve's home territory. Just as there was an enemy in the garden of Eden, there are enemies in our nations—enemies of corruption, poverty, racism, hatred, murder, etc. When God created our forebearers and placed them in the garden of Eden, He meant this garden to be a colony of Heaven for His children, a prototype for spheres and nations. It was created as perfect in the beginning.

Though most of our countries are not perfect today, we can still see Heaven released in them! We are empowered to disciple our nations to see God's Kingdom manifested in the earth. Of course, we know that there is a present kingdom and a future Kingdom. Our job is to steward the days we live in and the land we inhabit.

The Hamills instruct us how to take care of and "tend" our gardens in prayer. They relate and protect us by showing possible entry points where satan could try and take us down while we are securing our perimeters.

One of the revelations that God has given many prayer leaders today is we have the power to make decrees over our governments (see Ps. 2:7–8). We are living in days of intense spiritual warfare, and we need to learn to live like Daniel. He was a man of great wisdom and tact. Each of us should seek God on how to be a person of an excellent spirit. Jon and Jolene, in this hour, have the wisdom of a "Daniel and Daniela"!

Their writing is personable. It is both full of admonitions and comfort. This is not a dry and sterile book of "how-tos" but a fascinating read.

The Hamills have held many meetings of intercession from their own home that overlooks the historic and iconic sites of Washington DC. I have stayed with them in their prophets' quarter and gazed out at an inky, black night, lit by the White House, the Lincoln Memorial, and the US Capitol Building.

In fact, the first time that I stayed with them and walked out on their enclosed veranda, the first words out of my mouth were, "Oh, wow!" (The story of how God did a miracle for them to obtain such a treasured piece of real estate in Washington DC is another miraculous testimony, but that is theirs to tell, perhaps, another time.)

I hope that I have whetted your appetite to delve into this remarkable book! Yours truly read it and loved it, and I have read quite a few books on the subject of intercessory prayer.

Standing on guard for the nations!

CINDY JACOBS
President, Generals International
First night of Passover 2020

"WATCHMAN, WHAT OF THE NIGHT?"

THIS book was written between Thanksgiving 2019 and Passover, with the edited manuscript released over Pentecost 2020. On Pentecost Sunday, we hosted a nationwide prayer call, seeking the fire of God's Spirit in revival. To our astonishment, we were met instead with a fire of violence as smoke began to billow from the White House complex. It was visible from our home. For the second night in a row, a peaceful protest against police brutality and racial injustice had devolved into a riot.

I mention this because the substance of our introduction was written on Thanksgiving evening 2019 with the aim of finishing the manuscript within a month. At the time, the greatest anticipated crisis was a potentially divisive election. Thank God for prophetic friends who suggested Jolene and I slow down as a "centerpiece" of the book had not yet even been perceived. Then came the coronavirus crisis, followed by the nationwide upheaval. Our nation and world forever changed.

America is called by God to reflect Heaven's substance—with every race and ethnicity experiencing the liberty, justice, innovation, and prosperity that come when a nation aligns covenantally with Him (see

Rev. 5). For this reason, the core message of *White House Watchmen* has already proven prophetically relevant for this hour. Maybe it's even more emphatic. *A new movement is now breaking forth as God raises up watchmen on the wall to catalyze His restoration.* We have a limited window to rebuild a nation in covenant with God, perpetuating His freedom to successive generations. And you are invited to become part of His move.

Thanksgiving 2019

As ministry leaders in Washington DC, Jolene and I have been privileged to pray into this freedom movement, including the most comprehensive governmental turnaround in recent American history.[1] The turnaround has included an economic resurgence; the restraint of the scourge of abortion; and the restoration of alignment with Israel, with the historically reluctant State Department even leading the way.

President Trump has proven to be an amazing catalyst of God's intended turnaround. Ever since he stepped into office—at an energetic seventy years of age—he has brought the fight back into the White House and into the conservative movement.

There have been missteps and mistakes for sure, sometimes with dire consequences. But as you will see, President Trump—in all of his complexity—has been uniquely commissioned by God to lead America at this time. And the results have been astounding!

Perhaps more than any time in recent American history, prayer has helped to fuel this governmental turnaround. Forerunning prayer. Prophetic prayer. Governmental prayer. Watchman prayer that has produced documented results that many times were spoken into existence beforehand through God's mysterious, sometimes unsettling, gift of prophecy.

———————————

Our home is a watchman's perch which overlooks all of Washington DC. Prayer from this perch is usually a favorite pursuit for Jolene and me. The sweeping views never cease to inspire. The Capitol. The Supreme

Court. The Potomac. The Lincoln Memorial, my favorite monument. And even the White House.

Yet, this Thanksgiving evening, with familiar landmarks now shimmering against the shadows, inspired prayer is proving elusive. A tangible oppression seems to defy the twilight of holiday sentiments. My spirit is on alert. *"Watchman, what of the night?"*

The tradition of Thanksgiving was handed to us through unimaginable sacrifice as the Pilgrims moved through a dark night of their journey. November 2020 marks the four-hundredth anniversary of their arrival. My forefather Richard Warren was among the unlikely band of forerunners who launched this freedom movement we now call *America*. From the onset of their journey to the first Thanksgiving, the Pilgrims encountered virtually every setback known to humankind.

It was a miracle they even lived.

They were not actually known as Pilgrims but Separatists. Having read the Bible for themselves, they saw with clarity how the Church of England's unchecked institutional corruption, connected to the highest thrones of power, was bringing subjugation to multitudes that Jesus had invested His life to free. *"Come out from among them and be separate"* was the direction they received (2 Cor. 6:17 NKJV).

While in exile in Leiden, Holland, the Separatist community received a fresh vision from the Lord. Similar to the Jews under Pharaoh, the Pilgrims sensed the Spirit of God directing them to flee dictatorial governances, cross the waters, and establish a beachhead for freedom in the "Promised Land" of the New World. On July 22, 1620, propelled by prayer nourished with many tears, the first group departed.

But what was supposed to be a brief stopover in England turned into a deadly delay. Similar to many Washington DC offices today, one of their ships suffered continual leaks. Winter was fast approaching. It was decided the *Mayflower* should venture out alone.

The *Mayflower* was a cargo ship, not a passenger vessel. Only eighty feet long, its quarters were brutally cramped for the 102 passengers and their pared-down provisions. North Atlantic storms pummeled them, slowing their journey greatly. Then as they approached the East Coast, a vicious nor'easter arrested the tiny ship some 220 miles north of their original destination. The storm-tossed Pilgrims sought shelter on the tip of Cape Cod.

Against all odds, the Pilgrims kept true to their mission. Shortly after arriving, in the hull of the *Mayflower* on November 11, 1620, they signed a sacred compact concurrent with their calling—and forged a nation in covenant with God.

———————————

Historians note that the establishment of a "civil body politic" in the Compact forged the beginnings of democratic governance in the Western Hemisphere. Perhaps it was divinely inspired because, by their own words recorded in the document, the Mayflower Compact was written "in the presence of God and one another." The compact also conveys how the Pilgrims established a colony "for the glory of God and the advancement of the Christian faith," in which they were free to finally worship according to their convictions.[2]

During the ensuing winter, the Pilgrims lost almost half of their community to malnutrition and disease. Their first Thanksgiving feast became a bittersweet expression of worship to God. Gaining inspiration from our Jewish forefathers, they patterned their celebration after the Feast of Tabernacles, where the harvest for the year is celebrated before the Lord and the sojourn from bondage to the Promised Land is rehearsed.

A highlight of this covenant meal was honoring the native Wampanaog tribe, whose intervention made their survival possible. The tribe had also suffered devastating loss. In the years prior, a regional disease borne by rats had killed countless members. Wampanoags and Pilgrims found themselves in an unlikely partnership, grieving while rebuilding their respective communities together. A covenant of aid and protection was made between them.

And the Gospel was shared. Wampanoag, by the way, means "people of the first light."[3] Not coincidentally, they were the first tribe to receive the light of Jesus Christ. A move of God swept through the region, and villages of "praying Indians" soon rose up with Native leaders pastoring.[4] From the beginning, it was God's desire for Native and Pilgrim to walk together, forging a new nation in covenant with God. Successive generations really messed things up. But the root remains holy.

Note that the Pilgrims were not merely missionaries planting a church. Instead, they were *planting a government*—a government in covenant with God.

And a freedom nation was born.

Today America, and perhaps the world, finds itself in a similar position to the Wampanoags and the Pilgrims. Our task together is to rebuild a freedom nation—a nation under God.

White House Watchmen

Through some of the most improbable circumstances, Jolene and I have become torchbearers in Washington DC of the covenantal legacy the Pilgrims forged. Directing a ministry called *Lamplighter*, we have a driving focus to see government align with God's covenant.

Prophetically, I've known for many years that what we decide in 2020 impacts our nation in a way that few other times in history ever have. Like the Pilgrims' original voyage, our country is at a threshold from which there is no return. Will America choose to defy God openly? Will a vicious storm drive us off course or even reverse the vulnerable progress we've made? Or will we honor the covenantal foundations entrusted to us and complete the turnaround that secures our inheritance for decades?

That is what is truly at stake. I am praying large naive prayers that we, like the Pilgrims, will overcome our challenges to secure God's intended destiny.

In the pages ahead, you're going to be equipped with principles to grow as a White House watchman. You will discover dramatic, firsthand accounts of God's turnaround in action, including prayer times in the White House and other halls of government, in historic locations considered foundational to American freedom, and in revival movements across the nation. The securing of God's miraculous turnaround even ushered us to Jerusalem and throughout the land of Israel—including the very precipice of Armageddon.

Some of the most exhilarating moments of watchman prayer occur behind the scenes rather than in the limelight. They also seem to bear greater fruit. The reasons are simple. First, in a town which eternally seeks an audience with the president, we have found that standing before the eternal King unleashes His influence into these spheres far beyond our own capacities. Jesus is much more effective in persuasion than we are. The fact that He sometimes uses you and me as voices of His persuasion still rocks my world.

Second, in a town which views relationships as commodities to be leveraged, we have simply befriended people without expectation or demand. Further, our commitment to them is long term through both challenges and victories. Connecting with people in this way has gained unimaginable access and influence even though it has not been our goal or strategy. As Christians, we just walk in true relationship with those around us.

Third, the true nature of the battle over DC is spiritual. The enemy has made tremendous inroads. Events and meetings engineered to gain influence certainly have their place. It's how DC rolls. But photo ops generally won't dislodge principalities while special ops will—at least special ops prayer.

I'm so grateful for team players willing to join in relative anonymity on prayer assignments to demolish spiritual strongholds, rescue people held hostage by the enemy, and resurface before anyone even knows they were there. It's made all the difference.

What Is a Watchman?

Before we go any farther, this is a good question to answer. When thinking of watchmen, stereotypes abound, like the restless intercessor who continually challenges the pastor to pray more or the prophetic vision- ary whose sole capacity for conversation centers around their visions and dreams. Others picture a bearded shofar blower, draped by a Jewish prayer shawl, sounding an alarm on God's holy mountain.

Praying. Prophesying. Sounding the alarm. Aligning with our Jewish roots, the covenant roots of our faith. All are valid expressions of a watch- man's call. But you could equally consider Jesus at Gethsemane, virtually begging His overwhelmed disciples to press through their stupor and keep watch with Him. You could also see Joshua acting as a watchman when he served as a spy, standing up to his ten peers because he discerned God's timing to take the Promised Land when everyone else was afraid. Then there's Isaiah who penned the perennial words of his sixty-second chapter, introducing watchman prayer as the most essential catalyst of Zion's restoration. And we must not forget Daniel.

From his youth, Daniel was observed by kings as possessing compe- tence, maturity, intellect, and integrity far superior to his peers. Daniel was devoted to God, loyal to each king he served, and prone to prophetic experiences. The word of the Lord was with him, never tainted by either accusations or personal vendettas. He sounded the alarm when necessary. But he always tackled challenges first by covering them in prayer.

The fact that Daniel's counsel was welcomed through many regimes is particularly remarkable when you consider an accepted practice was to behead the advisors of former kings.

Daniel is a great prototype for the watchman prophet today. That said, experiencing God, loving Him, and serving Him were the overarching passions which fueled his life from youth to old age. One all-encompass- ing assignment remained constant as well. That was intercession for the restoration of God's covenant people from subjugation in Babylon back to their covenant land.

Most watchmen receive prayer assignments from the throne of God. They then are tasked with carrying them through until God mani- fests His promised answer. This is such a key facet of the watchman's call. Great responsibility is involved in these commitments. Sometimes, even the destiny of a nation hangs on them. But the rewards are beyond description.

With this in consideration, let's answer the question. What is a watchman?

From our perspective, a watchman is a person in covenant with the Lord at His direction, a person who unleashes God's Kingdom redemption within an assigned sphere of authority—first through prayer. From Isaiah 62:

> *For Zion's sake I will not keep silent, and for Jerusalem's sake I will not keep quiet, until her righteousness goes forth like brightness, and her salvation like a torch that is burning…. On your walls, O Jerusalem, I have appointed watchmen; all day and all night they will never keep silent. You who remind the Lord, take no rest for yourselves; and give Him no rest until He establishes and makes Jerusalem a praise in the earth* (vv. 1, 6–7).

Dividing the Eagle

A week before Thanksgiving, Jolene and I were treated to a special lunch at the White House galley. A friend had experienced a major breakthrough, and she wanted to convey her gratitude for our small role in intercession.

The visit marked our fourth time in the West Wing but our first time for a meal. Decorum was elegant and appropriate, with the White House seal—an eagle with wings outstretched, holding arrows and olive branches—displayed on the walls, plates, flags and saltshakers. It was even engraved in the butter. White House butter—what's the protocol? Should we even touch the seal? Which wing should we cut off first—the left or the right?

And is it proper to divide the presidency in order to simply butter your own bread?

Some in Washington DC obviously think so because, as we dined at the White House, members of the House of Representatives were just beginning hearings to impeach President Trump. Somehow, we happened to be on-site—publicly enjoying lunch, privately decreeing God's covering over the principals and all that the seal represents.

That said, especially as *White House Watchmen* launches in the election year 2020, a few disclaimers are appropriate. We compel you to vote for candidates aligning with biblical values. But this book is not a voting guide. Nor are we trying to persuade you to swear allegiance to a political party. No king but Jesus!

Further, our role as White House watchmen should by no means imply a relational connection with the president or an ability to grant you access to either political leaders or faith advisors now inhabiting the power corridors of Washington DC. We're just not that well connected. And, most importantly, your success is not dependent on connecting with the Oval Office but accessing God's throne with a heart of integrity and then simply following through in obedience to what He shows.

Put those together, and your prayers will eventually define history. If you can embrace this calling, then the pages ahead will equip you to be successful.

It's vital to emphasize the very same biblical principles that have shifted the White House can also be applied to shift your house significantly. To be honest, securing your house, your business, or your sphere of authority is as important as the White House for the legacy of freedom to continue.

A Midnight Cry

Three years ago, facing the same window to our world, Holy Spirit quickened to me that by 2020 our nation would enter a midnight hour of history. In a moment, I knew we would face down perils similar to those which the Bible attributes to the final days of an era known as the end times. Both the challenges and the victories in our era would even become a prototype for their watch in history.

Aspects of our future became very clear. From this prophetic experience came our book *The Midnight Cry*. Much of what was prophesied within its pages is already in play today. A midnight crisis. A midnight watch. A midnight cry. The good news is, in the midst of our midnight crisis, the Lord is offering our nation a turnaround that brings a long-term course correction securing His best intentions for our land.

During the American Revolution, a watchman named Paul Revere saw two burning lamps in the upper room of the Old North Church. This pre-arranged signal conveyed it was time to alert the Continental Army for the fight of their lives. Revere rode through the midnight hour to awaken them. Their victory in this existential fight for freedom birthed our nation and redefined our world.

We are engaged in a hauntingly similar battle for freedom in this hour. It cannot be emphasized enough that completing the turnaround is predicated on you and me heeding the awakening alarm God is now sounding.

A Freedom Movement

Freedom in Jesus is the fire that propelled both Pilgrims and Revolutionaries to give their lives for a movement called *America*. Immigrants fled brutal dictatorships, empowered in the unseen realms by an antichrist spirit which had claimed their lives, their property, their privacy, and even their offspring. They sought, in turn, to establish a nation forged in freedom, founded by covenant with God, as a beachhead against antichrist dictatorships.

This priceless gift is at the core of America's celebration each Thanksgiving. It is at the core of our national identity. And yet even the covenant they made remains under relentless assault. Why?

As a theme in this book explores, maybe it is because in both the spiritual and natural realms the right to rule is ultimately determined by covenant and covenants establish thrones of governance.

Note that, in each successive generation, God faithfully posted watchmen on the wall to bear witness to His covenant. From the Pilgrims came the Patriots. Then the awakeners. The pioneers. The abolitionists. The suffragists. The greatest generation. William Bradford and William Penn. Jonathan Edwards and Charles Finney. Paul Revere and George Washington. Abraham Lincoln, Harriet Tubman, William Seymour, and Martin Luther King, Jr. General George Patton, Ronald Reagan, and

Reverend Billy Graham. The humble Rosa Parks, known as the mother of the civil rights movement. And millions of others known but to God, whose hearts and legacies were also fueled by sacred fire from another realm. They faced down seemingly insurmountable challenges to preserve and perpetuate freedom, having only limited vision of the consequences and limited windows of opportunity to act.

It is no different in our hour. Will you keep the flame? Or will the Body of Christ slumber while the rest of the nation succumbs to deceptive agendas weaponized to destroy the very cornerstone of our constitutional freedom?

"Watchman, what of the night?" It's a midnight hour. Really, no viable solutions are available apart from the intervention of God. Completing the turnaround entrusted to us remains the great invitation of our time.

So, light your lamps. Sharpen your voice. Let the watchmen of this nation now arise!

Jon & Jolene Hamill
Washington DC

2015—Vision of a White House Turnaround

I felt the Lord wanted us to focus our eyes of faith way beyond 2016—actually to 2020—because this year God is opening a limited window for national turnaround, in which He desires to lay new tracks for our future.

It's not about politics. It's about a move of the Spirit that will impact the thrones of this land.

What does this turnaround look like?

Nov. 11, 2015. Holy Spirit spoke very simply, "Look at the 1970s." A panoramic vision unfolded of Richard Nixon resigning. Soldiers coming home from Vietnam. The Cold War in full swing, and we were losing. The economy spiraling downward. OPEC sanctions bringing gas lines across the nation. Respect for America globally at an all-time low.

Then came Iran. Holding fifty Americans hostage for 444 days.

Then a turnaround window opened! When Ronald Reagan came on the scene, everything changed. Honor was restored to the presidential office. The hostage crisis ended on Inauguration Day. Our economy began to rebound. Hope, faith, and a renewed patriotism began to overtake our shame. And finally, communism toppled with the Berlin Wall.

For seven years, the downward spiral continued. But in year eight, a turnaround window opened that affected every sphere. And, friends, that's exactly what the Lord is offering our nation today.

JON & JOLENE
Glory Train—Heaven at Your Gates!
Prophetic Word for 2016[5]

BLOOD MOON AT MIDNIGHT

CHAPTER 1

THE CONFLICT OF CROWNS

*For thus has the Lord said to me: "Go, set a
watchman, let him declare what he sees."*
—Isaiah 21:6 NKJV

TWO crowning movements made their global appearance on New Year's Eve 2019, both with the intent on conquering our world. The World Health Organization (WHO) received its first report of a previously undocumented coronavirus after "urgent notice on the treatment of pneumonia of unknown cause" was issued at the Wuhan Municipal Health Center.[6]

Corona, of course, means "crown." The word *coronation* derives from it.

Meanwhile, half a world away, a prophetic vision came on New Year's Eve while we were hosting our Revolution conference at the Trump International Hotel. A friend received a "vision of a crown descending from Heaven over the National Mall." We'll explore this more in a moment. But a real-time interpretation came that God was crowning and commissioning a movement of spiritual awakening and watchman prayer. Our government, nation, and world would be impacted.

Throughout the span of the coronavirus pandemic, Americans have been turning to God for support. Praying Psalm 91 and receiving communion have now become national trends. Sunday sojourners are becoming seekers in the secret place. Warriors in the Spirit are sharpening their swords. Our own weekly calls doubled in attendance, and Zoom calls have flooded the earth. Even many who never breathed a prayer before are reaching out to God because they want to receive the protection only He can give.

In short, America has awakened in prayer! And we have finally united together to fight an existential threat. President Trump called it a war against an "invisible enemy."[7] I believe this description is more apt than he knows. Within the context of these words, both the destiny of our nation and the lives of our loved ones are at stake.

How do you win the "conflict of crowns" against an invisible adversary? That's a great question. Regarding the pandemic, social distancing and washing your hands both provide vital protection.

But viruses are not the only invisible enemy we are facing—not by a long shot. The greatest devourers of humanity's potential are spiritual. The Bible makes clear that *our struggle is not against flesh and blood, but against the rulers, against the powers, against the world forces of this darkness, against the spiritual forces of wickedness in the heavenly places* (Ephesians 6:12). In both the Old and New Testaments much is shared about the necessity of overcoming these invisible forces to secure true life and freedom for humanity.

This is true for your home, your family, your church, and your spheres of responsibility. According to the Bible, it is especially true for government. And watchman prayer is vital to gain victory.

White House Watchmen is not so much a collection of platitudes as it is a field guide to help you maximize your potential. In the pages ahead, you're going to move beyond religious exercise and into a dimension where the stakes are high, revelation is real time, and the results are tangible. We want you to see Jesus' divine destiny for you realized in your life and world.

Fair warning—some of what will be exposed may be uncomfortable. But if you're a disciple of Jesus, it also may set you free. At the very least, you will have a better understanding of the true scope of our challenges. And you will be provoked to grow into a calling which, for us anyway, has become the greatest adventure of our lives.

One thing's for sure—God in His nature and character is always experiential. And He is never boring.

If the Lord is calling you to "come up higher" in your relationship with Him, if you care about our nation and want your prayers to make a difference even in the highest halls of power, if you want to grow in watchman prayer, then the pages that follow will empower you! Now let's begin our journey together.

Revival at the Trump International

As mentioned, when the vision of the descending crown came on New Year's Eve 2019, Jolene and I were hosting our seventh annual Revolution gathering at the Trump International Hotel in Washington DC. It was our second year in a row in the gilded ballroom. The hospitality shown to our attendees and volunteers surpassed the hotel's legendary reputation.

Our watchmen gathering was held in part to pray for the Trump administration. But our first and overarching priority was simply to enthrone Jesus in wholehearted worship because we have found that as we enter into His world, He revolutionizes ours! As the Lord said to Zerubbabel, *"Not by might nor by power, but by My Spirit"* (Zech. 4:6).

As an act of worship to enthrone the Lord, and as we were moving into both a new year and a new decade, we also sought to dedicate our new season to the Lord with a special consecration service for our Capital and nation. Jolene and I had asked conference attendees to bring two "memorial stones" with them. One stone would be used to build a symbolic altar of covenant to the Lord, rededicating our Capital and nation to Him.

The second rock was to be taken back to serve as a cornerstone of their respective altars to the Lord over each state. Again, these were meant to serve as a symbol of covenant alignment with the Lord Jesus Christ.

Here's a backstory. After we secured the hotel for Revolution, Dutch Sheets shared an amazing dream that a friend of his, prophet Clay Nash, submitted to him. Dutch actually shared the dream on Yom Kippur at a service we were facilitating with Jamie and Redonnia Jackson, host pastors of Remnant Church in Brunswick, Georgia.

In the dream, an angel of the Lord was standing in front of the Trump International Hotel in Washington DC, declaring, "Mercy," a seventh time. "Mercy that establishes God's covenant!"

As Dutch shared, I felt we had an invitation to build an altar of covenant to the Lord in the spirit realm, somehow synergizing with this angelic host in worship to the Lord, and declaring His mercy over the nation, over the New Year, and over the decade.

New Year's Eve at the Trump International—what a great time for a marriage!

But neither Jolene nor I had any idea what the plea of *mercy* in context with this altar of covenant would soon mean. Watchman prayer is always a journey of discovery with God. He knows the end from the beginning. Our acts of obedience sometimes don't make much sense until our journey finally unfolds. With this in mind, keep these stones and the plea accompanying them in your remembrance.

From the beginning of the gathering, the atmosphere was thick with expectancy. Becca Greenwood, the co-founder of Christian Harvest International and Strategic Prayer Action Network (SPAN), spoke, and then we led in prayer together for the glory of God to come. This was familiar territory for me. I had prayed a similar prayer probably a hundred times before. But there was something unmistakably different this time.

Cindy Jacobs ministered on the morning of New Year's Eve, and I asked her to impart an anointing for awakening. Early in her ministry, she had been one of the forerunners of a massive revival in Argentina, kindling a holy fire which spread across the globe. We wanted that kind of revival in America. As she considered my request, the renowned prophet looked up briefly, then nodded. She forcefully prayed something like, "Lord, let Your revival anointing come now. Now, Jesus!"

To the surprise of everybody, maybe even Cindy, the response from Heaven was immediate. A move of Holy Spirit literally filled the house.

Behind this plea were seven years of nonstop intercession for God's governmental glory to be restored to Washington DC and the nation. In pursuit of this, our "Glory Train" project had carried us from Washington DC to historic wells of awakening and covenant throughout the original thirteen colonies in 2014, then through all fifty states in 2016—mostly by train—and then throughout our nation in ensuing years. We had been to Israel seven times, as well as epicenters of historic revival in England and Wales in 2019.

Why all the effort? Very simply, we yearned for two things: governmental turnaround and another historic move of God.

That morning after Cindy Jacobs prayed, it was as if the train of God's glory had pulled into the station at the Trump International Hotel. The Spirit of the Lord came in a way similar to descriptions from the First and Second Great Awakenings. People were spontaneously touched, deeply and personally. Some laughed. Some wept. Others entered into ecstatic experiences with Holy Spirit. Many had visions. Virtually everyone testified to the awe and heartfelt conviction that seems only to come when God's majesty is unveiled.

The afternoon service brought more of the same. Chris Mitchell Jr., an African American, apostolic leader from Virginia Beach, shared profoundly on how covenant restoration uncaps wells of historic moves of revival. I tagged onto his message. Pastor Jamie Jackson then got up to speak.

Jamie was visibly shaken. Tears flowed freely. His knuckles became white from tightly gripping the podium for stability. About seven times, he opened his mouth to speak but simply couldn't. Out of an abundance of caution, Chris Mitchell positioned himself close by to catch him. Finally, Jamie shouted, shook violently, and then collapsed under the weight of God's power. In what looked like a lightning strike, Chris instantly toppled as well.

And the presence of God again flooded the room—to the extent that few wanted to leave, even after several hours. Plans for elegant New Year's Eve dinners, meticulously planned weeks beforehand, were simply abandoned as God was visiting His people.

Crown of Glory

During this time on the floor at the Trump International Hotel, Jamie Jackson received a vision. He mentioned it to the crowd later in the evening. Jamie saw a crystal crown coming down from Heaven over the National Mall in DC. Everything the crown touched became crystal-like in substance, including the White House, the Capitol, the Supreme Court, and other governmental structures. Even the Lincoln Memorial became crystalline. Jamie's vision reminded me immediately of a passage foundational to everything we were pursuing.

> You will also be a crown of beauty in the hand of the Lord, and a royal diadem in the hand of your God. It will no longer be said to you, "Forsaken," nor to your land will it any longer be said, "Desolate"; but you will be called, "My delight is in her," and your land, "Married"; for the Lord delights in you, and to Him your land will be married.... On your walls, O Jerusalem, I have appointed watchmen; all day and all night they will never keep silent (Isaiah 62:3–4, 6).

To us, through both the outpouring and the vision of the descending crown, God was using very clear language to convey something very personal in nature. Jolene and I, along with a few friends, had launched the annual Revolution gatherings seven years beforehand to empower the Body of Christ in a new movement of governmental worship and prayer that the Lord was birthing in the earth. It is called *Crown & Throne*. Our first book carries this title and serves as an equipping manual that apostolically frames out key aspects of the movement. It's a field guide, if you will, for spiritual revolution.

And it is this movement, brought by God's hand at a desperate hour for America, which has propelled us into the firsthand experiences with the extraordinary governmental turnarounds, including many that were prophesied beforehand in our midst and now define our world.

While in prayer after the conference, the Holy Spirit showed me that the sudden outpouring and vision of the descending crown at Revolution were very intentional by the Lord. They together conveyed a crowning, or coronation, of this movement in our land. No king but Jesus!

Corona Outbreak

Again, none of us had any idea that, on the very same day half a world away, another "coronation" took place. The virus in Wuhan had reached a threshold where the WHO had to be alerted, acknowledging for the first time the potential for the virus to encircle the entire world and cause a global pandemic.

Thus, two crowning movements were set in motion to usher us into 2020. Note that crowns bear witness to their respective governments, whose authority they represent. One is a crown of devastation that seeks to destroy life from the inside out. The other is a crown of glory. It's a watchman's crown, and it has been sent by God to release His governmental authority in a manner that empowers life, union, honor, and restoration.

And from its beginning, 2020 has already been largely defined by this conflict of crowns. One crown seems more dominant in the earth than the other, for now at least. But I have it on very good authority that is about to change!

Shelter in Place

After the gathering, ideas abounded on how we could immediately expand and promote the move of God. We thought we might build a church around it or gather our speakers and take it on the road through January 2020 for maximum impact. By no means did I want to be neglectful of a gift the Lord had given. Yet none of these ideas resonated as Kingdom promotion, just self-promotion and striving. In our current culture, it's sometimes hard to discern between the two.

When God moved at Revolution, He came in His majesty yet as a cherished friend. The moments together were sacred. The holiness of what we experienced still leaves me without words. To turn these moments into a commodity felt as though it would be a betrayal of His sacred trust. We would never do this with friends in the natural. How much more so with God?

With this settled in my spirit, we sought the Lord again over our schedule for the opening months of 2020. A firm directive came which totally surprised me.

"Shelter in place!"

"Lord?" I asked, thinking I may not have heard Him correctly.

I conferred with Jolene to seek confirmation. Really, I had hoped she would refute my revelation, something she has done on more than one occasion. But this time she didn't. Instead, the Scripture the Lord directed her to was even more direct: *"Go, my people, enter your rooms and shut the doors behind you; hide yourselves for a little while until His wrath has passed by"* (Isa. 26:20 NIV).

"Shelter in place. Shut the doors behind you. Hide yourselves for a little while. Lord, what gives?"

After seven years of running hard in Washington DC, then running hard across the nation in ministry engagements, a little downtime actually seemed very wise. We followed God's directive, cancelling virtually all of the limited engagements we had already agreed to.

We had no cognizance of the danger just ahead. To my knowledge, the coronavirus had not yet hit the news cycle.

Though the Lord had prepared us in advance for what was coming, we were totally unaware.

World on Pause

It was late January before the gravity of the Wuhan outbreak became horrifically apparent. For containment purposes, there was no worse time for such a virus to make an appearance. With the Chinese New Year at hand, much of the nation was traveling either nationally or internationally. Initial symptoms were virtually nonexistent, sometimes mirroring a minor cold. Soon, the novel coronavirus spread throughout the world, largely from airline travelers who had little to no symptoms to alert them at the time they flew.

The viral outbreak proved extremely contagious. Thousands were dying. After China, it spread almost immediately through South Korea and Iran. Entire cruise ships became quarantined. Then came Italy, Spain, and Germany. On America's West Coast, Washington State and California were hit severely. On the East Coast, New York became the epicenter of the spread.

By mid-March, entire nations were directed into quarantine by their government leaders. The world was effectively on pause.

Coronavirus—Prophetic Perspective

Did God warn us beforehand? In retrospect, yes. I've mentioned a few prophetic warnings we received already. From our watchman's perch, the Lord told us three years beforehand that a midnight crisis would occur by 2020, provoking a midnight cry, and eventually a midnight turnaround.[8] But we knew it would be a midnight hour for America. We just did not know why.

Over Thanksgiving 2019, I had sensed an urgency in my spirit I could neither define nor shake for weeks. Then during the first week of 2020, the Lord gave us a direct warning to clear our schedule and shelter in place, and the word was confirmed through the Scripture Jolene had received with a hauntingly similar message.

Overall, we, and perhaps the community of watchman prophets we run with, only vaguely perceived the crisis ahead. The lack is on us, not God, simply from running too hard. God spoke a sobering message to us all through the prophet Jeremiah.

> But who has stood in the council of the Lord, that he should see
> and hear His word? Who has given heed to His word and listened?

...I did not send these prophets, but they ran. I did not speak to them, but they prophesied. But if they had stood in My council, then they would have announced My words to My people, and would have turned them back from their evil way and from the evil of their deeds (Jeremiah 23:18, 21–22).

Then there's the issue of stewarding the perceptions the Lord had actually given to us. Jolene was very troubled by the lack of clear prophetic words before the looming crisis. Where were the warnings?

In a flash, Jolene was reminded of a visionary encounter in which the Lord had actually warned her about coming plagues. "I spoke to you two years ago about viruses coming which had never been seen before on the earth. What did you do with this message?"

Suddenly, she had a vision of a recent traffic jam that had turned a two-hour journey into four hours. The Spirit of the Lord continued, "I attempted to get you ahead of the curve in forerunning prayer for the solution to this issue. It is still available. But because you and the prophetic community at large are just getting on the highway I tried to direct you toward, you are caught in traffic instead of ahead of the curve to mitigate the outbreak."

Mercy, Lord. What a hard lesson, learned the hard way, on watchman prayer. Please don't ever take lightly the dreams or prophetic perceptions the Lord gives you. Record them. Write them down where you can reference them easily. The Bible says to test all things and hold fast to what is true. Seek the Lord over them! Then act on what the Lord has shown you, especially by engaging in watchman prayer.

After all, the stakes are too high to overlook the warnings God is now entrusting to His Body.

The Conflict of Crowns

God is seeking to move through the crisis at hand to bring a reset. But our invisible enemy is at work as well. When the Holy Spirit spoke to me about the coming "midnight cry," He made it clear that, through 2020 and perhaps beyond, we would face a series of crises similar to what saints would face in the final days of the end times. From the global spread of the coronavirus, to plagues at Passover, to the "conflict of crowns" even between ideologies, the word has largely proven accurate.

In *Midnight Cry*, I also commented prophetically on President Trump's leadership.

> President Trump is a revolutionary figure. From the beginning of his candidacy we've prophesied that he will be a Winston Churchill for our time. The most important question then becomes—Why does America need a Winston Churchill in this hour? What exactly are we facing?
>
> Maybe this is why the Lord is so emphasizing the midnight cry … Winston Churchill's fierce leadership through World War II was accompanied by a "burning lamp movement" of 24-7 prayer led by Welsh intercessor Rees Howells. I know the Trump administration desperately needs this magnitude of prayer as our nation confronts the challenges of our time. We need a midnight cry …beginning at the White House![9]

What was barely perceived in 2017 is now at the forefront of our reality, especially the call for White House watchmen to arise. The challenges of our time certainly demand this magnitude of prayer!

So, let's talk about challenges ahead.

Two years ago, when Jolene was warned about new viruses in the earth, the Lord made it clear that more than one plague would be coming. Today, we need to get in front of the curve on this in prayer.

Jolene also sensed that, just as God released three days of darkness in Exodus, there may be some days of physical darkness ahead. Will a strong storm knock out power? Will hackers attack our power grid? Trusted friends have also received repeated dreams about electromagnetic pulse (EMP) attacks intended to cripple our infrastructure. We simply don't know when or how this may happen, but we do know we need to pray.

On a broader level, as of 2020, a "conflict of crowns" is now occurring on a global scale. We are engaged against global forces in the spiritual realm seeking to bring America, Israel, and the nations into subservience. You didn't pick this fight. But you're in it whether you like it or not. These spiritual forces and the human agents aligned with them are seeking any means to gain the upper hand, including exploiting the coronavirus crisis, to catalyze further restrictions on our privacy, freedom, ownership of property, and expressions of our faith.

Globalist Agenda—Waiting in the Wings

This is actually nothing new. Leaders and government officials have long fallen for the seductive promises of globalism tied to the occult. For decades, a dark agenda has matured to subvert our constitutional freedoms. Perhaps this fact explains the unprecedented resistance faced by President Trump from the beginning of his campaign. Why else would the goals of re-securing America's sovereignty and making America great again be so hotly contested within media and within our government itself?

According to the Bible, the global expression of this conflict of crowns will only increase, ultimately crescendoing in an existential battle for humanity and transpiring in a valley in Israel known as Armageddon. We're not in this hour yet. But let me be clear. In every step of this coronavirus crisis, leaders aligned with a globalist agenda have been waiting in the wings.

It's our job in prayer to make sure their opportunity is denied, and the time is redeemed.

The Plague Stops at the Threshing Floor

Now let's return to New Year's Eve at the Trump International Hotel. The revival anointing that broke out earlier in the morning carried us through the final service. Just after midnight, some of the most extraordinary moments of the gathering began to unfold.

Isaiah 62:4 holds out a promise that *"to Him your land will be married."* Some four hundred people crossed over into 2020 by dedicating the New Year and new decade to the Lord Jesus Christ. And in a way similar to the Pilgrims' plea four hundred years prior, we asked the Lord for His hand in marriage to this nation.

After the children of Israel had passed over into the Promised Land, you may recall how Joshua commanded that an altar of remembrance be built to the Lord with stones from the Jordan River. As we crossed over into the New Year and new decade, reaffirming covenant with God in the opening moments of 2020, an altar of remembrance was built with the stones each attendee had brought. The second stone was dedicated and sent home with them to serve as a cornerstone of their own altar of remembrance.

Many wrote on their stones special sayings or favorite Scriptures. *Healing* was the word on one rock. *Love* was written on another. That makes for a great cornerstone, right?

"Blessed is the nation whose God is the Lord," read one small stone which caught my attention. I agree. It was right above a stone that read, "Hephzibah." From Isaiah 62, it means "the Lord delights in you." And it's to Him our land shall be married!

So together we renewed covenant. We built an altar of remembrance. Afterward, we received communion together to seal this work. It was a great way to enter into 2020.

And then God pushed pause. The word of the Lord came to shelter in place. News broke of massive numbers of people dying from a new virus in Wuhan, China. It was a virus that had never before been seen in the earth. The coronavirus spread silently to the nations, in most cases with no telling symptoms until well after those infected had become contagious. Soon, the entire globe was engulfed in perhaps its greatest crisis since the Second World War.

On March 10, at approximately 1:30 a.m., apostolic leader Chris Mitchell Jr. awoke from deep slumber, speaking to God in prayer. The Lord directed him to review the biblical recounting of a plague that had occurred during the days of King David's reign. It's described in 2 Samuel 24:18–24 and 1 Chronicles 21:18–26. We sent out a posting with Chris's insights on the same day. They are recorded below.

The Lord is calling us back to the threshing floor, to separate the clean from the vile....

...As my friend Jolene Hamill spoke, from Revelation 18, this is an hour in which the Lord is calling for His people to "come out" of alignment with every Babylonian system. I believe what the Lord highlighted to Jolene through this is of vital importance.

Prophetically, the threshing floor is the foundation of His governmental house (Solomon's temple was built on the threshing floor of Araunah as mentioned below) and mixture cannot be tolerated.

"And I heard another voice from heaven saying, 'Come out of her, my people, lest you share in her sins, and lest you receive of her plagues'" (Revelation 18:4).

In Second Samuel 24, as response to David's sin, the Lord allowed a plague to come upon Israel. David began to lean on the strength of his army, and the abundance of his resources more than his intimacy and covenant with God. As the destroying angel moved through Israel, God in His mercy commanded him to stop at the threshing floor of Ornan/Araunah.

"Then Araunah said, 'Why has my lord the king come to his servant?' And David said, 'To buy the threshing floor from you, to build an altar to the LORD, that the plague may be withdrawn from the people.' And David built there an altar to the LORD, and offered burnt offerings and peace offerings. So the LORD heeded the prayers for the land, and the plague was withdrawn from Israel" (2 Samuel 24:21, 25).

...I believe we will see breakthrough concerning the coronavirus to the extent that we yield to God in these areas. This is a defining moment for the Bride, we must cooperate with the hand of the Lord in this, then we will see Haman scheme become his own demise.[10]

The plague stops at the threshing floor. But notice Israel's greatest king had to take the lead. When the angel of the Lord hovered over this property with his sword outstretched to slay Jerusalem, King David was the first to step in to repent and plead for mercy. What was essentially a spontaneous national day of prayer immediately ensued.

With dire reports pouring in, the hour was just as urgent.

A day after posting, I contacted officials in collaboration with the White House Faith Initiative. The conversation was warm and encouraging. I recounted the midnight cry Chris Mitchell experienced with the Lord, which led him to record these thoughts on how the plague stops at the threshing floor as the king—or in our case, president—takes the lead.

And I learned in response that many similar proposals for President Trump to call a National Day of Prayer were also coming in. It would definitely be considered!

Shortly after this, another Chris Mitchell called. *Jerusalem Dateline* anchor Chris Mitchell, who covers the Middle East for the Christian Broadcasting Network (CBN), is also a close friend. He called me with a similar burden for the president to call a day of prayer. He promised to pray from Jerusalem, the site of the original threshing floor!

Two days later, President Trump officially designated the coronavirus pandemic as a National Emergency. He then designated Sunday, March 15, as a National Day of Prayer.[11]

Immediately, I saw the Lord's plan for those seemingly insignificant rocks we had received during the opening moments of 2020. The plague stops at the threshing floor. Like David, our Lamplighter community was being summoned to present to the Lord a covenant altar. Every state had now become a threshing floor. And we were called to build altars of mercy, prepared in advanced for just this moment.

It was decided that the first hour of our Sunday call would be yielded to the One Voice Prayer Movement. Jolene and I serve on the leadership team for the One Voice Prayer Movement, along with Intercessors for America director Dave Kubal. Together, we decided our "building an altar of mercy" call would immediately follow.

To our utter astonishment, some 4,500 people from across the nation joined the calls. With literally One Voice, we united in a plea for mercy from the Lord and sought forgiveness for our sins. Then from Israel to England to the White House, the Capitol, the Supreme Court, the Lincoln Memorial, and all fifty states, we presented the Lord with a covenant altar and invoked His mercy for our deliverance—because the plague stops at the threshing floor.

Was the plague eradicated? Not immediately. But we did see the beginnings of a turnaround. Within two days, a discovery was made public that a combination of malaria-fighting drugs and antibiotics had been successful in treating the worst cases of the coronavirus.

Here's a final story on this. CBN correspondent Chris Mitchell had read our posting featuring Chris Mitchell Jr.'s encounter and decree. Though they are not related in the natural, they are similar in spirit. On the morning of the National Day of Prayer, Chris Mitchell called me again from Jerusalem. This time, he was at the Western Wall. A virtually empty courtyard directed a faithful remnant to the large ashlar stones at the base of the Temple Mount. It was the very area of the threshing floor where David had built his altar to the Lord, and the plague had been stopped.

Solomon had built Israel's Temple on this threshing floor where the plague had been stopped. At the dedication of the Temple, he was given a sacred promise. Perhaps it is familiar to you.

> *If I shut up the heavens so that there is no rain, or if I command the locust to devour the land, or IF I SEND PESTILENCE among My people, and My people who are called by My name humble themselves and pray and seek My face and turn from their wicked ways, then I will hear from heaven, will forgive their sin and will HEAL THEIR LAND. Now My eyes will be open and My ears attentive to the prayer offered in this place* (2 Chronicles 7:13–15 emphasis added).

God will heal our land. According to the passage, this promise extends to all His children through all generations who call on His name, especially when connected to the threshing floor which became an altar. Note this altar became a place of encounter for all generations to come. I feel prophetically the Lord desires to grant the same for our nation, for many states, and for you. The threshing floor becomes an altar of encounter. This is a promise from the Lord!

But back to our story. Chris—along with Rick and Patricia Ridings, founders of Succat Hallel—joined our call from Jerusalem Sunday night. But first, Chris put together a brief video at the Western Wall for *Dateline Jerusalem*. Eyes moist with tears, Chris presented to the Lord the proclamation from President Trump seeking healing on the National Day of Prayer. In a haunting way, President Trump's plea met with King David's at the same threshing floor. A printed copy of the plea was then placed in the cleft between the rocks of this giant stone altar now known as the Western Wall.

And on the paper recording Trump's plea were the following handwritten words: "The plague stops at the threshing floor."

For Review

Please take a moment to reflect on what you've just read. We suggest taking notes as you answer questions below.

1. What are the greatest concerns you have been praying about in this season?

2. On a national level, America has endured a threshing-floor experience. What have you learned? How have you grown? Where is more healing needed? Where is the threshing floor becoming an altar in your life?

CHAPTER 2

THE TRUMP TURNAROUND

ON January 7, 2020, a tractor trailer wound its way along an empty road in western Iran, its headlights shining on a deserted highway. Suddenly, burning streaks of fire appeared in the night skies above. It was on. The Iranian Revolutionary Guard had launched a barrage of missiles targeting US bases in Iraq. It was a revenge strike for Iranian master terrorist Qasem Soleimani's sudden takedown—which had been approved by President Donald J. Trump.[12]

A video loop of the soaring missiles played endlessly through the night on US networks. Talking heads raged over the legitimacy of taking down the Iranian general. Was President Trump crazy? Was the action legal? Was it necessary?

Few in public view jumped to Trump's defense. But, privately, many intelligence leaders considered Qasem Soleimani to be the most ruthless and effective terror leader alive on the planet. Over decades, he had relentlessly targeted both Israel and America.[13]

The general had just orchestrated an assault on the US Embassy in Iraq, seeking to replicate the hostile takeover of the US Embassy in Iran exactly forty years beforehand. His proxies had just killed an American contractor. He pioneered the use of IEDs during the Iraq War, which killed more than six hundred Americans and maimed countless thousands of US soldiers. Soleimani had grown Hamas and Hezbollah into the strongest terror networks still in operation globally, and even successfully planted sleeper cells in the United States.[14]

Further, intelligence was clear that Soleimani was relentlessly pursuing nuclear warheads with the dark ambition of destroying Tel Aviv, Haifa, and even cities in America.

At the risk of war with Iran, President Trump made an extraordinary decision. It was time to take Soleimani down.

Sparking Armageddon?

When Iran's revenge strike was finally launched, a hostile American press invoked a harrowing term: *Armageddon*. Usually reserved for late-night discussions on pandemics, nuclear war and end-time preppers, Armageddon became a clarion reference point by talking heads seemingly convinced President Trump had just catapulted America into the biblical end-time battle for all humanity.

As for the commentators, their collective opinion was clear. Taking down General Soleimani had carelessly sparked World War III.[15]

Our view was completely different. A year earlier, divine intelligence on a coming conflict with Iran was conveyed by the Lord in a way that completely arrested our attention. We will explore this comprehensively in the next chapter. For now, just know we were being summoned to pray for a turnaround. Over an eleven-month period, our intercessors focused on breakthrough for America, as well as for a coming conflict with Iran and the ancient principality the Bible identifies as "the Prince of Persia." On December 12, 2019, the moment came when the Lord confirmed in an unmistakable way that the breakthrough had been granted and victory secured. We knew this turnaround would soon play out in current events.

Thankfully, the future aligned with the Lord's desire rather than the observations of the press. Armageddon had been postponed.

Iran saved face, of course, by sending the rockets. But Reuters and other news organizations analyzing damage assessments concluded the Iranian government had directed their missiles to avoid mass killings of American soldiers and diplomats.[16] As noted by President Trump, instead of engaging in World War III, the Iranian government deliberately chose to deescalate the situation.

It was an extraordinary turnaround and a dramatic win for President Trump. At the right time, against improbable odds, he took a calculated risk. And, characteristic of wins that have defined both his life and presidency, what looked like a doomsday scenario suddenly turned to victory.

Also characteristic, he made it look easy.

Of course, thousands of intercessors across America would hotly debate the "ease" of this turnaround. In fact, many collapsed from battle fatigue the very next day, which is also very typical of every Trump turnaround. Especially this one.

The truth is even many administration officials have noticed an uncanny parallel between Trump administration victories and a relentless push of watchman prayer. A dimension of governmental intercession has been fueled by prophetic revelation which directs our course to breakthrough. The parallel is not coincidence.

Watchman Prayer in a Time of Rebuilding

It's important to make this clear at the outset. To me, it is inexcusable that leaders within our nation continued to carry through their assignment to divide our nation and sabotage the administration even in the midst of national crisis. Their efforts to destabilize began the day the American voter elected President Trump, and they have continued unabated ever since.

What if these leaders had succeeded? For instance, if President Trump had been impeached, our national government would have been completely destabilized, and our nation even more divided, just as the coronavirus pandemic was breaking out.

Every state of our nation, and every nation of the earth, has now been horrifically affected by the coronavirus pandemic. From the beginning of the outbreak, President Trump has earned high honors overall for guiding America through the crisis. Though few in the press gave him any credit, the fact remains that innovative, hands-on leadership demanded the best from both government and the private sector to bring relief to healthcare professionals and all Americans. As a result, relief came at a speed and comprehensiveness few previously thought possible. It's privately referred to as *Trump speed*.

President Trump's business acumen has proven invaluable throughout many challenges. He thinks like a businessman. He builds like a businessman. He relates with business leaders in a way few presidents ever have, because he understands the needs of both giant corporations and the small businesses that keep America prosperous.

The united response to this crisis began to resurrect true greatness of America's potential. Then came the tragic death of George Floyd at the hands—or actually the knee—of an abusive Minneapolis police officer. A nation in healing suddenly erupted over the horrific injustice and abuse, on display for the world to see. We wept. We marched. And then we wept some more as a pure justice movement became co-opted by Antifa, anarchists, and others with vastly different goals. Riots, vandalism, and looting broke out nationwide. Calls to defund law enforcement, or even eradicate it completely, dominated the national discourse.

We have endured great hardships already. Let's take a moment to look down the road. In this vulnerable season, we will either restore our covenant nation and the freedoms we have enjoyed, or we will succumb to outside opposition, lawlessness, and false ideologies from within, which could ultimately restrict these very freedoms. By rehearsing past challenges, and the turnarounds we have witnessed right before our very eyes, we can gain a reasonable perspective on the potential for the future. And we can plot a new way forward together.

I for one predict a turnaround. Let's rebuild! And as part of the rebuilding, let's mobilize a vast army of White House watchmen to pray through the extraordinary challenges we continue to face.

Trump as Catalyst of America's Turnaround

Even among the prophets, few in the faith community looked positively on newcomer Donald J. Trump as he burst into the 2016 presidential race. He was far too controversial. Chuck Pierce had prophesied about a hidden "Trump Card" God would use to overcome demonically empowered resistance.[17] Lance Wallnau famously perceived Donald Trump as "America's Cyrus."[18] And, while serving as the forty-fifth president of the United States, Trump would fulfill in our day much of what was prophesied concerning Cyrus in Isaiah 45.

But by and large, Donald J. Trump was the least favored among the contenders, even by the prophets. A private roundtable with high-level prophetic voices made this clear. All are now in full support of the president. But they were not then by any means. My support for Trump proved very controversial, but I could not deny what had been shown to me.

On January 5, 2016, just at the start of the election year, the Lord identified Donald Trump in a dream as His choice for our nation's highest office. I honestly did not believe it at first. Surrounded by Republican giants like Senator Ted Cruz, Senator Marco Rubio, and Governor Jeb Bush, Trump seemed to be positioned strategically as the ostracized troublemaker, the bad cop in a field of kinder, gentler, good cops. He appeared useful only to speak inconvenient truths nobody else would dare to speak and face consequences nobody else could bear to face.

"Make America Great Again" (MAGA) was his campaign slogan. And his platform? America first. Rescue the nation from a globalist agenda. Bring jobs back home. Build the wall. Restrain government-funded abortions. Negotiate with strength. Fix Veterans Affairs. Drain the swamp.

I believe this last mandate especially is what unleashed the terrified resistance of the Washington DC elite so vehemently opposing him from the beginning of his term. "Before Trump was even sworn into office the Deep State went into overdrive to thwart his presidency," noted former Rep. Jason Chaffetz. "In agency after agency, the threat to big government posed by Trump changed all the rules."[19] Note that, when this resistance ruled, Christians were deliberately marginalized both within the spheres of government and in the nation. Israel was intentionally denigrated. Propaganda which promoted open defiance of God's heart and Word was not only generated, but forced upon the American people virtually as law.

The Turnaround Verdict for Presidential Elections

As a watchman in covenant with God over the nation, the Lord had promised a turnaround. Further, He had made a very personal promise to me that the next president would serve as His chosen catalyst for the governmental turnaround He was desiring to release to America.

I'll never forget the moment. In March 2015, we spent ten days in Jerusalem contending for an election turnaround in favor of Prime Minister Netanyahu. The Obama administration had pressured Israeli citizens against the Prime Minister due to his opposition to the Iran Nuclear Accords, even sending President Obama's campaign manager to help with the opposition.[20] As governmental prophets from Washington DC, the Lord asked us to minister, prophesy, and pray on-site in Jerusalem for His sovereign choice to prevail.

All of our friends in Jerusalem wanted Netanyahu to win. Due to US pressure, nobody believed he would. But as God often does, He showcased His covenant land before the world and then brought the impossible into reality.

A little background is appropriate. On July 22 the previous year, the Lord actually called us to convene a special gathering to receive Daniel 7:22 as verdict from His throne for the US and Israel.

> *I kept looking* [watching], *and that horn was waging war with the saints and overpowering them until the Ancient of Days came and judgment was passed in favor of the saints of the Highest One, and the time arrived when the saints took possession of the kingdom* (Daniel 7:21–22).

The verdict brought judgment in favor of the saints, restraining the enemy and releasing the saints to possess the Kingdom, including the governmental seats of authority for nations.

I am aware this may sound unusual, but again the verse was actually presented by the Lord as a verdict from Heaven's Court for this hour. Because of the unprecedented turnarounds that have been catalyzed ever since, we now call this passage *The Turnaround Verdict*. We will explore it much more thoroughly in the pages ahead. But it is vital for you to grasp now to fully appreciate all that has since transpired.

The turnarounds we are experiencing right now are by no means random or haphazard. The opposite is actually true. There is a dramatic consistency to their frequency, their quality, their comprehensiveness, and the long-term blessing they secure. Again and again, we ourselves have seen impossible situations turn on a dime as we stand on this ancient courtroom decision.

On the day of Israel's elections, God met us with a promise of a turnaround in the US presidential election. Jolene and I were actually on the ramparts of Jerusalem at the time. As was noted earlier, Isaiah 62 speaks of "watchmen on the walls" of Jerusalem who will never hold their peace until God makes His covenant city a praise in the earth. Our friend Linda Wyatt had felt strongly impressed to commission us on these ramparts as "watchmen on the walls" both for Jerusalem and our nation's capital. It was a sacred moment for us.

And on the ramparts of Jerusalem's walls, the Holy Spirit spoke to me a sacred promise, "As you have stood with Me for My elections in My covenant land, so I will stand with you for a turnaround in your 2016 presidential elections."

Against all odds, Prime Minister Netanyahu was declared the winner. The Turnaround Verdict prevailed. To Jolene and me, this was much more than a victory in politics—*it was actually a manifestation of a verdict from God's throne*. It was an initial fulfillment of a global prayer assignment conveying how God is rendering judgment in favor of the saints, granting unprecedented turnarounds in our lives and world.

"You're Hired!" Trump Identified as God's Catalyst

Based on these promises, Jolene and I embarked on a fifty-state "turn-around tour" throughout 2016. We actually visited every state, seeking the restoration of God's governmental glory and the presidential turn-around He promised. On January 5, 2016, while we were making final preparations, the Lord awakened me from an extraordinary dream that identified Donald Trump as His chosen catalyst for this turnaround.

In the dream, Donald Trump was handed the contract to restore the Department of Homeland Security. He got to work immediately to repair a portion of the campus far from public view, which had been neglected to the point of complete dilapidation.

While he was making this repair behind the scenes, a procession of seemingly hundreds of black and Hispanic women came shouting and dancing through the gates of Homeland Security, singing praises to God. I kept hearing Trump's voice in the background, saying, "You're hired! You're hired! You're hired!"

President Trump then walked through the gates with his entourage. He looked at me and nodded coolly. I pointed to him and said the follow-ing, "Sir, you must restore Christmas!" Then I awoke.

From this surprising dream, I knew President Trump was called by God not only to be president, but to restore the security and prosper-ity He desired for our homeland. I also knew that the blessing from this restoration would extend to all Americans. Every tongue, tribe, and eth-nicity, for the glory of God.

Which brings me to a delicate subject, especially given the present environment. Many now claim President Trump is racist. But even a brief look at his actions, past and present, strongly indicates that he has con-sistently used his wealth and power to benefit minorities. He has worked relentlessly to bring solutions and results that benefit African American communities and families. Opportunity Zones are revitalizing econom-ically oppressed areas. The First Step Act has become a tremendous first step in criminal justice reform.[21]

And when Trump purchased Mar-a-Lago in 1997, one of many private, all-white clubs in Palm Beach, he mandated opening the club to blacks and Jews. To do this required a bold stand, including a $100 million lawsuit against the town. Mar-a-Lago became the first club to open to African Americans in Palm Beach.[22]

I personally agree with the assessment of Trump cabinet member Ben Carson. "What will help the nation heal is if we engage in dialogue together," he said in a June 2020 interview with CNN. "Let's not make the solution be a Democrat solution or a Republican solution. Let's make it be an American solution, and recognize our country is extraordinary."[23]

Final point from the dream. By the Spirit, I also knew the black and Hispanic women moving through the gates represented Christians returning to the halls of government where they had been ostracized and marginalized by previous administrations. This has also happened at an unprecedented magnitude, now reshaping the very culture of our government.

Greatest Turnaround in Modern US History

Three years after this dream, explosive job growth propelled America into the recovery of our greatness. According to statistics, people of color prospered greatly in both financial independence and societal influence. Unemployment among blacks and Hispanics hit a historic, record-shattering low. Food stamp rolls declined by 7.7 million people since Trump took office.

Meanwhile, the stock market broke all records. The economy muscled through credible warnings of impending recessions. Even the *Washington Post*, traditionally negative toward the Trump administration, took notice: "US economy shakes free of recession fears in striking turnaround since August," declared the headline from December 15, 2019.[24] And even the press declared the turnaround!

Our nation's military, diplomacy, and homeland security are being restored with honor. Even a new branch of the military, the Space Force, has been launched.

One of the greatest turnarounds is occurring within the judicial branch of our government. According to figures provided by the White House, in just his first term in office, President Trump has already seated two Supreme Court justices and 189 federal judges. In contrast, President Obama only seated 50 federal justices in eight years.

The record-breaking appointments have already shifted one of the most contentious, federal judiciaries in the land, known for liberal activist judges who rule according to their own preferences. The Ninth US Circuit Court of Federal Appeals in San Francisco actually overruled a lesser court to uphold the Trump administration's legal right to restrict and defund Planned Parenthood.

The extraordinary legal efforts to restrict government-funded abortion mark a dramatic turnaround in policy from former administrations. But America's strongest pro-life president has not waited on courtroom verdicts to take action regarding abortion. When forming his administration, Trump hired a presidential advisor whose primary role was to eradicate abortion from government policy, department by department.

It is now time to complete this turnaround and see the full shift in American government from a covenant of death empowering a culture of death, to a covenant of life empowering a culture of life. Especially in light of the conflict of crowns with the coronavirus, this is an overarching assignment for 2020–2024. And it can be achieved!

A driving force behind every turnaround mentioned is actually believers in Christ who have been welcomed back into the highest halls of US governance. From President Trump and Vice President Pence to Secretary of State Mike Pompeo, Attorney General William Barr, Secretary of Education Betsy DeVos, Secretary of Housing and Urban Development Ben Carson, and on to a multitude of equally extraordinary but lesser known leaders populating every facet of the administration, many of the highest seats of power in our nation are being stewarded by authentic Christians competent in their spheres. We have been privileged to become friends and partners in prayer with many.

And where religious freedom was suppressed both within our government and across the nation during previous administrations, it has now become a celebrated pillar of the Trump administration and a hallmark of US diplomacy. In his address to the 2019 Global Ministerial on Advancing Religious Freedom, Secretary of State Mike Pompeo noted that the ministerial was the largest humanitarian gathering hosted by the US State Department.[25] Led by Ambassador to Religious Freedom Sam Brownback and Secretary Pompeo, the annual gathering provides an unprecedented forum for the voices of persecuted Christians, Muslims, Yazidis, and others to be heard by leaders of nations. According to Ambassador Brownback, coalitions of nations are now being formed to advance religious freedom globally.

Nationally, President Trump loosed the governmental chains imposed on school prayer and expression of faith within our education system. This rollout was in conjunction with a month's-long collaborative effort across departments of government to secure and empower religious freedom for the American people. And at the very beginning of his first term, Trump signed an executive order overruling the Johnson Amendment, which had sought to prevent ministries from speaking out on political issues.[26] The voice of America's prophetic conscience was finally welcomed to influence government again, and to influence her citizens regarding government, just as our founders had intended.

And we together are bearing witness to the greatest, most comprehensive governmental turnaround in recent American history.

Jerusalem Turnaround—A Christmas Story

Of all the priorities on my heart for America, compelling the future president to "restore Christmas" would rank pretty low on the list. And yet I did—at least in my dream. Amazingly, not long after posting this word, President Trump spoke of a new mandate he was committing to prioritize in his administration. Very simply, to "Make Christmas great again!" And in the 2020 election year President Trump has re-emphasized this mandate.

Here's a Christmas restoration story you may not be aware of. It begins with a tragic mistake.

On December 23, 2016, President Barack Obama made the extraordinary decision to vote in favor of a United Nations resolution declaring much of Jerusalem—including the Western Wall, Judaism's holiest site, and the Jewish quarter of Jerusalem's Old City—as Palestinian land illegally occupied by Israel.[27]

Until that time, America had largely stood by Israel. Now, America joined nations hostile to Israel in demanding the Western Wall, the only remaining structure of the historic Jewish Temple area, be turned over to the Palestinians. Were the mandate to be followed through, Jews would even be restrained from praying at their holiest site.

This action was President Obama's final prominent act of diplomacy. Note that it came two days before Christmas—and only a day before the Jewish celebration of Hanukkah—which is really important to note because Hanukkah celebrates the retaking of the Temple, including the Temple Mount.

The Maccabees went up against the strongest army in the known world, the Seleucid Empire, to retake their covenantal heritage from the globalists of their day. Their temple had been defiled with sacrifices to Baal and Zeus, polluting even the Holy of Holies. The Maccabees relit the Temple menorah to reconsecrate the sacred space to the Lord, divorcing it from the idolatry that had claimed it. The Maccabees only had oil to keep the lamp burning for a single day. Yet, miraculously, the flame burned bright for eight days straight! Amazingly, the final act of rededicating the Temple to God occurred on December 25, 165 BC.

Can't make this stuff up.

Always remember this. True globalism is always yielded to gross idolatry and empowered by gross idolatry. The Hanukkah story serves as a reminder to us all of the true source of all human subjugation, as well as the true cost of keeping freedom's flame burning. We must keep vigilant. We must keep watch.

That said, the claiming of the Western Wall by Israel's fiercest enemies, empowered by American diplomacy with the full agreement of the United Nations, was the ultimate slap in the face of Israel. Two days later, a defiant Netanyahu embraced the calling of his Maccabee forefathers, lighting a special menorah at the Western Wall.

Not long after, Donald Trump was inaugurated as president. And on December 6, 2017, President Trump proved once again to be God's chosen catalyst for turnaround. This time for Jerusalem.

> "When I came into office," Trump intoned, "I promised to look at the world's challenges with open eyes and very fresh thinking. We cannot solve our problems by making the same failed assumptions and repeating the same failed strategies of the past. Old challenges demand new approaches.
>
> "Therefore, I have determined that it is time to officially recognize Jerusalem as the capital of Israel. Jerusalem is today, and must remain, a place where Jews pray at the Western Wall.... Today, we finally acknowledge the obvious: that Jerusalem is Israel's capital. This is nothing more, or less, than a recognition of reality. It is also the right thing to do."[28]

Here was the turnaround that reversed a dark nightmare from the previous Christmas. Whereas Obama sought to defraud Israel of her holiest sites, President Trump declared Jerusalem to be the capital of the covenant nation.

That was three weeks before Christmas. And on the Jewish calendar, only a week before Hanukkah!

The magnitude of these examples of decisive action birthed out of forerunning prophetic intercession is hard to comprehend. From Heaven's vantage point, prayer and action must be inseparable. Together, they have helped to set a new course not only for our nation, but also Israel and the nations of the earth. No wonder competent prophetic intercession is even being appreciated and welcomed by our nation's highest offices.

All of this may seem like an unusual pathway for achieving goals or affecting policy or turning a nation back to God. But remember that the Lord has promised to choose the foolish things to confound the wise. There's no doubt the wisest among us are rightly confounded by both the methodology employed, and the consistent results which now define many successes of this hour.

I want to emphasize again that this book is not primarily about politics. God has opened a limited window of opportunity to complete the national turnaround He invited us to embrace. This turnaround is not based on the political popularity, capacities, affiliations, or inherent strengths or flaws of any of our leaders. The reality is no man can truly take credit for it. Because this turnaround is based on the restoration of God's covenant with our land. It is literally a move of God.

Through the rest of this book you're going to receive clear biblical principles guaranteed to empower breakthrough in your own life and sphere. You're going to gain more understanding of the move of God's Spirit in our day, and the terrible conflict of crowns which relentlessly seeks to abort God's intended purposes.

And, hopefully, you're also going to become a catalyst and protector of the national turnaround which the hand of the Lord is entrusting to us all. It's important for you to know that, down the tracks, this is all leading to awakening, revival, and harvest. If for this reason alone, we must complete the turnaround.

With this in mind, let's now take a deeper look at our first example mentioned—postponing Armageddon.

For Review

Please take a moment to reflect on what you've just read. We suggest taking notes as you answer questions below.

1. The Trump presidency has undoubtedly been tumultuous. What are your feelings about President Trump? How have you been praying for him? For his family?

2. What aspects of the turnaround have touched your life personally? Make a list of the answers to your prayers which have come to pass during this season.

3. How do you feel the Lord is calling you to grow in prayer? In intimacy with Him? In hearing Him? Writing down specifics will really help you advance.

4. What does the term *watchman* mean to you?

5. In what aspects of your life do you feel the Lord wants to bring a personal turnaround? What circumstances need to change?

CHAPTER 3

POSTPONING
ARMAGEDDON

EVER since birth, Donald Trump has been gifted at making a dramatic appearance. On June 15, 1946, the night the future president was born, a blood moon appeared in the skies over Jerusalem. Jewish revolutionaries known as the "haganah" took the celestial event as a sign from God. After thousands of years, it was time for Israel to be reborn.

And as you will see, another meaning of this sign was on God's heart as well. Donald Trump was literally born to become a "Cyrus" for his era.

On January 20, 2019, in the skies above Washington DC, a bright full moon succumbed to the earth's shadow until it seemed almost to have been erased. Nature had accomplished a perfect lunar eclipse. At once, the moon started to glow a deep orange, illuminated by the reflection of sunlight which other regions of the earth experienced as either sunrise or sunset. A blood moon at midnight appeared over the nation's capital.

Like all blood moons, this eclipse found its genesis in a vast orchestration of time and physics set in motion billions of years beforehand. That's what made its timely appearance over the Capitol especially intriguing.

To the very day, this blood moon marked the third anniversary of Donald Trump's inauguration as president of the United States.

After appearing in the sky on January 20, the blood moon came to fullness just after midnight, at 12:12 a.m. on January 21, marking the third anniversary of President Trump's first day at work.

Blood Moon Over Washington—a Sign?

God as Creator is extremely intentional in His creation. Therefore, it is no surprise that ancient prophets received startling messages related to this phenomenon's appearing. The book of Joel conveys that a blood moon will serve as an end-time sign of extreme turbulence among the nations, as well as a massive outpouring of Holy Spirit on all mankind.

> *Let the priests, the Lord's ministers, weep between the porch and the altar, and let them say, "Spare Your people, O Lord, and do not make Your inheritance a reproach, a byword among the nations...." Then the Lord will be zealous for His land.... "It will come about after this that I will pour out My Spirit on all mankind; and your sons and daughters will prophesy, your old men will dream dreams, your young men will see visions ...I will display wonders in the sky and on the earth, blood, fire and columns of smoke. The sun will be turned into darkness and THE MOON INTO BLOOD before the great and awesome day of the Lord comes. And it will come about that whoever calls on the name of the Lord will be delivered. . ."* (Joel 2:17–18, 28–32 emphasis added).

Extreme turbulence. Major moves of repentance. An outpouring of Holy Spirit accompanied by visions, dreams, and revelations. Deliverance for Zion. A blood moon as a sign. We have already witnessed firstfruits of every one of these manifestations during President Trump's time in office.

I personally don't believe this blood moon at midnight represents the fullness of the time identified by Joel. But, in our book, it's a harbinger. Truly. Because as you know, our book *Midnight Cry* prophesies about a series of midnight crises by 2020 that will serve as a foretaste of the end-times both in the scope of challenges and the scope of victory.

A midnight hour. A midnight watch. A midnight turnaround. Something about the appearance of the blood moon at exactly 12:12 a.m. on the third anniversary of Trump's inauguration, compels me to believe we're on the right track.

For this reason, our Lamplighter family connected nationwide via conference call to watch and pray through the midnight hour as a blood moon marked the third anniversary of President Trump's inauguration. We prayed for the president. We received communion together nationwide. And we launched a yearlong prayer watch directly from the playbook of Daniel, contending for today's "Armageddons" to be postponed.

Here's the backstory.

Third Year of Cyrus

Three weeks before the blood moon appeared, Jolene and I traveled to Saint Simons Island for rest and ministry through New Year's Eve. Pastors Jamie and Redonnia Jackson arranged for us to stay at a special home on the southern Georgia island.

And in yet another cosmic orchestration known but to God, the townhome they secured for us happened to be owned by a man named Gabriel Speaks. Jolene took the man's name as more than a sign—it was an invitation from God.

The Bible records the dramatic impact of the archangel Gabriel's words upon humanity. The births of both John the Baptist and Jesus of Nazareth were foretold by him. And six hundred years prior, Daniel received prophetic revelation via this angel which prophesies even to our day.

Before I could even haul in the luggage from the car, Jolene had claimed the most comfortable chair in the house, switched on the lamp, and started her quiet time. Her Bible literally fell open to the book of Daniel, the scroll from which Gabriel speaks to humanity. And by the time I made it up the stairs with the first load of luggage, she had already discovered a passage that would come to define the year. She called to me from her chair, "Honey, have you read Daniel 10? You should really read it. Like, right now!"

A few more muscled trips, and I was finally able to take her advice. Flipping to Daniel, I began to read—and gasped. The presence of God immediately fell.

> *In the third year of Cyrus king of Persia a message was revealed to Daniel, who was named Belteshazzar; and the message was true and one of great conflict, but he understood the message and had an understanding of the vision* (Daniel 10:1).

As mentioned before, Donald Trump was prophesied as a Cyrus even before he began his campaign for the presidency. From God's perspective, again, a blood moon over Jerusalem the night he was born conveys that he was literally born to fulfill this role! And when the "third year of Cyrus" was highlighted in Daniel 10, Jolene and I both knew Holy Spirit was emphasizing Trump and his third year in office—all of which make the actions recorded in the rest of the chapter extremely relevant to our day.

Daniel served as a counselor to Cyrus, King of Persia. Behind the scenes, he was a watchman prophet both for God's restoration movement and for Cyrus personally. In our terms, he was the original "White House watchman." And it was precisely this calling which prompted Daniel to pray in the third year of Cyrus.

Daniel 10 records how the prophet dramatically engaged in fasting and prayer for twenty-one days during the third year of Cyrus's reign, until a supernatural force the Bible calls the *Prince of Persia* was restrained and an angel of the Lord broke through. The message brought by the angel prophesied into eras to come, even to the end times. Further, the breakthrough itself helped jumpstart the fulfillment of Cyrus's decree for a "freedom movement," restoring the Jews out of subjugation in Babylon.

I knew immediately that, during the third year of America's Cyrus, God was promising a breakthrough of similar magnitude for the freedom movement of our time. But as with Daniel, the breakthrough needed to be contended for until it came.

When did President Trump's third year begin? Having attended his inauguration, the date remained very clear in my mind. I googled "January 20"—and gasped again. Sitting on the couch at the house of Gabriel Speaks, across from my prophet wife immersed in the book of Daniel, I suddenly realized a blood moon at midnight was about to mark the third year of America's Cyrus.

And Gabriel was seriously speaking.

Let's put these two occurrences together for you. Some 2,600 years ago, during the third year of Cyrus's reign, a breakthrough came via the intercession of the prophet Daniel. It framed our future and restarted a freedom movement. Further, it conveyed the potential that God is granting to His "White House watchmen" in this very hour, whereby a man prophesied as a Cyrus for our time has now become the forty-fifth president of the United States.

God's exclamation point to the above sentence could not be clearer. Through an orchestration of creation set in motion millions of years before, a blood moon appeared in the night skies over Washington DC, on January 20–21, precisely marking the third anniversary of President Trump's inauguration.

Talk about divine intentionality. It's actually a little intimidating. You simply cannot make this up.

"The message was true, but one of great conflict." That sure proved true for Trump's third year. The message in Daniel 10 was given in no uncertain terms. Warning—conflicts ahead!

Jolene and I knew immediately that, just as with Daniel, God was calling us to contend in intensive prayer for breakthrough throughout the entire third year of Trump's presidency, and beyond, of course. First, we were to pray for the president and his God-given mandates to gain breakthrough from the internal resistance which could symbolically be described as an internal governmental Armageddon. Sure felt like it.

Second, we were to contend for the Prince of Persia to be restrained, postponing, as it were, a literal Armageddon.

That said, it is no coincidence that President Trump's toughest challenge on both fronts would come during his third year. More on this in a moment. For now, let's take a look at Daniel's vigil because there's vital revelation in it for us.

Pray Until God Moves

You may have engaged in a Daniel fast. But it's important to note that Daniel didn't simply select twenty-one days to fast and pray, as many practice today. Instead, Daniel had become grieved by the extraordinary obstacles to fulfilling the mandate Cyrus had announced—restoring Jerusalem and restoring his covenant people back to their land. The prophet fasted and prayed until an angel of the Lord showed up and tangible breakthrough was secured.

The words *prayed until* are extremely important. Quitting or continuing would have made all the difference in Daniel's day. And it absolutely does in ours. Jesus said you will have what you hunger and thirst to obtain. You will have what you contend for. Pray until!

Spiritual Warfare in Government

When the angel finally showed up, he gave Daniel a surprising message.

> *Then he said to me, "Do not be afraid, Daniel, for from the first day that you set your heart on understanding this and on humbling yourself before your God, your words were heard, and I have come in response to your words. But the prince of the kingdom of Persia was withstanding me for twenty-one days.... Now I have come to give you an understanding of what will happen to your people in the latter days"* (Daniel 10:12–14).

I want you to see two things here. First, it was while serving as a governmental leader that Daniel was shown perhaps the greatest revelation on spiritual warfare in the entirety of the Old Testament. Ephesians 6, the classic passage on spiritual warfare written by the apostle Paul, can basically be described as an exposition of Daniel's experience in wrestling against principalities and powers. Here's how the great apostle summed it up:

> *Put on God's complete set of armor provided for us, so that you will be protected as you fight against the evil strategies of the accuser! Your hand-to-hand combat* [wrestling] *is not with human beings, but with the highest principalities and authorities operating in rebellion under the heavenly realms. For they are a powerful class of demon-gods and evil spirits that hold this dark world in bondage. Because of this, you must wear all the armor that God provides so you're protected as you confront the slanderer, for you are destined for all things and will rise victorious* (Ephesians 6:11–13 TPT).

This wrestling, by the way, is an inherent call to every believer. But don't miss this fact. Daniel was shown the mystery of spiritual conflict *as a believer functioning within government.*

Through every era, in every nation, the sphere of government is a primary battlefront for intense and intentional spiritual warfare. Do you serve in this sphere? Whether you're in diplomacy, intelligence, policy, or advisory, God holds you responsible to grow in competence in governmental prayer. As with Daniel, the success of your mission depends on it!

Secondly, Daniel's words were heard before the throne of God the very moment he set his heart in prayer. The angel was immediately dispatched in response to his words. Sometimes, you and I are praying for exactly what God showed us to seek, yet we experience no manifestation or answered prayer. Just as in Daniel's case, there's probably more going on than meets the eye.

Learn this, and you will be successful. Keep focused on fresh direction from the Lord. And pray until God's movement breaks through!

Restraining the Prince of Persia

The resistance to Daniel's answered prayer came from a supernatural being identified as the Prince of Persia. This demonic prince or principality was so empowered that he was able to completely block the angel's passage through the heavenly realms. The archangel Michael had to join the fight in order for the answered prayer to make it through.

Hell's blockades are no match for Heaven's firepower. But the level of resistance sometimes exposes the level of significance each answered prayer carries in releasing Kingdom advancement. Your Spirit-empowered prayer projects are a threat to the enemy. They are far more important than you know!

When reading the passage at the home of Gabriel Speaks, we knew by the Spirit that 2019 would mark a confrontation with the Prince of Persia. Ancient Persia is modern Iran. We saw how, if it were not mitigated in prayer, this conflict of crowns could even trigger World War III.

Conversely, we also knew that the Lord was moving powerfully among the people of Iran. For a few years now, an underground revival has been sweeping the land with the underground church of Iran growing exponentially. They suffer relentless persecution for their faith.[29] But we saw by the Spirit that, if war were to break out, the conflict could be used as an excuse by the regime to slaughter the Christians just as the Nazis slaughtered the Jews. Wouldn't it be just like the enemy to provoke America, a Christian nation, to engage in a war in which emerging believers in Jesus become the first casualties!

Prophetic leaders Rick and Patricia Ridings, recognized Mideast prayer leaders, received a similar directive from the Lord. During our 2018 Revolution conference, Rick had shared a dramatic vision. Rick saw the restraining hand of the Lord holding back an ungodly alliance between Iran and other nations to take over Jerusalem's Temple Mount. Rick felt that intensive prayer was needed throughout 2019 to see the vision come to pass and the harvest of the region preserved. *"Let My people go!"*

After much intercession and consultation, we sensed the Lord was opening a limited window of opportunity in this third year of Cyrus to see the Prince of Persia restrained, with a freedom movement catalyzed instead of another holocaust!

Persia, the Nazis, and Iran

Yeah, about that. In case you consider the word *holocaust* an exaggeration, let me point out two facts. First, ancient Persia changed its name to Iran at the request of the Nazi party. The Persian ambassador to Germany met with Nazi officials, who invited an alliance and even suggested a name change to reflect their collaboration.[30]

The Nazis venerated the Aryans as a superior race chosen to rule the world. Interestingly, Aryans originated from Persia. And Iran is simply a variant of their name, which makes the Prince of Persia far more than a minor regional power. Daniel was up against a brutal force determined to take out his entire race. This force resurfaced a generation after Daniel, empowering a brutal Persian counselor named Haman to plot the destruction of the Jewish people.

Here's a spiritual principle we will cover thoroughly in future chapters: *Covenants in the natural realm open doors in the spirit for principalities to impose their evil upon humanity.* There is no doubt the Prince of Persia was greatly empowered by Iran's newfound alliance with the Nazis. And it's no coincidence that, within only a few years, Hitler's "Final Solution" sought the eradication of the Jewish people from the entire face of the earth.

Beloved, this was the very force Daniel was up against during his twenty-one days of contending for answered prayer. He did not even know it.

And the same holds true today. A clear manifestation of the Prince of Persia's influence over the Iranian government can be seen in its resolute vow, repeated many times, to "wipe Israel off the map." Moreover, Israel is considered the "little satan" and America the "great satan."[31]

It's no coincidence that, within the third year of Trump's term, a confrontation with Iran brought us to the brink of World War III. Collaborative prayer among Israel, America, and many other nations was mobilized to catalyze a significant breakthrough which would see the Prince of Persia restrained. I personally believe that, when General Soleimani was taken down at the beginning of 2020, the principality empowering his military advancement was also restrained.

And Armageddon was postponed.

Launching the One Voice Prayer Movement

A global collaboration in forerunning prayer helped to secure a break-through regarding Iran. We realized that to overcome challenges on the national front, we also needed a united front of intercessors from across the spectrum of the Body of Christ. In short, we needed a Daniel movement here. Our cry for this movement would soon be answered in an extraordinary way.

I first met Paula White-Cain at the Global Ministerial to Advance Religious Freedom. As pastor to President Trump and leader of his Faith Initiative, Paula White-Cain is renowned for her poise, intellect, and pioneering work. But, until that event, I had no idea of her fierceness in prayer. She privately told me that the spiritual warfare she encountered in her role far superseded any she had ever encountered.

And it was very apparent she was determined to see God's breakthrough.

Pastor Paula's resolve was soon set in motion through the One Voice Prayer Movement (OVPM). On the July fourth weekend of 2019, Pastor Paula became stirred in her spirit that the time had come to birth a nationwide governmental prayer movement. She envisioned the non-partisan movement combining the strength of apostolic authority with real-time prophetic insight to bring breakthrough in the spiritual realm.

Todd Lamphere, chief of staff for Paula White Ministries, called a last-minute meeting. Dave Kubal of Intercessors for America, Jolene, and I were asked to lead the OVPM under Paula and Todd's direction.

Remember how Daniel birthed a prayer movement in the third year of Cyrus? In a strikingly similar way, the One Voice Prayer Movement was launched during this third year. Its very existence is a sign of God's intentionality in the thread of Daniel 10. The mandate of One Voice is best captured by Pastor Paula's own prayers from a White House ceremony on the 2019 National Day of Prayer:

> Now we lift up our president. You declared in Jeremiah 1:5 that
> before he was ever formed in his mother's womb, that you had
> set him apart and you had ordained him. You ordained all of

his days before one of them ever came into being, so not one day takes you by surprise....

I declare and decree that the White House is holy ground. We are not wrestling against flesh and blood but against principalities, wickedness and darkness, so we declare every demonic network is scattered right now! We declare right now that there is a hedge of protection over our president, first lady, every assignment, the purpose they carry and the mantle![32]

You can probably feel the anointing on this prayer. Please decree it yourself right now.

Cyrus—Make Israel Great Again

Fueled by Daniel's prayers, Cyrus launched a program to "make Israel great again." The efforts began with a now-legendary decree establishing his intentions and setting them into action.

> *Now in the first year of Cyrus king of Persia, in order to fulfill the word of the Lord by the mouth of Jeremiah, the Lord stirred up the spirit of Cyrus king of Persia, so that he sent a proclamation throughout all his kingdom, and also put it in writing, saying: "Thus says Cyrus king of Persia, 'The Lord, the God of heaven, has given me all the kingdoms of the earth and He has appointed me to build Him a house in Jerusalem, which is in Judah. Whoever there is among you of all His people, may his God be with him.... Every survivor, at whatever place he may live, let the men of that place support him with silver and gold, with goods and cattle, together with a freewill offering for the house of God which is in Jerusalem'"* (Ezra 1:1–4).

The essence of the Cyrus decree was to restore the desolate heritage of the land, which in Israel's case was the Temple in Jerusalem. It meant the rebuilding of the walls of Jerusalem so the city identified as the footstool of God's throne could not be plundered anymore. Finally, the decree included restoring the Jewish people back to their ancient homeland.

Sound familiar? It should because, within the Cyrus decree as recorded by Ezra, you will find essential elements that, if enacted, would also make America great again: first, to restore the desolate heritages of our land—spiritually as well as constitutionally; second, to rebuild our walls or restore the homeland security of our nation; third, to generate an economy sufficient to fund this restoration, both for the nation and for renewal in the Body of Christ; and, fourth, to empower the further restoration of Israel, God's ultimate covenant land.

The Resisters and the Watchmen

In response to Cyrus's decree, a delegation of Jews was sent back to Jerusalem to establish the restoration work. For a few years, the work went on uninterrupted. But, soon after, everything Cyrus set in motion came to a standstill.

> *Then the people of the land discouraged the people of Judah, and frightened them from building, and hired counselors against them to frustrate their counsel all the days of Cyrus king of Persia* (Ezra 4:4).

Ezra recorded how opposition by Israel's enemies forced the progress to cease. The "deep state" of the era hired lawyers and lobbyists to stall the entire process through lies, deception, and bureaucracy.

Lawyers, lobbyists, and lies—sound familiar? It should. We are in the same type of rebuilding process right now as in the days of Cyrus. And, by understanding the dynamics they faced, we can better perceive God's pathway to victory, including deep-aastate deliverance.

More on all of this in the next chapter.

The Global Call to Religious Freedom

Religious freedom nationally and globally is a key aspect of covenantal heritage that is being restored in our hour. In America, the Pilgrims and others founded our nation in covenant with God to empower religious freedom. On the four hundredth anniversary of the Mayflower Compact,

God is breathing on these covenantal foundations with fresh restoration winds worldwide.

Not coincidentally, the Pilgrims, along with other believers through the centuries, gained inspiration from King Cyrus and his decree.

Cyrus pioneered a new way forward. Previous to the Cyrus decree, ruling empires obliterated the religious structures of conquered lands and imposed their gods and culture upon the conquered people. Scholars view the Cyrus decree as the first documented, broad-scale effort by a ruler to secure religious freedom within the governed empire.[33]

Maybe it's not a coincidence that America's Cyrus has made religious freedom such a pillar of his administration. And as with Cyrus of old, maybe it's a reason why Trump has been so vehemently opposed.

One such time, President Trump became the first president to ever host a summit on religious freedom at the United Nations General Assembly. To my knowledge, it is the first event of its kind ever held during the UN General Assembly. In collaboration with Secretary of State Mike Pompeo and Ambassador of Religious freedom Sam Brownback, Trump gave voice to the voiceless from across the world who have been persecuted, violated, and abused simply for practicing their faith.

Again, it was stunning to discover that, until this meeting was convened, no gathering had apparently ever been held at the UN General Assembly to empower religious freedom and hold nations accountable. It was the first time their struggle had been validated within this hall.[34]

"Today, with one clear voice, the United States of America calls upon the nations of the world to end religious persecution!" Trump intoned. "Stop the crimes against people of faith. Release prisoners of conscience. Repeal laws restricting freedom of religion and belief. Protect the vulnerable, the defenseless, and the oppressed!"[35]

Trump continued by compelling "the governments of the world to honor the eternal right of every person to follow their conscience, live by their faith, and give glory to God."

But the global initiative never got the press it deserved. Instead, the press focused on a widespread rumor that House Intelligence Chairman

Adam Schiff was preparing to formally declare his pursuit of impeachment. The announcement would be made the next day as President Trump again addressed his peers.[36] This time, the entire world watched his address to the UN General Assembly.

"The future does not belong to the globalists!" Trump intoned in his General Assembly address. "The future belongs to the patriots!"[37]

The reply by Adam Schiff and House Speaker Nancy Pelosi came the same afternoon. "Impeach!" And watchman prayer in the third year of Cyrus was about to directly confront the deep state.

For Review

Please take a moment to reflect on what you've just read. We suggest taking notes as you answer questions below.

1. How has the message of Daniel 10 affected you? Please read the chapter for yourself and take notes on your impressions.

2. When news broke of rockets from Iran being fired at the US base, did you think it was the beginning of an Armageddon-like war? How did you pray? How are you praying now?

3. What stood out to you in comparing President Trump to Cyrus? Do you agree? Who are the Cyrus leaders in your immediate sphere? Who are the Daniels?

4. Have you ever experienced encounters with the Lord where revelation from His Word flowed freely? Describe the experience. What did He show you? How has it been applied to your life?

CHAPTER 4

DEEP STATE DELIVERANCE

SURROUNDED by many who sought to impeach him, President Trump closed out his roaring, poignant State of the Union address for 2020 with a defiant declaration. It was the night before his Senate trial was set to end with a dramatic acquittal. In a fashion extremely atypical for the president, he refused to pick a fight. Therefore, he did not reference the impeachment trial once; instead, he simply focused on the accomplishments that defined his presidency.

Trump's message to his colleagues and our nation closed with a confident tone, especially given the next day's deliberations. "The best is yet to come!" Trump simply declared. "God bless the United States of America!"

The chambers of the House of Representatives roared with applause. Immediately, House Speaker Nancy Pelosi, who launched the impeachment efforts with colleague Adam Schiff, picked up her copy of the speech and held it out for all to see. Behind Trump's back, while Senators and House members, Supreme Court Justices, administration officials, and thirty-seven million Americans watched, the Democratic leader ripped each page in half.

It is said that hell hath no fury as a woman scorned.

Personal vendettas aside, though, the real damage from the impeachment efforts was actually suffered by constitutional governance itself. A few of America's top leaders had essentially attempted a hostile takeover of the presidency, openly defying the votes of the American people.

Further, they chose to politicize institutions which should never be utilized as tools for partisan gain. First, the US intelligence community actually became weaponized by these leaders against the president. Second, for perhaps the first time in American history, the constitutional provision of impeachment also became weaponized as a tool for political conquest.

The facts alone suggest at least an unconscious correlation between Trump's dramatic stand against globalism and the immediate engagement of a hostile takeover of our national governance.[38] But by whom?

To answer this question, consider a dream pastor Jamie Jackson received in March 2016. President Trump was still candidate Trump, just a face in a crowd of Republican contenders. Few had ever heard of the deep state or its alleged influence. Our pastor friend from Brunswick, Georgia, certainly was not among them.

> I'm sitting in the presidential limo with our current president, which was then Barack Obama. In the dream there are a total of four men in the limo including myself, the president, the driver and one other person. None of the other men did I know or have ever seen with exception of President Obama. The driver turns to the president and says, "No one's here."
>
> The president says, "Let's wait a few minutes," and we just sit there.
>
> Then in the dream I looked at the president and said, "Can I ask you a question?"
>
> And he said, "Absolutely."
>
> I asked, "After you leave office, how many of your staff will remain in place in the government?"
>
> President Obama paused, and then said, "72%."

We then came to this pool. It had a shallow end and a deep end. At the moment, I had no idea why, but I stepped out of the car and did as he asked me to. I looked at him to see if he was going to get out of the limo, but he did not. At that moment, he told the driver to drive the limo into the water. The driver did as the president asked and drove the limo into the deep end of the pool.

I remember seeing that at the back of the pool there was a dark overshadowed place that seemed to be perfect for the car to fit in. This is where the driver parked the car, and at this point the limo became a part of the darkness and non-visible to the eye.[39]

Note that in the dream, the deep end of the pool became the place where President Obama was able to hide in plain sight. Symbolically, I believe it represents the deep state.

Since the time of this dream, it has become widely acknowledged that a covert alliance has been collaborating over many years to subvert the administration.[40] But that's the small part. In reality, officials over many decades have sought to capture America's freedom governance to extend their dark agenda and perhaps even to claim it as their own.

During the previous administration, much of their covert achievements seemed focused on marginalizing our Judeo-Christian foundations. Conservative institutions and the faith community both became targeted. And in a new low for weaponizing institutions to achieve political goals, the IRS was actually employed as a tool—even against the Billy Graham Evangelistic Association.[41]

For this reason and others, I personally believe a devotion to idolatry is woven into the very core of this alliance. Historically and even presently, political leaders seek to gain power by entering into covenants with entities the Bible conveys as principalities and powers. The Bible identifies them as covenants with death and hell (see Isa. 28:18).

Take a look at how Jesus was tempted. "Bow your knees to me, and all this can be yours" (see Matt. 4:9). There would be no cause for temptation if this practice yielded no results. Thank God, the verdict has already been rendered by the Lord. Covenant with death and hell is annulled!

Perhaps not since the days of Hitler has Western civilization been so publicly affected by such a cabal. From a biblical perspective, similar to Hitler, the ultimate goal of this alliance seems to be the cultivation of a global dictatorship, sourced in the occult, uniting nations under their influence. The book of Revelation actually prophesies their emergence. Some have called this alliance the *deep state.*

———————————

With this shared, I want to clarify again our wrestling is against forces of darkness in the spirit realm, catalyzing oppression and deception (Ephesians 6:12). You might be surprised that, as a watchman assigned by God over the White House, the president I have prayed for the most remains Barack Obama. Shortly before President Obama's first inauguration, the Holy Spirit shared His heart in a way that compelled us to fervent prayer. He impressed to me how our forty-fourth President stood between Moses and Pharaoh—hesitating between two opinions—and that he would choose one legacy or the other. In a vision, I looked toward the White House and saw the president wearing the mantle of Pharaoh, stretching forth his rod in extreme pride, defiance, and anger against the Lord. Immediately following, I saw the president on his knees in the Oval Office. Pride was gone, and he was weeping and crying out to the Lord. We continued to contend over this potential throughout both terms.[42]

Early Warnings

A stunning email came to us in June 2018 from friends in Israel. Due to the sensitivity of the issue, they wish to remain anonymous. "Israeli investigators have discovered evidence suggesting strategic plans to remove President Trump from office," warned the author. "Please pray with us Israeli believers for his protection and deliverance from any such evil scheme."

The warning got even more dire:

A reputable Israeli journalist revealed that PA President Abbas has maintained close ties with the previous Obama-Kerry administration. Recently, John Kerry met with a top confidant of Abbas.… Kerry reportedly told Agha to inform Abbas that Trump will not remain in office for long, with a good chance he would leave the White House within a year. He advised Abbas to stay strong against Trump and "play for time." Kerry offered both American and international help to the Palestinians.

The journalist our friends in Israel were referring to was Ben Caspit. He had written an article regarding Kerry and Abbas that appeared in the *Jerusalem Post*.[43]

Could it possibly be that former Secretary of State John Kerry actually passed on to Palestinian leader Mahmoud Abbas that President Trump would soon be removed from office? Remember this was 2018. What was in play?

Maybe it was not a coincidence that George Soros later echoed these same sentiments while speaking at the Davos Economic Forum in Switzerland, even while President Trump was in the next hall.

"I consider the Trump administration a danger to the world," globalist investor Soros intoned, as reported in a *Bloomberg* article. "But I regard it as a purely temporary phenomenon that will disappear in 2020, or even sooner."[44]

Or even sooner?

> "Let me tell you, you take on the intelligence community, they have six ways from Sunday at getting back at you," [Senator Chuck] Schumer told MSNBC's Rachel Maddow.
> "So even for a practical, supposedly hard-nosed businessman, he's being really dumb to do this."[45]

On January 3, 2017, Senator Schumer accused President Trump of making war against the intelligence communities by disputing accusations of alleged Russia collusion during the 2016 presidential campaign. Schumer's public "advice" seemed to be no favor. Instead, it seemed to be a warning shot for the Trump administration. Looking back at the nonstop assault through accusations of Russia collusion, the Mueller Report, and the impeachment attempt, these coercive warnings proved largely true.

Interestingly, on March 4, 2020, Senator Schumer fired another warning shot—this time against Supreme Court justices who were considering a case that could unravel the legalization of abortion through Roe v. Wade. In a vehement violation of the separation of powers, he actually made these threatening remarks by the steps of the Supreme Court—while the jurists were hearing the case, "I want to tell you, Justice Kavanaugh and Justice Gorsuch, you have unleashed a whirlwind, and you will pay the price," Schumer said as the judges heard the case's opening arguments. "You won't know what hit you if you go forward with these awful decisions!"[46]

Exactly what price was the New York senator warning they would be forced to pay?

And by whom?

Upholding Our Intelligence Communities

Both Supreme Court Justices and President Trump were targets of Senator Schumer's threats. But it was the reputation of our intelligence community that took the bullet. Every controversy the administration faced has now become saturated with suspicion of deep state collusion within our intelligence communities. What about the leaks of Trump's phone conversations? Illegal and illicit leaks to the press? Threats of a potential "heart attack"?

Was the impeachment accusation a manufactured crisis designed to take him down?

Let's make something clear. The intelligence community does not alone constitute the deep state. Some in the deep state work within the ranks of government, including the military, diplomacy, and intelligence, true. But also within the fields of entertainment, the media, health, finance, education, etc. Some are national, some international. My guess is that, behind the scenes, our intelligence communities are working hard to expose what essentially amounts to the intentional subversion of our government.

Part of our calling is to pray for the intelligence world. They are our counterparts as watchmen in the natural—our Joshuas and Calebs, Gideons, Mordecais and Esthers. Most are incredible patriots who give their all every day to keep America safe and strong. Their greatest victories are never celebrated publicly because to do so would make them vulnerable. And, for the same reason, their most heartbreaking setbacks are largely faced alone.

Or maybe they're not alone, at least if another watchman is praying. Let's undergird them!

Deep State Deliverance—Verdict from Heaven's Court

Now that we have a basic perspective, what exactly is the deep state? The term has come to refer to officials across the spectrum of government and culture, who are loyal to an outside entity such as a previous president or a foreign power, and they actively seek to undermine the governance of a legitimate administration to further their goals.

Biblically, think of Sanballat and Tobiah's influence against Nehemiah. They couldn't defeat Nehemiah from the outside, so they set up residence within Israel's very Temple.

That said, in our nation, disempowering covert sabotage from the deep state is key to empowering the rulership of legitimate constitutional governance.

In the early hours of January 29, 2018, I saw a response from Heaven's Court regarding the continual threats against the president and against American governance itself. I literally awoke praying a passage from Acts 4:29, *"Behold their threatenings: and grant unto thy servants boldness"* (KJV).

From this visitation, I knew the corporate cry of God's covenant people had actually been entered into Heaven's Court as a united plea. Our cry defined not only the injustice against us, but the very verdict we sought to receive. And we obtained it. Based on Daniel 7:22, this "turnaround verdict" has been rendered in favor of the saints, restraining the beast, and releasing the saints to possess the Kingdom.

> *"Why did the nations rage, and the people plot vain things? The kings of the earth took their stand, and the rulers were gathered together against the Lord and against His Christ.... Now, Lord, look on their threats, and grant to Your servants that with all boldness they may speak Your word, by stretching out Your hand to heal, and that signs and wonders may be done through the name of Your holy Servant Jesus." And when they had prayed, the place where they were assembled together was shaken* (Acts 4:25–31 NKJV).

In like fashion, God has brought our corporate cry before Heaven's Court. A verdict has been issued. The Lord is usurping the deep state where the deep state has planned to usurp His covenant and His covenant people.

The Lord is overcoming the "deficit of justice"! This phrase was Holy Spirit-breathed to me in the early hours of June 15, 2018. Just before dawn, I stepped onto our perch overlooking a spectacular blood-red sky over Washington DC. Note that it is highly atypical for me to watch a sunrise. But the Spirit of God was emphasizing something. He is awakening the dawn of a new day of justice in America. Then I heard the Holy Spirit clearly speak to me, "I will overcome the deficit of justice!" I knew this was referencing both the Department of Justice (DOJ) and specific justice issues across America. Since this time, the DOJ has made major strides in exposing the targeted, covert targeting of the Trump administration.[47]

The tremors of His movement, releasing a sweeping river of His redemptive justice, have already been felt. God's river will sweep the nation. But the waters covering the deep state will recede, no longer covering the actions of these sharks. They will be sidelined and stranded.

Our Deep State

Before we seek to deal with the deep state in government, I believe we should seek deliverance from the spiritual deep state seeking to undermine our personal lives. Some spiritual influences are present because of our own sin and compromise and some because of generational sin. These forces are literally aligned with "foreign powers," seeking to destroy our lives and freedom. Ultimately, these forces seek to sabotage the governance of King Jesus in our lives.

Thank God, Christ died to redeem us. We can be delivered from the false governance of the "deep state" within! It's important to note that the same principles that usher individuals into transformation also apply to bringing our respective spheres into transformation.

Genesis 1:2–4 gives us a great picture:

> *The earth was* [became] *without form and void, and darkness was over the face of the deep. And the Spirit of God was hovering over the face the waters. And God said, "Let there be light," and there was light. And God saw that the light was good. And God separated light from the darkness* (ESV).

Darkness was on the face of the *deep*. Note that God is not scared of the darkness in the deepest parts of your heart and spirit, where the real you resides. Jesus gave His life to redeem you—to separate light from darkness. That's the greatest "deep state deliverance" we can obtain.

Note also that the Lord made declarations over the areas of darkness in which Holy Spirit was moving. Let's identify where His Spirit genuinely is operating and then move with Him in our prayer and declarations. This paradigm—identifying where the Spirit is moving and then simply moving with Him—has proven extremely effective both in personal ministry and in governmental prayer. It is amazing how quickly our efforts are met with His spontaneous results—quite literally, at light speed!

As pictured in Jamie Jackson's dream, darkness is truly over the surface of the deep, keeping hidden what lies beneath. But the Spirit is again brooding over the waters of the deep state. The light is beginning to shine in a whole new way. And God is bringing genuine freedom. *Let there be light!*

The Resistance

Long before the impeachment hearings, America was thrust into a three-year storm of unceasing accusations over alleged Russia collusion by President Trump. This comprehensive effort was launched from the moment it became clear Trump won the elections. Accusations were validated both to government and the media by James Clapper and John Brennan, the highest officials in former President Obama's intelligence world.[48]

That's a lot of clout. And, in a new low for journalism, the American media broadcast these false claims as absolute truth.

Amazingly, these same allegations were later proven false by the report issued by FBI investigator Robert Mueller. Trump was exonerated. Interestingly, the Mueller Report was issued on April 18, 2019, the anniversary of the date Paul Revere rode to launch the American Revolution.

Yet, from that moment on, many of the same leaders sought new allegations to foment into a crisis mandating impeachment. It was found by Representative Adam Schiff, Chairman of the House Intelligence Committee, with a CIA whistleblower alleging improper conduct by President Trump on a conference call to the Ukraine. Accusations against President Trump revolved around a high-level call made between Trump and the nation's president. The CIA whistleblower later warned officials about a potential abuse of power.

For Representative Adam Schiff to make the case against President Trump, he had to actually expose a much clearer example of governmental abuse of power regarding the Ukraine—by the Democratic frontrunner for the 2020 presidential elections.

> Until this time, few Americans knew of former Vice President Joe Biden's role in the Ukraine, let alone that he openly shared on video about his demands from the Ukraine of an apparent quid pro quo deal. *"You're not getting the billion dollars.... If the prosecutor is not fired, you're not getting the money!"*[49]

Amazingly, this prosecutor in question was investigating a Ukraine energy corporation for which VP Biden's son Hunter served as a board member. According to reports, he was hired right after his father was tasked by President Obama with overseeing diplomacy in the nation. Note that Hunter Biden had no previous experience in the energy industry. Yet the former vice president's son was taking in tens of thousands of dollars per month in compensation.

Quid pro quo? You be the judge.

Further, it was soon discovered the CIA whistleblower had worked with VP Biden on the Ukraine. He remained at the White House with the Trump administration until being transferred back to CIA headquarters, apparently over concerns of leaks.

The narrative reads like a spy novel. You really can't make this stuff up.

House Impeachment Launches on Halloween

Perhaps it's telling that Representative Schiff chose Halloween as the date to start the formal process of impeachment with a vote on the House floor. Whether he knew it or not, Schiff's selection of the date synergized with occult practitioners across the nation who vowed to "curse President Trump until he is bound and removed from office." Their words, not mine. The *Washington Examiner* ran a story on their efforts on October 18, a few weeks before Halloween. "Participants in the ritual, which has been performed regularly since Trump's inauguration, are taking particular encouragement from Democrats' recent launch of an impeachment inquiry," according to the *Examiner* story, "which they see as a sign their efforts are working."[50]

I know I keep saying it, but you really can't make this stuff up!

Perhaps this explains why simply praying for the president has been at times so overwhelming. A former veteran now working for the administration privately described it as "more intense than the front lines of Afghanistan." That's sobering.

The impeachment effort which began with the House Intelligence hearings was then transferred to the House Judiciary for final hearings.

Amazingly, the effort which began on October 31 was culminated on December 13. This all transpired, then from Halloween to Friday the thirteenth. Two occult high holidays essentially served as bookends to the House impeachment trial.

But God would not be defied.

The Gavel Falls! Impeachment Turnaround Secured

A small group of leaders took a prayer tour through the three branches of government on Tuesday, November 5, a year to the day of the 2020 elections. We were closing our time at the US Capitol when the Lord arrested me with a momentary prophetic experience. Its brevity betrayed its true importance.

Before us was the actual cornerstone of the US Capitol, laid by President George Washington. Many consider it symbolic of the cornerstone of American democracy, faults and all. In the laying of the cornerstone, a Masonic ceremony committed both the stone and the institution built upon it to a deceptive mixture of God and idols.

As we were praying, I turned and saw something that in the natural simply wasn't there. Much like Daniel's vision of the handwriting on the wall, a judge's gavel appeared from a wall and struck with fierce intentionality. The sheer magnitude of authority expressed in the vision made me tremble. I heard the words, "Covenant with death and hell annulled" (see Isa. 28:18).

We had just made some potent declarations: covenant with God divorced from idolatry secured, restraining order against demonic powers issued and enforced, and forces empowering deception overthrown. We had decreed turnaround and declared that Jesus be seated as the cornerstone of our national governance—in all three branches of government.

And the gavel fell as if in response, sealing Heaven's verdict of turnaround.

When Parties Openly Defy the Lord, the Gavel Falls

What does the turnaround look like?

In September 2019, the Lord gave me a prophetic experience conveying the potential of a *sweep for life* in the 2020 elections. I'm not seeking to be political here or tell you how to vote. Both parties have severe faults. Also, there are aspects of God's intended turnaround conditional and dependent on the obedience of leaders entrusted to the office.

But many aspects are not.

I wrote in September, "I also sensed one particular party had so openly defied the Lord, in word and in deed, that He was ready to bring the gavel fully down."[51]

In truth, I had totally forgotten this perception when, on November 5—again a year from the 2020 elections—the vision came of the gavel falling in the Capitol.

Prophetic Perception on 2020 Elections

The post which prophesied the gavel falling ran on September 25, 2019.[52] In a vision, a bridge to the White House appeared. I walked across the bridge and went tentatively through an open door. At that moment the Lord spoke to me clearly, "I keep moving to open doors you keep trying to shut!"

I wholeheartedly repented.

In the vision, President Trump was at the top of stairs with crimson carpet in his private residence, kneeling as if praying and pondering. He signaled to me, inviting me to enter into prayer.

His hands were on a miniature sculpture of the Capitol. Interestingly, it was brown.

In the vision, I was a little taken aback. Was President Trump seeking to reshape the Capitol? Immediately, the word of the Lord came, "What I desire to do next in this nation requires peace between the two offices!"

This prophetic perception is a direct reference to Zechariah 6:13, *"Yes, it is He who will build the temple of the Lord, and He who will bear the honor and sit and rule on His throne. Thus, He will be a priest on His throne, and the counsel of peace will be between the two offices."*

But I also knew intuitively the Lord was speaking about a sweep in the 2020 elections which would give Trump's political party the majority in both the House and Senate.

I was frankly astonished. Friend, if you know Jolene and me, we are governmental, but we are definitely not political. No king but Jesus! So, for this prophetic perception to even cross my mind was totally out of my wheelhouse.

I sensed in this experience that the Lord is shaking the highest seats of authority across the political spectrum, bringing much-needed correction and redemptive exposure. But it was in this experience when I also sensed one particular party had so openly defied the Lord that He was ready to bring the gavel fully down.

Life Prevails Over Covenant with Death

Finally, the vision shifted, and I was looking over Capitol Hill. I saw a back door open from the Senate to the Supreme Court. A person walked from one building to the next. Then the entirety of the area became a giant womb. A beautiful child was within the membrane of this womb, sucking his or her thumb.

I knew this represented the prevailing of life over the covenant with death and hell which empowered abortion in America.

What does the "gavel falling" truly look like?

Seems to me it looks like a sweep, catalyzing the very thing Trump's opponents are trying hardest to prevent. It's the full completion of the turnaround for life in America.

But if that's true, how much of this is conditional? How will it happen?

Given the current state of conflict in Washington DC, I cannot but wonder what lies before us that would so infuriate Americans that the masses would vote to completely eradicate the influence of a particular party. I also have to wonder if things would be different if leaders were to truly repent and realign with the Lord.

Let me be clear on something: In the prophetic experience, I saw President Trump on his knees, praying. He was in a place of repentance, humility, and prayer, with a genuine cry coming forth from his heart. To me, this conveys that the summons of *teshuvah* (repentance) is vital for all leaders, even including President Trump, to secure God's best in this season. That's the alignment the Lord is seeking.

There are those whose top priority, even during this coronavirus crisis, remains to "bind the president until he is removed from office." But by verdict of Heaven's Court, turnaround has been decreed. The details of how this will be and is being played out, I do not know.

But the handwriting is on the wall.

12/12: The Midnight Turnaround

Yorktown, Virginia, is ground zero for America's freedom. During the American Revolution, the riverside battlefield marked the surrender of the British and, therefore, the securing of America's future. Over many years, I have sensed that a time would come to connect with saints on this very ground and declare *victory* in the revolution for our day. And, in December 2019, the moment finally arrived.

The impeachment fight was at its height, and the spiritual conflict was overwhelming. But the Lord had spoken to me the date—"12/12"—as the pivot point.

My spirit leapt as God seemed to be conveying a double-portion breakthrough for this time. The number twelve represents both government and apostolic ministry. Further, the date seemed appropriate given that a blood moon coming to fullness at 12:12 a.m. on January 21, 2019, had launched us into this yearlong travail of prayer. God was speaking in very personal language to confirm His direction.

We had no idea then that the date 12/12 would also play host to a lunar phenomenon, with a full moon reaching its fullness at exactly 12:12 a.m. Nor did we or anyone else know that the entire House impeachment hearings would culminate the following day, on Friday the thirteenth of December. God had scheduled His Victory Day for the culmination of this spiritual revolution waged over 2019. It was time for His midnight riders to be released for turnaround. And for this dramatic moment, we were summoned to the very ground where freedom was first secured for our land.

And as if this were not enough, God gave us another sign to fully convince us the project had been successfully completed and His turnaround secured.

Our prophetic friend Lynnie Harlow had decided to join us for the journey. We traveled as a team from Washington DC to Virginia Beach. Chris Mitchell Jr. secured rooms for us at the Founders Inn on the campus of the CBN and Regent University. Given the work ahead, everybody was seeking afternoon naps.

Lynnie didn't get one as, suddenly, an angelic host appeared in Lynnie's room at the Founders Inn, just by her doorway. According to Lynnie, the angel appeared similar to a Roman centurion, with a robe that was white and gold and a spear of gold. The most important thing about this angel was that he was continually kneeling, head bowed in reverence to the Lord.

I know the sudden appearance of an angel of the Lord may sound far-fetched for some, me included. Lynnie is genuine, honest, and extremely accurate prophetically. In all our years of friendship, never had she shared with us about any such experience. It was totally new territory.

Further, please remember that the Lord used the appearance of an angelic host to Daniel as a sign of victory in the spiritual battle he had faced. Sometimes, we forget that, through Jesus, we have a better covenant than even what Daniel and the patriarchs operated in. They longed for the access and experience with God we often take for granted.

The word of the Lord came to Lynnie that this angelic host was an angel of revelation. Holy Spirit then spoke the following to her: The full moon at 12:12 a.m. on 12/12 is a sign of this nation's rapid turnaround, as well as a rapid turnaround for Israel, for Britain, and other nations.

Lynnie then felt impressed to read Job 37:12. Not being a student of Job, she had to look it up. The passage says, "It changes direction, turning around by His guidance, that it may do whatever He commands it on the face of the inhabited earth."

At God's command, *turnaround.* The appearance of this angel was a sign to us. God's covenantal deliverance had been sealed in victory.

Ministry that night at Chris Mitchell's church was off the charts. Then a full moon began to appear as a giant celestial ball, hovering just above the skyline, glowing a muted orange. As it ascended, it progressively shed its orange hue and huge, pretentious stature. Shining with greater intensity, the moon reached its fullness at precisely 12:12 a.m. on 12/12. To us, its hovering prophesied as a sign of the victory and rapid turnaround the Lord was granting.

More than six hundred people from fifty-four states and three nations joined for a special "Midnight Shining" prayer call during this time, similar to the call during the Blood Moon eleven months earlier. Lynnie Harlow shared her "rapid turnaround" experience. James Goll shared a word on midnight riders. As 12/12 was election day in the United Kingdom (UK), friends from England led us in prayer for a Boris Johnson victory. Later in the day, it happened.

The next day, Friday the thirteenth, the House Judiciary Committee held its final hearings in an impeachment effort that had begun officially on October 31. The House later voted in favor of removing President Trump from office, whereupon the impeachment trial shifted to the Senate.

Then on the afternoon of 12/12, our team gathered on the Yorktown battlefield to re-present the declarations for turnaround God had given us. It was finally time to release the sound of victory.

On February 5, a day after President Trump's dramatic State of the Union speech, the Senate acquitted him. The gavel had indeed fallen. In fact, Chief Justice John Roberts, who presided over the hearings, was presented with a Senate gavel as a gift. Proceedings thus closed, Chief Justice Roberts made his way back from the Capitol to the Supreme Court, precisely following the path seen in the vision.

Between the midnight moons and during the third year of America's Cyrus, a year of unyielding intercession bore tremendous results. Armageddon was postponed. The hostile takeover of the Trump presidency was restrained, and a victory for freedom was secured. Our Revolution conference even brought the crowning of a move of God.

Then came the global pandemic.

For Review

Please take a moment to reflect on what you've just read. We suggest taking notes as you answer questions below.

1. What are your perceptions on the deep state? Is it real? Is it a threat? What aspects stood out to you in this chapter?

2. How have you perceived the resistance against President Trump? Is it fair? How have you prayed?

3. God wants to grant "deep state deliverance" in our own hearts. List areas of your life where generational patterns of sin or sabotage have challenged you. Seek the Lord over these issues. Seek counsel and healing prayer as needed. It's worth it all!

4. Have you been praying for our intelligence communities? For our military? In many ways, they are the counterparts in the natural to watchmen in prayer. Ask the Lord how you can help them keep watch!

CHAPTER 5

FORGED IN THE VALLEY

Yea, though I walk through the valley of the shadow of death, I will fear no evil; for You are with me.

Psalm 23:4 NKJV

THE *Drudge Report* headlines of 10:45 p.m. on April 3, 2020, read:

One thousand US deaths in a single day. America may never be the same. DC Mayor: 1 in 7 could be infected. Kissinger: pandemic alters world order.

Economy in shambles, Trump scrambles for new 2020 message. No masks for Trump. Nation facing hunger crisis as food banks soar. Record number of Americans NOT in labor force. Payrolls drop 701,000 in March. Thirty percent of mortgages will default? Quarter of Americans have no emergency savings.

Virus hits Boris Johnson hard; they've barricaded the doors at number 10. After ignoring warnings, Israeli ultra-Orthodox hit by virus. Wuhan residents line up for hours to buy graves. Creeping authoritarianism has finally prevailed.[53]

And that's just one moment from one evening, in a three-month vigil that promised to stretch into at least early summer.

Once again, I've begun to take regular prayer walks circling the White House, praying for President Trump and his team. In this delicate balance between crisis mitigation, recovery, and the preservation of our freedom, our intercession is needed more than we could possibly understand. On the first few journeys, I sensed little to nothing, outside the discomfort of a cold mist that chilled me to the bone. But discerning the spiritual climate has now become almost second nature. It is strange, though. Many times, when my internal alarm is at its highest, the briefings from President Trump are conveying the opposite.

One thing is clear. America is truly at the threshing floor. And there is far more going on than meets the eye.

Forged in the Valley

No headlines warned of their plight. But the virus, especially when combined with other diseases, viciously demanded a tithe.

Then came the virus. Over thirteen hundred soldiers died from it.

True freedom—God's way at least—is forged in the valley more than the mountaintop.

Many, many years prior, on a very different land, during Passover, Joshua crossed the waters of the Jordan Valley. His army was eager to conquer the Promised Land. Instead, the Lord instructed Joshua to honor covenant by circumcising all of his troops who had not yet been circumcised (see Josh. 5). The skin of their manhood severed, virtually every soldier was completely incapacitated at a time when their camp was most vulnerable to attack.

God paired Gideon's army down to three hundred in the shadow of Mount Gilboa (see Judg. 7).

David fought Goliath in the valley of Elah. Little shepherd boy versus a man-beast. The odds were certainly against David, yet he prevailed (see 1 Sam. 17).

Elijah transferred his mantle in the Jordan Valley, near where Moses passed (see 1 Kings 19).

John the Baptist returned to the same region to turn a nation to her Bridegroom.

Jesus was baptized by John in this valley, then was thrust into the wilderness to be tempted by the devil. He returned to this valley of baptism just before embracing the cross.

As noted, the Pilgrims overcame excruciating trials to forge a nation in covenant with God. And 150 years later, tasked with carrying out their legacy, George Washington faced down impossible odds at Valley Forge.

Prophetically, Valley Forge is America's Jordan Valley. And, as of Passover 2020, America is camped there.

In a prophetic experience back in 2012, I saw a vision of George Washington as a general. He was standing tall in a refined colonial uniform. He had a fierce countenance, courageous but clearly unsettled. Then Washington turned to me, and with tears in his eyes said, "I only saw in part."

Immediately, I knew the Lord was showing me Washington's heart regarding freemasonry. His participation always puzzled me. Even then it was overt idolatry, abhorrent to God and detrimental to mankind. But in Washington's generation and in ours, sometimes we are simply blind to blatant sins which have been embraced as societal norms.

The vision continued. The Father of our nation turned to me again and spoke to me with great intensity, "I am again praying by the river."

Washington praying? It literally took a vision from God for me to see our first president's humanity, and his genuine reliance on God.

Repenting, I searched for more information. It turns out that area farmers reported how Washington often prayed by the Schuykill River and sometimes with loud cries. Morning by morning, he would intercede for his troops—for their welfare, the success of their training, their provision, the Lord's intervention to preserve this freedom movement in its most vulnerable state.[54]

From the vision, I knew we were facing a similar period of history where our freedom could be imperiled. A cloud of witnesses was contending from beyond the veil. We had been summoned to the same sacred task.

The troops gathered at Valley Forge in Washington's day were not trained soldiers. They were tradesmen, farmers, blacksmiths, and dockworkers, with a few doctors and diplomats thrown in to bolster legitimacy. Against all odds, probably in the midst of prayer, Washington made a dramatic decision, and Valley Forge became the camp where infected and forlorn troops were trained to become the strongest fighting force in the known world. The tide of the revolution soon turned. American forces, in partnership with France, conquered the global empire holding them in subjugation. *And a freedom movement became a freedom nation.*

Again—from God's perspective—true freedom is forged in the valley.

One more note on Valley Forge. The British army had actually used a plague spreading through the thirteen colonies as a force for their advantage. English doctors inoculated their troops against smallpox, making them largely immune to its devastating effects. Meanwhile, the Continental Army could have been completely incapacitated through its spread—without a single bullet being fired.

Maybe driven by another fervent prayer time, Washington made a very controversial decision. At Valley Forge, he moved to inoculate his troops as well. It likely preserved the outcome of the American Revolution.

China's Numbers

It now appears that the magnitude of coronavirus casualties was grossly underreported by China's government. The entire world was misled.[55] Leaders initially refused to even indicate the outbreak was real. Was it negligence? Was their motivation simply to save face? Or was a decision made that, if China were to suffer a potentially overwhelming crisis, retaining a balance of power demanded the rest of the world suffer too?

Whatever the motivation, China's actions crippled any initial hope of containment. In late March, US intelligence confirmed a cover-up.

Meanwhile, the entire Western world had prepared for a severe thunderstorm when a Category 5 hurricane descended and decided to stay.[56]

Chuck Pierce prophesied back in 1986 that "starting in 2020, China makes its biggest move toward economic domination worldwide."[57] Could their response to the coronavirus have that effect? Chuck also warned that, if America did not take a strong stand in the Lord, by 2026 China would not only lead the global economy but have a prevailing leverage over our nation.

Religious freedom is virtually nonexistent in China. In the age of digital surveillance, persecution of Christians and other religious minorities has rarely been so intense—or so comprehensive. Not only are followers of Jesus punished, but with the "social credit score policy" their families are too—whether or not they are believers.[58]

Imagine what could happen if this totalitarian expression were to gain a prevailing economic dominance globally. The rise of a global surveillance state seems almost inevitable. So does worldwide persecution.

Good thing God is birthing a freedom movement concurrently. A global Moses-Joshua movement is now at hand. The mandate today is similar to the days of Exodus. And it is truly Passover time. *"Let My people go!"*

The Freedom Movement

The United States has now surpassed China as the global epicenter of the pandemic. New York City, arguably the global capital of finance, is facing an unimaginable crisis. My thoughts turn again to the evening three years ago, overlooking the broad cityscape of Washington DC, when Holy Spirit spoke to me about a "midnight crisis" coming by 2020. It's amazing how the novel coronavirus first showed up on the WHO's radar on New Year's Eve 2019.

If the warning on the midnight crisis proved accurate, then the rest of the sequence the Lord showed me will prove so as well—including a midnight turnaround with a freedom movement breaking loose that secures our inheritance for generations to come, even for the unborn.

Back in 1983, prophet Bob Jones was shown that a defining movement was coming which would marry the miracles of Exodus with the miracles of Acts. "Let My people go" would be joined with the restoration of God's glory (Acts 2), the release of the miraculous, and a rebirth of the Church. Multitudes would come to Jesus. Bob described this movement as the greatest move of deliverance that had ever been seen on the North American continent.

We describe it as a spiritual revolution. For this reason, in 2013 we even launched our yearly Revolution gatherings from Valley Forge. In our hearts, there was no ground more sacred to set a course for victory.

Moses and Joshua

President Ronald Reagan noted that "freedom is a fragile thing and it is never more than one generation away from extinction. We didn't pass it to our children in the bloodstream. It must be fought for, protected, and handed on for them to do the same."[59] For this reason, the passing of the torch from generation to generation is a matter of life or death. Just as every Cyrus needs a Daniel, every Moses needs a Joshua.

In a visitation two years ago, the Lord showed Jolene and me in a very personal way that He was now initiating a transition in leadership from Moses to Joshua. Great importance was placed on the year 2020. The word showed how, as we crossed the threshold of the four hundredth anniversary of God's covenant with our land, a great inheritance is poised to be released, defined by a promise made to Moses that was carried through by Joshua.

Be strong and courageous, for you shall give this people possession of the land which I swore to their fathers to give them (Joshua 1:6).

This promise is good news as we move through the challenges of 2020. But here's what I'm struggling with. None of us realized that a virus from China would especially target the Moses generation of this hour. In many cases, there is no other option but for Joshuas to arise now.

From the ashes of World War II to the explosion of digital technology, our fathers and mothers redefined our world. They faced down communism, secured civil rights, overhauled government, and oversaw the miraculous rebirth of Israel.

There are still a few among us who survived Hitler's concentration camps. I grieve over every loss as the coronavirus robs us of their voices.

On the negative side, rebellion against God became a celebrated virtue for many in this generation. Sexual immorality, abortion, drugs, and divorce crippled the lives of millions. Witchcraft and even satanism were popularized. Saul Alinsky even invoked Lucifer as a role model for community activism. Both Hillary Clinton and Barack Obama claimed Alinsky as a mentor.[60]

But God raised up a movement to turn the tide. Many of our fathers and mothers were born again in the Jesus Revolution. Their pioneering spirit birthed the apostolic and prophetic movements, and the prayer movements which run concurrently with these. Their hard-won wisdom framed them to endure.

Note that the Moses generation has never been behind. Actually, quite the opposite. Almost always you can count on them to be several steps ahead. My personal prayer remains that Moses and Joshua will have many more years together, so emerging leaders can at least have a chance to catch up! I mean this in all sincerity.

From painful experiences, I also know that many Moses leaders deeply yearn for a Joshua to carry on their legacies but find few genuinely willing to embrace the call. Everything shared here goes for ministry and government. A generation raised on entitlement is eager to receive. But beyond the fleeting glory of an inherited mantle, precious few have proven willing to embrace the forging process which comes in the valley. Integrity has faltered. And the crisis of leadership has proven devastating.

As uncomfortable as these subjects are, they must now be explored. In reality, the coronavirus crisis initiated a process that was already at hand in the decade of the 2020s.

With this at heart, the commissioning experience you're about to read is one of the most sacred experiences we have ever had. I believe it serves a signal to the Body of Christ. The time is at hand for Joshuas to arise.

The chronicle of the commissioning is taken from our posting on August 18, 2018.

Joshua Arise! Visitation and Commissioning

On 8/8/2018, the Lord granted an amazing visitation during a prayer time focused on receiving communion. Pastors Jamie and Redonnia Jackson had given us a silver communion fountain with eight cups. I felt led to receive the Table of the Lord from each of the eight cups.

I suddenly became aware of a high-ranking angelic host in our living room. His wings were feathered and brilliant white. They encompassed me, literally enfolding around me. Within my spirit, I heard the voice of the Lord.

"Moses My servant is dead. Now therefore arise." The words of Joshua chapter one continued to flow. "Now therefore arise, go over this Jordan, you and all this people, into the land that I am giving to them, to the people of Israel."

All at once I became cognizant of a sword resting on my left shoulder, then my right shoulder. It was a similar sensation to a treasured ministry commissioning we received a few years previously from apostle John Benefiel. Our old rank was removed, and a new rank conferred.

I wasn't seeking anything more than to give myself afresh to Jesus through communion on August 8, but the Lord had other plans. Two questions immediately came to mind. First, what just happened? Second, exactly who was the "Moses" who had died?

The second query was answered first. In a vision, I saw a cloud of witnesses. And in the cloud of witnesses, I saw two people: our friend Bob Jones and our friend Jill Austin. Both were mighty prophets who had gone on to be with the Lord, leaving a portion of their legacy to us.

It was just a flash, but deep was calling to deep. And I knew the Lord was activating deposits of His heart, His covenant, and His anointing that had been imparted through these amazing leaders. They are now in the immediate presence of the Lord. We are tasked with walking out the covenant dream they lived for and gave their lives for, including the prophetic expression of God's Spirit, angelic release, and even the Glory Train movement which Bob had prophesied.

I actually experienced this during the visitation. Suddenly, I felt myself *moving through* the gates we had just warred to see opened. Momentum is being recovered. The Glory Train, this freedom movement, is now rolling through the gates.

Jolene came home from her prayer meeting that same afternoon after a similar encounter with the Lord. She heard the Lord say the date 8/8/18 represents "double portion 8:18." Deuteronomy 8:18 declares that God gives power to gain wealth to establish His covenant. We have now moved through these gates!

What was the Lord initiating through this commissioning? Ponder the movement Joshua inherited. A Moses movement, fueled by four hundred years of prayer for deliverance, ushered the people of God from bondage to freedom. Even though Moses' journey was cut short, *the movement was not*. The angel of the Lord who partnered with Moses was released by God to partner with Joshua to complete the turnaround!

Immediately, I thought of the prophetic word our friend Anne Tate of Glory of Zion released to our home group just weeks before. Anne prophesied the Lord was releasing a "finishing angel"— to complete the work He had begun in Washington DC, even generations before. Anne's ministry to our home group, overlooking all of Washington DC, was pivotal. I really believe the "finishing angel" she saw weeks before actually brought this new commission. Heaven perpetuated the blessing she deposited!

I think it's so amazing that the year 2020 marks the four hundredth anniversary of America's covenant with God. It's time for 20/20 vision. There's an assignment, started by our fathers and mothers, that God wants this generation to complete. May you receive the fullness of your commissioning in a new way even as you read these words, *No king but Jesus!*

That's where our post from August 2018 ends.[61] And it's where the book in your hand actually begins. *"Now therefore, arise!"* Because it's time to complete the turnaround. Both the responsibility and the opportunity are yours.

New York—Exodus, Abortion, Awakening

On a personal level, both the scope of our assignments and the effectiveness of our ministry increased substantially after our commissioning. This was imperative in light of the next assignment given.

A major turnaround that God is summoning our nation to complete is overthrowing the scourge of abortion. Scripture is clear that unjust bloodshed invokes God's judgment. The cause and effect are as immutable as gravity. And, in April 2019, the Lord spoke a specific warning to Jolene regarding New York, abortion, and a coming loss of life that would be similar to the Exodus Passover.

Jolene and I were ministering in Houston at the time. Earlier in the day, we had prayed over the largest abortion clinic in the nation. In light of the coronavirus crisis and its prevalence in New York, some of what we share here may prove controversial. It's not meant to be. But Jolene did receive this word, and she shared it on our online post on April 17, 2019:

> I saw during worship how God has been dealing with abortion in America in a way that's similar to how He dealt with abortion in Exodus. He's doing the same with the idolatry behind it.
>
> And it's now a Passover moment to deal with the 10th plague, the spirit of death. The Lord highlighted the 9th plague, where we've been in the midst of darkness so tangible that it can be felt. And we're moving into the 10th plague which is dealing with the spirit of death through abortion.… You have to understand we're going into an extended season of Passover, not just a week of Passover. It means God's work is going to be through an entire time period until He is done dealing with this spirit of death through abortion in America!

Exodus 12 covers the Passover. In Exodus 13 Israel's firstborn are consecrated. When God's dealings in this Passover season have been completed, then there will be a consecration of the firstborn in our nation similar to the consecration of the first-born in Exodus![62]

The rest of the April 2019 posting focused our upcoming Glory Train journey to shift America from abortion to awakening.

Back on Christmas morning in 2018, the Lord had given me clear instructions for this in a dream. New York was highlighted in the dream. In it, I was standing at the base of the Washington Monument on August 8, having just launched the Glory Train tour on July 22 at Faneuil Hall Boston. I sat up in bed to pray into the dream, and immediately revelation came. We were being summoned to Faneuil Hall to receive the next phase of execution of God's Daniel 7:22 verdict for this hour. Then for the northeastern part of the journey, we were to follow the angelic pathway outlined in a legacy vision chronicled below, from Albany and Lowville, New York, to the Washington Monument in Washington DC. This portion of the trip would have a focus on shifting America from abortion to awakening.

Babies in the Sky—Vision of New York Awakening

On 08/08/08, or August 8, 2008, Jolene and I found ourselves in an open field in the small town of Lowville, New York, surrounded by worshipers and intercessors seeking to uncap a legacy well of the Second Great Awakening. The brief narrative of a nearby gravestone explained it all. It read simply, "Daniel Nash, laborer with Finney, mighty in prayer."

If you're unfamiliar with American revival history, Charles Finney was a primary catalyst of the Second Great Awakening in Upstate New York. He was one of the first evangelists to ever "hire" a full-time intercessor. It was a smart investment because his friend Daniel Nash would be sent as a forerunner ahead of the legendary evangelist to cities earmarked by the

Spirit of God for awakening. His main job was to prevail in prayer. Once breakthrough was secured, Daniel Nash would send for Charles Finney, and they together would reap what was described as the greatest harvest ever seen since the book of Acts.

Note that Finney and Nash were not just evangelists but abolitionists. Their stand against slavery was well known. Eventually, the currents of God's "awakening river" even shifted America out of the scourge of slavery.

On 08/08/08, with leaders Bill and Rita Gamela, we were seeking the Lord to uncap this historic well of forerunning prayer for awakening. Bill and Rita had just purchased the property over Passover, sensing from the Lord that the title deed had to literally be secured before this sacred well could be uncapped.

As we walked the land, we saw how a Masonic obelisk demarcated the exact location where Daniel Nash had had his church. This was a surprise to me because Finney and Nash actually attributed the outpouring of the awakening to entire denominations recanting of masonry. We were asking the Lord how to move forward when all of a sudden I had a vision.

The first thing that happened was the ground began to shake. I thought it was an actual earthquake and looked around to see the reactions of friends. To my astonishment, nobody else felt it. Then I saw a geyser burst forth from the ground, and I knew this well of the Second Great Awakening had been uncapped.

As the vision continued, the earth began to break apart from Lowville, New York, all the way through to southern New York and Valley Forge as well as other Pennsylvania towns, eventually heading toward Maryland, and straight to the Washington Monument in DC. And everywhere the earth broke apart, I saw babies shooting out of the earth and into the sky!

All creation was travailing for the manifestation of these sons and daughters of God. In the vision, the babies were being caught by angels.

From the vision, I prophesied that the uncapping of this awakening well would shift us from a covenant with death empowering a culture of death to a covenant of life empowering a culture of life. In short—a seismic shift for justice, an American exodus moving us from abortion to awakening.

And three years later, when the Washington Monument cracked in an unprecedented earthquake, we took it as a sign!

We know Passover as God's response to the injustice of slavery against His covenant people. But have you ever seen the correlation to abortion? Exodus 1:22 describes how Pharaoh mandated all the firstborn of the Jewish people were to be aborted. Pharaoh's clear intention was to subjugate God's people through the imposition of horrific trauma.

According to Exodus 2, God responded by bringing the groanings of His people into a courtroom hearing and rendering a verdict which would speak into each successive generation. *"Let My people go!"*

Here's a pattern you may have never seen. Roe v. Wade was passed on 1/22/1973. The date correlates to the very scripture—Exodus 1:22—recounting the horrific loss endured by the Jews under Pharaoh. Maybe it wasn't a coincidence that on January 22, 2019, the forty-sixth anniversary of Roe v. Wade, the New York legislature led by Governor Andrew Cuomo legalized abortion statewide right up through birth. That's infanticide. The vote occurred within a month of Christmas, when the Lord called us to the Glory Train journey through New York.

In light of New York's current status as the global epicenter of the coronavirus pandemic, Jolene's warning over Passover 2019 has brought us often to tears. The way through the crisis remains unclear. Our earnest prayer is that the embrace of forced death from womb to old age will be repudiated in New York and across the nation. It is time for this gate of sabotage to be shut governmentally. As we posted in April of 2019, "The mandate stands—for New York and for our nation. A higher Court is trumping the decisions of the Empire State. The heavens over New York are shaking, and all creation is groaning for the sons of God to be revealed. It's time to shift from abortion to awakening. *Let My people go. Let My children go!"*[63]

Immediate Sign of Breakthrough

On August 8, we finished our northeast Glory Train journey with a private prayer time at the base of the Washington Monument. This was after launching at Faneuil Hall on July 22. The results were immediate and proved monumental.

On Friday, August 16, President Trump's request to defund Planned Parenthood was upheld. San Francisco's Ninth Circuit Court of Appeals made the precedent-setting decision. It was completely unexpected, especially given the court's legacy of left-leaning judicial activism. And the pro-life movement saw one of its greatest breakthroughs since Roe v. Wade was enacted.

Note that this turnaround occurred in the third year of America's Cyrus—the most pro-life president America has ever had.

The decision to impeach President Trump followed almost immediately. The spiritual conflict surrounding Representative Schiff's pursuit was by far the strongest we had experienced since the 2016 elections. As noted, it seemed directly synergized with the occult. In the midst of this sudden battle, our prophetic warnings regarding Passover, abortion, and New York were tucked away in the archives, all but forgotten, that is, at least until I started writing this chapter. Just a few days before Passover 2020, I rediscovered the word we were given one year ago. The Exodus story suddenly became very real with the entire globe sheltering in place and making a collective plea for mercy to triumph over judgment, and for the death angel to finally pass over.

Return to Valley Forge

As mentioned in the beginning of the chapter, as of Passover 2020, America prophetically is again camped at Valley Forge. In the midst of a pandemic crisis, we are staging for the battle ahead to complete the turnaround and secure our freedom for future generations.

The assault has been relentless. Liberties enjoyed by our nation are again hanging in the balance in a way few can barely perceive. Meanwhile, open defiance of God continues to be normative, even during the coronavirus crisis with abortion clinics counted among the essential services mandated to remain open.

As with Joshua in the Jordan Valley, or Washington at Valley Forge, there is only a limited window of opportunity to complete the turnaround the Lord has initiated. We must access it now, because one way or another, 2020 is a point of no return.

In late February 2020, we were asked by Dutch Sheets to join a small team of leaders journeying to Valley Forge and back to Washington DC. Prophetic dreams had conveyed clear direction from the Lord. At the time, they did not seem to relate specifically to the coronavirus. The clear mandate seemed to be unlocking God's freedom for this new era by Passover.

Dutch had no idea about our previous history at Valley Forge as we had started the Revolution movement and then revisited the encampment this past summer. We stayed largely silent on the matter. And we immediately accepted the invitation.

God's timing was conveyed through the dreams. The governmental prayer journey was to be carried out while the cherry blossoms were still in bloom in Washington DC. That gave me hesitation as most DC roads become parking lots during this spectacular event. And for those trying to find hotels, prices are exorbitant. But Dutch's team was willing to pay the price, literally and figuratively, to make this happen.

Order—Shelter in Place

Within weeks, preparations to confront the coronavirus took a dire turn. Orders to shelter in place began to come across the nation. Highways became deserted. The cherry blossom festival was cancelled with metro police even blockading roads of access to the Tidal Basin. Dutch made the hard decision that the team should remain home.

I thought the journey was simply going to be postponed. But Dutch called me just over a week before the scheduled journey, feeling compelled by God's Spirit that he should still undertake it during the time of the cherry blossoms. He really felt he needed to do it because it was what God had said.

Since we lived so close, Dutch welcomed Jolene and I to join him if we'd like. The rest of the team agreed to connect via conference call.

Most other times my response would have immediately been *yes* once again. But in a moment when even going to the grocery store seemed to risk our lives, Jolene and I needed to pray about it. By unanimous vote, our caution soon turned to *yes*.

Shortly afterward, the Valley Forge National Park officially closed.

The War Has Turned—Angel at Valley Forge

Clay Nash, a prophetic leader from Arkansas, saw the following in a dream. He shared it with a small group on a text thread.

> Dutch I dreamed that while at Valley Forge the Angel who spoke "mercy" six times appeared to you. You were on a walking trail. He presented to you twelve stones which he said had come from the Delaware River. He instructed you that as you continue your walk to complete your assignment, you would come upon a very unique tree, distinguished by its shape. It was bent over near the base—many Indians used this art to mark the way for others to follow. You were to place the twelve stones under the bent over part of the tree as a memorial that the angels are released, and the war has turned....
>
> As you walked the trail, a man stepped from behind a tree. It startled me as I never saw him. He was dressed in clothes of a much earlier era. He spoke to you and informed you he was William Penn, and because you were a man who kept your word—even when it cost you—God was releasing to you the stewardship ability of Elijah. You would speak your words, and God would honor your words from His covenant with you. He disappeared, and you walked by out the trail.

Note that in Clay's dream the angel who spoke "mercy" appeared—just as at the Trump International Hotel—this time with twelve stones to build an altar of covenant.

You might remember it was Clay who had had the dream shared on Yom Kippur that the angel of the Lord had been released to declare "mercy" the seventh time over the United States of America. It's mercy that secures God's covenant! As recounted in chapter 1, we framed our Revolution 2019–2020 conference at the Trump International around the promise of this dream.

Then we all sheltered in place.

And as we also discussed in an earlier chapter, Chris Mitchell soon reminded us how, when a plague was about to sweep through Jerusalem, David had been instructed to build an altar at the threshing floor and seek God for mercy. The plague stopped at the threshing floor.

With this thread, I suddenly saw how Valley Forge was a threshing floor for America. Similar to David's plea, George Washington's prayers mitigated the plague from this ground and turned the tide of the Revolution.

"I am again praying by the river." I didn't push this on Dutch, but in my mind there was only one place in the entire park where God would want us to pray. That was by the river, near a simple two-story stone house that had served as Washington's headquarters. The problem was that, as the park was officially closed due to the virus, we had no access.

On Monday morning, March 30, we showed up anyway.

Jamie Fitt of the Philadelphia Tabernacle of David joined us with stones from the Delaware River. He had actually gone to Penn Treaty Park, site of the original covenant between Penn and the Native Americans, to pull them out of the river.

Due to the many "no parking" signs nearby, Jolene decided to remain by the vehicle while Dutch, Jamie, and I scoped out the area. Two National Park Service cars immediately pulled up. "The park is closed. You cannot park here!" we were told.

Cautiously approaching a park service guide, I could almost hear Dutch's thoughts, *Jon, don't do this.*

But we had come too far to stop now. I had to at least ask. "Sir, we have come from Washington DC, and South Carolina," I began, "because we felt strongly to pray here for our nation in the midst of this crisis. We felt it imperative to pray from the same location George Washington had prayed to counter the virus in his day, which even helped secure our freedom. He prevailed through prayer. Sir, if you allow us, we will prevail too."

I mentioned by name the guide we met the previous summer. He had shared Washington's story with our team. To our amazement, a special exception was made. No need to clarify—we just walked on.

When we approached Washington's headquarters to pray, it hit us all hard that our nation's first president actually turned the tide of the revolution from the home we were staring at. He lived there. It seemed a perfect place to pray.

Instinctively, Dutch moved away. He followed a narrow trail down a brush-laden embankment concealing the river nearby. *"I am again praying by the river."* No need to clarify—we just walked on.

And the synergy of the ages soon united Heaven and Earth as our pleas merged with George Washington's at the very same "threshing floor"— by the river, outside his headquarters, where area farmers described the father of our nation as having prevailed in prayer.

We prayed, "Lord, stop the plague. Heal our people. Heal our troops. Bring miraculous provision. Equip and prepare your covenant people for the battles ahead. Raise up re-founding fathers and mothers. As in Washington's Day, grant us a turning point. Because we must win this revolution.

"And bless President Trump because his leadership, and our nation's, is now being forged in the valley."

Finally, it was not missed by us that the same angel of the Lord assigned to speak mercy seven times—mercy that secures God's covenant—had now shown up at Valley Forge.

We began 2020 at the Trump International by receiving a national resetting of covenant, building an altar to the Lord at His instruction, and declaring, "Mercy," over America seven times. A nationwide call for mercy at the threshing floor soon followed, as we built our altars of covenant nationwide. Then just before Passover, an altar to the Lord was built at His instruction on the threshing floor at Valley Forge to complete this work.

Once again, mercy was decreed over the land seven times—mercy that turns the tide, mercy that secures God's covenant for the future.

CHAPTER 6

ANOINTED FOR VICTORY! TWENTY PROPHECIES FOR THE 2020S

WE have explored how watchman prayer in the third year of America's Cyrus became a primary factor for setting a new course for 2020 and beyond. The gavel fell. The storm of a global war abated, and a hostile takeover of our nation was cut short by an extraordinary impeachment turnaround. Now the coronavirus has reshaped our world. America and the nations are being forged in the valley.

Clearly, the victory intended for our nation at this time is extremely vulnerable. Liberty must be guarded as well as expanded in our time of rebuilding.

In his 2020 State of the Union Address, President Trump declared, "The best is yet to come." These words are met with much greater sobriety now. Yet we still wholeheartedly agree.

Here are twenty prophetic priorities we feel God is emphasizing for the 2020s in our "State of the Union Address." Please take them to heart.

1.   White House Watchmen

The fiery intercession which started this turnaround is again mandated to complete the turnaround. It's time for a great army of watchmen to take their place on the wall.

Every Cyrus needs a Daniel. A blood moon over Jerusalem on the date of President Trump's birth confirmed that he was literally born to be a Cyrus. And the blood moon over Washington DC on the third anniversary of Trump's inauguration emphasized the importance of this partnership. Following the pattern of Daniel 10, prayer mobilization helped secure great victory for our nation. Everything turned.

Prophetically, just as Daniel prayed for the restoration of his homeland, from 2020–2022, the Lord is calling for a three-year watchman vigil to undergird the rebuilding of our nation. This three-year window is also tied to the restoration of God's governmental glory.

That said, watchman prayer is vital through this distinct window of vulnerability—so that Jesus' plans for America can be established and not aborted!

2.   New Way Forward

In August 2017 I received a vision. I was at a train station, above the engine of a large train that was beginning to move forward. As with my original vision of the Glory Train, the locomotive looked like it was made of pure gold. There was a platform on either side of the train. I looked to the right of the train engine, and saw a group of people literally wearing white sheets and pointed hats, like the KKK. I looked to the left of the train engine, and saw people dressed in all black, like Antifa. All of a sudden, steam shot out from under the wheels of this gold engine. *And the train began to move forward.*

I believe the vision represents the Glory Train. This movement is now moving beyond both the radical left and the radical right. The passengers on this train were all aboard. And we, the body of Christ, were made up of people from every tribe, tongue and nation.

In this new season the restoration train is leaving the station! We are advancing beyond the confines the enemy established to both divide us and define us. Instead, honor prevails. Dignity prevails. Love, strength, justice and freedom prevails. And that's what this movement is all about.

3. New Era of Victory

Despite setbacks, in the core of my being, I know that victory has been secured for our nation. A covenant reset, strengthened by lessons learned and ground already taken, will take hold. I sense this also includes victory for the Trump administration. As a leader set in place by God for this hour, President Donald Trump carries an anointing of victory. The mantle God granted him is actually removing man-imposed limits to define this new era in victory. And perhaps more than ever in this century, we need this mantle to direct our future.

Part of this victory must be a turnaround for life—from a covenant with death empowering a culture of death, to a covenant of life empowering a culture of life. If the opportunity is stewarded correctly, I believe we will see a sweep politically that fully secures this potential.

Leaders who have continued in open defiance of the Lord are facing measured discipline. The trust of the American people has been severely compromised. In the pattern of Shebna and Eliakim from Isaiah 22, many keys and many crowns are going to be confiscated and redistributed in this season.

Obviously, the pathway forward must be undergirded by vigilant forerunning prayer, keeping humble because pride comes before a fall. And in balance, we must also remember that fearless confidence still carries a great recompense of reward.

4. Balance of Power—Original Intent

Keeping watch from our perch recently, I was amazed to see a bald eagle soaring over the Potomac. This majestic symbol of our nation spread its wings and glided past the Supreme Court, the Capitol, and the White

House. All of a sudden, the eagle caught an updraft and shot up higher, circling the area from a height I could barely see.

Note this wasn't a vision; it was real. Nevertheless, I sensed the Lord speaking prophetically through the experience. A clear word of warning to the Democratic Party—really to both parties—followed:

> The Lord says, RETURN TO ME! Dive into the cleansing water of My blue wave. Let My revelation cleanse you. Let the current of My river redirect you from the sewer your platform is spiraling headlong into. Open your eyes underwater, and let Me wash all defilement from your vision. Let Me release My waters and birth you anew.
>
> For I desire a left wing and right wing for My eagle of this nation, pure and strong, so that I may thrust this nation higher. But know that I have already rendered My judgment against the evil intentions and immorality you have propagated even to My children in this land. Therefore, I will not allow your defiled waters to redirect the course of this nation anymore.

Hear God's heart in this. He wants all of us—whatever political party or affiliation—to return to covenant with Him and return to the biblical values that provide the infrastructure for our greatness. He wants a left wing and a right wing *centered in Him* so we can soar higher. The other option is to fly aimlessly in circles and eventually be devoured by each other.

Final point. God wants the prophets to return to this same plumb line of covenant consecration to Him. We are not to be owned by the left wing or the right wing. Instead, we are to be the *eyes of the eagle*, having clear vision to guide and direct the nation higher.

5. America—From Jacob to Israel

Faneuil Hall is considered the historic womb of the American Revolution. What was birthed there was genuinely a freedom movement that changed the course of our nation and the nations of the earth.

On July 22, 2019 the Lord led us to return to Boston's historic Faneuil Hall to receive His Daniel 7:22 verdict for this hour. It was stunning to discover that Faneuil in Hebrew is Phanuel or Peniel, meaning "face of God." Freedom quite literally was birthed from the face of God.

And it still is for each of us today. This *pey* decade will be defined by Phanuel moments, destiny-shaping times before the face of God.

Jacob wrestled with God through the night at Phanuel (see Gen. 32:22-32). At daybreak, he received his breakthrough. A name change accompanied his blessing. No longer would he exist as Jacob, meaning "supplanter" or "deceiver." Instead, his name would be Israel, meaning "God prevails." His name would be the name of a nation in covenant with God.

The Lord showed us how, in this midnight hour, America has been in a similar season of wrestling before the face of God. Our name has gone before us. We have deceived and been deceived. The Lord is shifting our hearts and identity from Jacob to Israel—a nation in covenant with Him! And we are now crossing over to possess our inheritance as a nation.

Been mislabeled? Misunderstood? Overlooked? This process is occurring corporately, but the window is also open for you to shift personally through covenant reset with God. Leave the baggage behind and cross over!

6.   Pass the Test, Possess Your Inheritance

I prophesied in December 2019 that, as with Jacob and David, there will be great tests to pass through the course of these next years, one fiery trial in particular. But if we pass the tests and cross this threshold, beginning in 2022, a three-year period of vulnerability will give way to a deepening of breakthrough which perpetuates our Judeo-Christian foundations. Prophetically, it is as though the pillars securing our future will be driven deep enough to finally connect with our covenant roots.

Whether the challenges of the first half of 2020 represent that fiery trial or whether there are more of similar magnitude I do not know. What I do know is that *teshuvah*, or repentance, is still mandated at the threshing floor of our American experience. And fathering the nation—genuinely—is a test that God is intensively evaluating for all of us (see Isa. 22).

That said, the door is now open to possess our inheritance and see God's covenantal heritage forge our future. The Joshuas among us must now arise. As you will discover in chapter 15, breakthroughs in personal inheritances are coming as well. The magnitude of this opportunity cannot be overstated. Neither can the consequences of not following through.

7. Yom Kippur 2019—Mercy Secures God's Covenant

Over many years, the Lord has consistently met us on Yom Kippur, the Day of National Atonement, with prophetic revelation that frames our future. Jewish tradition holds that the "Book of Life" is opened on Rosh Hashanah, and after evaluation God pencils in His destiny for individuals and even nations. Between Rosh Hashanah and Yom Kippur, Heaven's Court is accessible for repentance to secure a better verdict.

I believe what transpired on Yom Kippur 2019 conveyed God's heart, not just for the year, but for the decade of the 2020s. You are already familiar with the first message. Because it was during our Yom Kippur 2019 gathering in Brunswick, Georgia, marking the completion of our Glory Train journey through the original thirteen colonies, Dutch Sheets shared the dream that *mercy has secured God's covenant.*

8. Yom Kippur 2019—Complete the Turnaround!

On Yom Kippur, I saw in a vision an old steam train rolling down the East Coast to Jekyll Island. It was carrying financiers who in 1910 established the Federal Reserve. The train vision shifted to the Glory Train rolling along the same tracks to Jekyll Island. This train accelerated even around a 180-degree turn and shot back the other way. Turnaround!

A gavel then appeared before me, seemingly over the train, and I heard the words, "Complete the turnaround!"

From this prophetic experience, I knew the Lord was granting grace to complete the fullness of the turnaround that He had initiated for us.

9.   Keep the Turnaround Window Open!

To keep the turnaround window open, continued obedience in the divine exchange of tithes and offerings is not an option (see Mal. 3). Because the promised blessing—the devourer rebuked, the windows of Heaven opened, a perpetual flow of provision—is needed now more than ever as we rebuild.

Let's keep the turnaround window open. Let's keep the promised blessing producing an overflow for multitudes. According to Deuteronomy 8:18, power to gain wealth is now being given to establish the covenant God swore to our forefathers!

10. American Passover

On Yom Kippur 2019, I heard the Lord emphasize Passover 2020 as an American Passover. Just as Moses was released into his freedom movement at the age of eighty, so the Hebrew year 5780 has brought us across the threshold into a freedom movement for America, Israel, and many nations. Moses brought his people across the Red Sea, creating Passover. Then the torch was passed to Joshua, who, during Passover forty years later, brought God's covenant people across the Jordan into the covenant land.

Note that 2019 was marked by the release of a "baptism revival" from Georgia to the nation. We became immersed. We became purified. Holy Spirit flooded us in the flood waters. And we crossed over!

This revival will certainly continue. But in this season, we are now crossing over to possess our inheritance!

This is where we are right now in this freedom movement. By Passover 2021, we are poised to possess the land! It's an American Passover. And as in Exodus 23, it will again be said that the hosts of the Lord are with us.

11. Watch Against Assassinations

Finally, on Yom Kippur 2019, the Lord gave me a vision that ultimately represented God's verdict for President Trump and our nation.

I saw President Trump underwater, struggling desperately to free himself. The water was murky and dark. His feet were chained to a large block of cement. I heard by the Spirit, "They tried to leverage him, but it did not work. So, they decided to throw him overboard!"

In the vision, we were able to break the chains. The president shot up to the surface and gasped for breath. I heard the Lord say, "The resurrection of Donald John Trump!" I don't fully know what the future holds. But I do know the Lord is freeing President Trump from the traps laid for him.

President overboard! Yet, in this baptism movement, the Lord has rescued him from many waters, including a midterm visitation, Father to son, patterned after Zechariah 3. It's a fresh start! Watch how Psalm 40 becomes an anthem for his presidency.

Please pray against assassination attempts. This is a major reason why more White House watchmen are needed on the wall.

12. The Governmental Glory of God

In 2020, we began a three-year window to see the governmental glory of God restored. Awakening and covenant consecration—what a way to cross the threshold into 2020! This movement will both redefine and accelerate God's freedom movement, especially in America, the United Kingdom, and Israel. Eventually, the movement is going to all nations.

This movement is sourced in Isaiah 6. A hallmark of the governmental glory is a restoration of genuine repentance for leaders and society. Watch for an anointing of holy conviction to penetrate all of our hearts in these next three years.

The first responsibility of a watchman is always to keep watch over covenant. Remember that 2020 marks the four-hundredth anniversary of our nation's covenant with Christ made by the Pilgrims. I don't believe it's a coincidence that a manifestation of God's governmental glory began to come through the gates as we shifted from 2019 into 2020 at the Trump International Hotel. After all, glory always follows covenant restoration!

And the years 2020–2027 will be marked by many nations entering into a covenant reset with the Lord. This will become a demarcation for the freedom movement which unlocks true identity, calling, and destiny in this new season. Dictatorships will fall. Nations will be born again! Entire regions will be lifted out of recession and poverty.

The key to all of this is covenant reset. And it is already turning the hardest of locks.

13. Thirteen Colonies Awakening

Ezekiel 43 shows how the glory of God fills the house by way of the gate facing east. Watch as the thirteen colonies, the geographic "east gate" of our nation and seedbed of most of America's original covenant roots, come alive with awakening and Kingdom advancement. It will be a sure sign that God is now filling the "house" of the nation!

Florida becomes a refuge of healing. Georgia, the reconstitution state, and the Carolinas are marked for awakening and revival. The virginity of Virginia is being restored. The sword of the Lord springs forth from Pennsylvania to circumcise our government and nation. Massachusetts and New England are crossing over. Newfound freedom breaks forth as Holy Spirit again becomes the "Spirit of America" during this four-hundredth year of covenant. The New England bride is rising!

Mid-Atlantic states, keep watch. Through this *pey* decade, your service as gatekeepers for the nation, and even for Washington DC, comes to the forefront. Beware that an enemy at the gates is seeking the path of least resistance.

New York, please choose life. Shut the gates of sabotage!

14. Apostolic Centers—Apostolic Covering

There's been a lot of hype surrounding apostolic centers with only a few genuine successes. When the initial words from Heaven came, many simply repackaged old religious structures and called them new. Yet as covenant restoration has been secured, an anointing to build and establish

God's new covenant covering for our future is now ready to be accessed. From a word on December 3, 2019:

> Watch now the movement of My glory for your future.... For mercy has indeed secured your covenant with Me. From this time My ark will both secure your way and secure your possession of My dwelling for your future.... And I say watch! Watch for I will visit you on your watch, even as I visited My servants of old. Watch even for new wineskins to form that will cover My remnant people. Suddenly it will appear!

15. Rise of Apostolic Diplomacy

Every Cyrus needs a Daniel. Let's keep in mind the prophet serving Daniel was a true statesman in his own right. This ancient father will have many modern protégés in many respects. As we mature in the watchman call, many will mature to excel in other aspects of Daniel's example and anointing as well. This means that a new era of apostolic diplomacy is at hand. So is the healing of nations.

16. New Invasive Technologies

With the invention of the internet, our world changed. Now in this decade, we will see the emergence of 5G wireless internet, robotic technologies, and even transhuman technologies featuring embedded computer chips connected to our minds and bodies. The world will change once again.

Opportunities are endless. Yet negative aspects are quite terrifying, especially as dictatorial nations are already harnessing new technology to invade personal privacy and exert control over their populations.

Where will this lead? How will this impact believers?

Better pray and act. Otherwise, a flood tide of religious persecution could be coming even to America.

17. Global Women's Movement

Two thousand years ago, Miriam became the handmaiden chosen by God to birth Christ's salvation into the earth. In similar fashion, a global women's movement is now helping to birth the revelation of Christ's nature, character, and power into the earth today.

Miriam devoted herself to God's call. So did Joseph. But it took a visitation from the angel Gabriel for him to embrace God's new move. Afterward, Joseph wholeheartedly covered, protected, and supported his new family in every aspect. He continued to receive direction from the Lord which preserved their lives. The world changed as a result.

Watch how many families and spheres now yield to a greater call—to host Jesus in the midst of their daily lives.

Miriams and Josephs together must lead this new movement today. In the decade of the 2020s, a window is opening for a fresh, Spirit-breathed synergy between couples devoted to Him. Even Holy Spirit encounters and supernatural interventions from His angelic hosts will occasionally occur.

And watch for Miriam's prophetic observation about her Son's calling to also come true. He brings down unjust rulers from their thrones.

18. Burning Lamps of Spiritual Revolution

Yorktown showed us that we had gained victory in one season of spiritual revolution. Our time at Valley Forge made clear the next phase of spiritual revolution has now begun. And it is ours to either lose or win. Victory will be marked by Heaven's fire on our altars.

The Jewish feast of Hanukkah memorializes the relighting of the lampstand, or menorah, to reconsecrate the Temple to the Lord after it had been defiled by hard-core idolatry. Led by Judah Maccabee, a group of spiritual revolutionaries took on the strongest army of their day and recaptured their desolate heritage to restore covenant with the Lord. Today, we remain in the fight of our lives to do the same—to recover our desolate heritage and relight the covenant flame.

Here's some good news. In this season, God's lampstands prevail.

Jesus stands in the midst of the seven lampstands before the throne (see Rev. 1:12). Is your lampstand there? It's time to prioritize genuinely becoming a burning lamp, shining strongly enough to illuminate your world.

19. The Revelation Road

For today's freedom riders, the King's highway is a Revolution Road which always leads to victory. And for 2020 and beyond, the King's highway is not only a Revolution Road, it is a Revelation Road. In the latter part of 2020 and beyond, revelatory scrolls are being released to guide the Body of Christ on a midnight procession. As Jesus prophesied—it's time to light your lamps and go out to meet the Bridegroom.

Our journey along this Revelation Road, this Revolution Road, will mobilize the Body of Christ in America to secure our inherited freedoms for our generations to come. Dry bones will come alive. The Breaker will break open!

Remember the journey of Joseph and Miriam. Once Jesus was birthed, there was a multiple-year window of vulnerability that threatened His life. Joseph was given direction in a dream, and a Revelation Road opened up for them to be protected. We are in a similar hour today. Watch for God's clear direction to direct your path!

Watch for the Lord to break forth in breakthrough revival along the Isaiah 19 highway which they traveled. The revelation of Jesus will be so profound that multitudes will come from across the world to experience His glory.

Watch also for crises to break out which even spark a mass exodus. The Body of Christ must intervene to turn these crisis highways to Revelation Roads.

Most importantly, along this Revelation Road many in the Body of Christ will gain an unveiling of Jesus Christ. This is the ultimate breakthrough revelation! We will see Him in every dimension of His majesty.

The Lion in His humility. The Lamb in His kingship. His unimaginable sacrifice for us and His eternal worthiness.

Further, I believe the book of Revelation will come alive to us in a way it never has before—living, breathing, burning scrolls to guide us along the way.

Who but God knows where this Revelation Road will take you. Finding out will be the adventure of a lifetime!

20. 2020 Vision—*Ayin* in the Decade of *Pey*

In Hebrew, the decade which began in 2020 is the decade of *pey* or the decade of *the mouth*. Many prophetic teachers have pointed out that, in the roaring 2020s, it's time to govern with your mouth. I love the imagery of a lion roaring! And truly it's time for the Body of Christ to regain our voice and speak.

Yet we still need 20/20 vision. The previous decade, *ayin* in Hebrew, was the decade of the *eye* or *vision*. And the Lord desires that we bring the revelation and authority we've gained from the *ayin* decade into this *pey* decade. Clear, authentic prophetic foresight from Jesus must be the source of the words filling our mouths. If we don't align our mouths with throne room vision, we will perish from presumption. And it will be said of us what was said of the prophets of old:

> *I did not send these prophets, but they ran. I did not speak to them, but they prophesied. But if they had stood in My council, then they would have announced My words to My people, and would have TURNED THEM back from their evil way, and from the evil of their deeds* (Jeremiah 23:21–22 emphasis added).

We want to bring the anointing of turnaround into the decade of *pey*, don't we? Therefore, let's prioritize standing in the council of God. Prideful presumption is a poor substitute for genuine breakthrough. In humble awe, let's keep watch before the throne and speak what Holy Spirit is saying. Only then will we rule with our mouths with authority to set His course for the future.

That said, it's important for prophetic roundtables to now access the council of God from region to region. It's a corporate expression of *ayin* in the decade of *pey*.

Below is a prophetic word I received while writing the "2020 vision" insights:

> The Lord says, "In this new era I am raising up new era watchmen who will keep their voices in alignment with My counsel and, therefore, change the course of nations. Even the wind you experience in this season shall be a sign to you. Come from the four winds, O Breath, and breathe on these slain that they may live!
>
> "For I am breathing on the ancient embers of awakening and revival from city to city and causing these to blaze again. I am even causing underground fires to surface as a sign that it's time to light your lamps and go out to meet the Bridegroom! Watch how the watch fires of My glory emerge. Kindle your own flame within My fire and see how I fashion you as a burning lamp in this season. For from region to region I am resetting My covenant lampstands and relighting the flame.
>
> "Where will you carry My lamp? Will you stand still long enough to gain and release My redemptive exposure? Will you proceed at My command to make a way for My glory? How are your eyes focusing on Me? For in this season I will grant many not only to sit on My throne with Me and watch, but to gain watchman eyes.
>
> "And a new impartation is coming to many," says the Lord. "My eyes of fire will indeed be released into the earth!"

Review

Please take a moment to reflect on what you've just read. We suggest taking notes as you answer questions below.

1. What prophetic perceptions stood out to you from this chapter? Make a list. You might even want to restate them in your own words to help you personalize them.

2. What has the Lord been speaking to you about 2020 and the new decade we've entered? How is it similar to what you've just read? How is it different?

3. How do you feel to mobilize for 2020 and beyond? What issues do you consider most important? How are you praying for the president and our government?

4. Describe the Revelation Road you are on right now. Where is it taking you? What journeys do you feel the Holy Spirit quickening you to take? What is the Lord showing you?

5. How would you describe the condition of your lampstand of prayer? Jesus wants you blazing and shining on your journey through this decade. Is your lamp burning?

EQUIPPING FOR VICTORY

CHAPTER 7

WHITE HOUSE WATCHMEN

"THAT'S really where it's at!"

The message, followed immediately by a man-punch on the arm in the middle of the White House Rose Garden, stunned me. Not because of the force applied or the affirmation or even the location. It was the source. Vice President Mike Pence had just compelled Jolene and me to keep praying for him with his firm yet friendly jab serving as an exclamation point. The story is worth noting.

Not long after the election, Jolene and I were invited to attend a last-minute speech by President Trump. Nobody, including our host, knew what the announcement was actually about. To our surprise, with great passion Trump announced the disengagement of the United States from the Paris Climate Accords.

The occasion actually proved to be a huge answer to prayer. The science of climate change clearly has merits. Years ago, however, we had been alerted that global climate-change efforts were being co-opted to form an infrastructure for global governance sourced in idolatry. Our national sovereignty was even at stake. Jolene and I, together with leaders nationwide, launched a year's-long prayer movement to overcome an historic expression of idolatry tied to this initiative.

And the unexpected invitation suddenly became a full-circle moment where we saw answers to our prayers unleashed. God never forgets the efforts of His watchmen.

"Foreign leaders in Europe, Asia, and across the world should not have more to say with respect to the US economy than our own citizens and their elected representatives," Trump declared.

"Thus, our withdrawal from the agreement represents a reassertion of America's sovereignty. Our Constitution is unique among all the nations of the world, and it is my highest obligation and greatest honor to protect it. And I will!"

After the historic announcement, President Trump waved, mouthed "thank you" many times, and then returned to the Oval Office. We rose from our seats to leave.

Jolene rarely pursues leaders after a gathering. Usually they gravitate to her. And if they don't come—she's pretty confident it's actually their loss. After years of observation, I have concluded this is true.

This explains why it was shocking when my beautiful wife suddenly made a beeline toward Vice President Mike Pence! After brief introductions, a smiling Jolene took the vice president's outstretched hand and actually pulled him close, signaling to whisper in his ear.

My immediate thought—*Who dares to whisper in the ear of the vice president?*

My second thought—*How will the snipers react?*

The vice president leaned forward. "My husband and I pray for you every day," a beaming Jolene whispered. "I just didn't want to say it too loud. You know, with all the press standing by. But it's our honor to pray for you!"

Pence smiled, nodded, and thanked her.

I decided to follow up, just to offer a confirmation. "Sir, it's true. We pray for you every day."

"Thank you both!" he said. Then his grip on my hand tightened, and he looked directly in my eyes, arresting my attention. "That's really where it's at!"

And that's when I got my man-punch.

A week later, Vice President Pence addressed a Catholic prayer breakfast with the following words. They convey far better than I ever could the urgency to serve as a White House watchman.

> I will tell you that the sweetest words the president and I ever hear are when people reach out at an event to grab a hand and say, "I'm praying for you." And we hear it a lot....
>
> I encourage you to redouble your efforts, but don't so much pray for a cause as for country. I've always been drawn to what Abraham Lincoln said when he was asked once if he thought that God was on the side of the Union Army in our great Civil War. Abraham Lincoln responded, "I'd rather concern myself more with whether we were on God's side than whether God is on our side."
>
> So just pray for America. Pray for this country because America matters.[64]

Pray for your country. Redouble your efforts! And make sure you're on God's side in this because America matters.

White House Watchmen

Let's examine a few characteristics of the biblical call to keep watch. You will gain clarity on both the responsibilities and the vast potential of the call.

Daniel is a prototype for White House watchmen today. Keeping in mind that every Cyrus needs a Daniel who will contend in prayer for their divine destinies to be fulfilled. Daniel kept watch over his king and administration, over his adopted nation, and also over the freedom movement his king began for God's covenant people. A spirit of excellence was evident in all.

I cannot emphasize enough that the assignment to serve as a White House watchman in this hour is exactly the same. Praying for the president, for his administration, for the nation, especially for awakening and revival. And contending for God's freedom movement in this hour of history which brings restoration for His covenant lands and covenant people.

Executive Branch Prayer

At the beginning of 2019, veteran prophetic statesman James Goll received a defining prophetic word on governmental prayer for the executive branch. The word is very similar to the mandate Jesus conveyed to us at the very same time—with a blood moon at midnight serving as an exclamation point. More on this in the next chapter.

What astounded me most about James's prophecy is that he gave details of a movement already advancing, a movement he knew nothing about.

> In June 2019 while ministering in Miami, Florida, at King Jesus Ministries, I proclaimed that soon *the greatest governmental prayer movement in the history of the United States* would begin—and that it would possibly be a model for governments of the nations.
>
> I was given dreams at the beginning of 2019 where I saw that a united prayer force would converge to intercede for all three branches of the US government and eventually cover every cabinet member in prayer. After waiting for the right location and time, I released this prophetic word in June at apostle Maldonado's School of the Supernatural.... Let's make history together![65]

That said, how much prayer does the White House need?

Nobody really knows. But the scope of responsibility is—to use a very Trumpian phrase—"Yuge."

Led by the president, the executive branch of the US government is responsible for all US diplomacy, military, and intelligence efforts. It encompasses all departments of government, including the Departments of Defense, State, Justice, Labor, Education, Commerce, Agriculture, Homeland Security, Interior, Housing and Urban Development, Veterans Affairs, and more. Here's a fascinating fact. You might be surprised to learn that Health and Human Services actually has the biggest budget of all the departments, surpassing even the Department of Defense.[66]

White House advisors and aides formulate policies that direct the course of these departments, and then they work to hold the departments accountable for their implementation. They are the true warriors on the front lines of this governmental turnaround. The resistance they face is often extreme. The spiritual warfare against them is often unimaginably fierce. And yet they are among the least prayed for, because outside of policy circles they are largely unknown.

Again, every Cyrus needs a Daniel.

Here's just one example. At the beginning of the Trump administration, our friend Katy was hired as a legal advisor to the president to eradicate abortion from government policy. Trump did not wait for Roe v. Wade to be overturned by the courts. Instead, wherever abortion was embedded as policy, from USAID and the UN to Health and Human Services and far beyond, she worked tirelessly with government lawyers to eradicate its promotion, funding, and practice.

The personal sacrifice Katy made on a daily basis was staggering. You can only imagine the spiritual intensity involved with this, including occult opposition from pro-choice activists who called to curse her on a regular basis. But she was driven by two things: a deep, mature love for Jesus and the prospect that every hour of her effort, and every victory won, equated to more babies saved.

Katy's dedication inspired us to help mobilize more effective prayer for government leaders because we earnestly believe every Cyrus needs a Daniel! And maybe you are an answer to a leader's prayer.

Shamar—Watch, Protect, and Defend

Watchman prayer is by nature a higher dimension of intercession. It brings both a greater level of responsibility as well as a greater expression of authority than simply making requests. It is generally assignment based. Here is some hard-won understanding for you to grow in this call, as well as to grow in the sphere God has called you to cover.

A primary Hebrew word for *watchman* is *shamar*. From the time when God first committed Himself to the Jewish people, He has been known as *Shamar Israel*, the Watchman over Israel—*"Shamar Israel—He who watches over Israel—never slumbers or sleeps!"* (see Ps. 121).

When we hear the word *watch*, we think primarily of seeing. And that is entirely appropriate. But one of the most basic meanings of *shamar* or *watch* is to guard or protect and defend. This was actually the original commission given to Adam and Eve. Tend the garden and keep it, or *shamar* it!

And the battle today is hauntingly similar.

But, beloved, you have gained an incredible benefit package as a part of your covenant with the Lord. He promises to serve as Watchman over your life in its entirety. He also makes this promise to nations and spheres that have genuinely aligned with Him through covenant. Further, He wants to accomplish the guardianship of His watch in partnership with you.

Note that seeing is definitely part of guarding or keeping watch, which is why in Israel intelligence assets and Secret Service agents are often referred to as *ayin* or *eyes*. All the strength in the world will not protect you from enemies you do not perceive. Nor will vast capabilities allow you to access opportunities you are unaware of. Thank God for His prophetic anointing, which communicates vision beyond our own capacities!

Keeping alert and watchful means to actively see, search, and perceive so the alarm can be sounded when needed to protect, defend, and advance God's people.

White House Watchmen—Secret Service

In the spirit realm, White House watchmen are similar to the Secret Service agents who guard the president night and day. These agents engage in many activities, often covertly, to *shamar* both the president and the nation. The Song of Solomon provides a great picture of this anointing in action: *"All of them are wielders of the sword, expert in war;*

each man has his sword at his side, guarding against the terrors of the night" (3:8).

A primary duty of US Secret Service agents is to prevent assassinations or assaults against the president, the vice president, their families, or other leaders the agents are assigned to protect. A secondary duty is to prevent unwanted infiltration into the sphere of their leaders. The scope of the Secret Service also includes running counterterrorism, safeguarding the US currency and our financial systems, and conducting criminal investigations, including identity theft and even child exploitation.

The operative goal of the US Secret Service is to prevent an incident before it occurs. Please hear me in this. In the Spirit, this is a primary mission of a White House watchman as well, keeping in mind that we don't *"wrestle against flesh and blood, but against principalities"* and powers (Eph. 6:12 NKJV). Your best day is when an enemy attack is averted or mitigated through your efforts to the extent that the gates of sabotage are shut, and those targeted are barely affected, if at all.

Needless to say, gaining a job at the Secret Service is a rigorous process. Background checks are invasive. Loyalty and integrity are paramount. Applicants must excel through extensive training and pass harrowing tests involving crisis situations. They must gain real-world discernment to quickly assess perilous situations and respond effectively.

The training for White House watchmen is similarly rigorous through the school of Holy Spirit.

Unwavering loyalty must be at the core of a Secret Service agent's character, not merely to the president but to the Constitution of the United States by which a president is set into office. Their commitment of loyalty is officially established through a covenant or oath whereby they enter into service.

The same holds true for White House watchmen in the Spirit. As we've mentioned before, covenant with God over your sphere is intrinsic to the watchman call, because covenant actually activates Jesus' watch of guardianship.

*The covenant that I have made with you, you shall not forget,
nor shall you fear other gods. But the Lord your God you shall
fear; and He will deliver you from the hand of all your enemies*
(2 Kings 17:38–39).

Above all, Secret Service agents must be willing to lay down their lives
for their mission. They must absolutely be willing to take a bullet for those
being protected. But, more importantly, they must embrace a lifestyle
dedicated to fulfilling their assignment with sacrificial diligence, precision, endurance, and sometimes hiddenness or remaining covert.

Secret in Service

One of the most extraordinary encounters with a Secret Service agent
came while I was leading a prayer group in front of the White House
during President Obama's tenure. Few people were around because of the
bitter cold. But prophetic declarations were flowing, with many perceiving that a turnaround mantle was being released over the seat of authority
of the presidency.

A homeless man limped over as if to join our group. In my haste, I
had not noticed him, but a team member told me he had been standing
nearby for a few minutes. I welcomed him. The man stood there for a
while, listening to our prayers. He then started raising his voice about all
things constitutional to the extent I had to step in. Gesturing toward the
uniformed Secret Service agents behind us, I told him he was free to stay
but needed to be more respectful or I would ask for their intervention.

Strangely, he smiled at me. I noted a glint in his eyes. Then he walked
away, limping and shouting. A moment later he had simply disappeared.

Two months afterward, I was praying at David's Tent on the White
House Ellipse during one of Prime Minister Netanyahu's visits. Secret
Service agents came through for a routine check. I was startled to see a
man on the team remarkably resembling the homeless guy. We talked.
When the agent smiled, I observed a familiar glint in his eye. He then
handed me a Secret Service pin. I wear it proudly in remembrance to
this day!

Perhaps this agent's most effective watch came when he was able to fade into the background as a homeless guy, unseen or simply ignored by those around him. This says a lot about our culture. To be effective, your service in keeping watch must sometimes remain absolutely discreet.

Can you step away from the spotlight and into the shadows simply to keep watch? It's time to learn.

Encrypted Communication—Praying in the Spirit

What if I offered you real-time surveillance that exposed plots of the enemy over your sphere, from anywhere in the world? What if I could also offer you strategy to stop these plots or mitigate their effects if already in play?

Even better, what if I could make you aware of incredible opportunities for advancement—and then administrate everything needed for the opportunity to be maximized?

And what if I offered all this to you in encrypted communication that was beyond enemy penetration?

To receive such a gift would undoubtedly prove invaluable. And that is exactly what God is offering you through the gift of praying in the Holy Spirit.

Let's face it, none of us fully know all of the dynamics of what to pray for. But according to Scripture, the Spirit Himself partners together with us to overcome on our behalf! Together, you and the Spirit make an unbeatable team as He knows every detail involved in seeing your answer to prayer come to pass. From Romans 8:

> *In the same way the Spirit also helps our weakness; for we do not know how to pray as we should, but the Spirit Himself intercedes for us with groanings too deep for words; and He who searches the hearts knows what the mind of the Spirit is, because He intercedes for the saints according to the will of God. And we know that God causes all things to work together for good…*(vv. 26–28).

Don't know what to pray on your watch?

The Spirit of God does, and He is present to help. So, with Holy Spirit's empowerment, you can at any moment pray with utmost precision for President Trump, your wife and children, your pastor, or the securing of your sphere from the enemy.

As with all gifts, a period of exploration and training is necessary to gain competence. But it is essential in your quest to keep watch, or at least the apostle Paul thought so. The man who wrote two-thirds of the New Testament, who thanked God that he spoke in tongues more than all of his peers, who labored in prayer over his spiritual children until Christ was formed in them, considered praying in the Spirit the most essential part of his watch. From Ephesians 6:

> *PRAYING always with all prayer and supplication IN THE SPIRIT, BEING WATCHFUL to this end with all perseverance and supplication for all the saints—and for me, that utterance may be given* (vv. 18–19 NKJV, emphasis added).

Notice Paul compelled believers to pray in the Spirit in the midst of all expressions of prayer. Praying in the Spirit completes the sentence. It perfects, protects, and seals your plea.

The old-timers knew this secret. They developed such keen sensitivity in interfacing with Holy Spirit that they sensed when a prayer assignment or burden was upon them and when it had been prayed through. You can absolutely cultivate the same sensitivity.

Throne Room Watchmen

As a watchman for Jesus, your first loyalty and focus must not be to the president, politics, current crises, or even church or family welfare. Your first loyalty and focus really must rest with the King seated on the throne.

Thrones of governance are established by covenant. Because of Jesus' blood covenant with you, from the moment you were born again you were granted what the apostle Paul described as a seat with Christ in heavenly places (Eph. 2:6). In other words, you have a throne before His throne! And in the words of the apostle John, it is time for you to come up higher.

> *After these things I looked, and behold, a door standing open in heaven, and the first voice which I had heard, like the sound of a trumpet speaking with me, said, "Come up here, and I will show you what must take place after these things." Immediately I was in the Spirit; and behold, a throne was standing in heaven, and One sitting on the throne.... Around the throne were twenty-four thrones; and upon the thrones I saw twenty-four elders sitting, clothed in white garments, and golden crowns on their heads. Out from the throne come flashes of lightning and sounds and peals of thunder. And there were seven lamps of fire burning before the throne, which are the seven Spirits of God* (Revelation 4:1–5).

Ponder this visionary experience. The presence-saturated awe of throne room worship. The heavenly light shows. The angelic hosts and redeemed human beings lost in reverence in this beauty realm of God. This is where you are right now, positioned with Christ!

That said, let's explore your seat. It is far more significant than a folding chair in a movie auditorium. Instead, your seat before the throne is similar to what is pictured with the elders. In a way resembling a president with his cabinet, you have been granted a seat at the table. From this seat, you are invited to worship the One seated on the throne, to fellowship with Him, to receive from Him, to influence Him. And you are invited to govern your sphere of authority with Him from your throne, keeping watch!

That was the secret to the prophet Elijah's success. One of Israel's greatest watchmen, Elijah, confronted Ahab over idolatry by releasing the governmental directives he received before the throne. *"As the Lord, the God of Israel lives, before whom I stand, surely there will be neither dew nor rain these years except at my word!"* (1 Kings 17:1).

Note that Elijah was granted a throne over his sphere of authority which no man could leverage, and no man could take away. It was given by God. To realign Israel with God's heart, Elijah's throne even prevailed over the governmental thrones that had become corrupted.

Elijah is a prototype of a throne room watchman we should all aspire to. He stood before the Lord as a lifestyle. He kept vigil before the throne, receiving clear prophetic revelation and apostolic directives. His authority to catalyze national turnaround came from his seat of intimacy and authority before the throne.

Maybe you don't know it yet. But the same is true with you.

Dimensions of a Watchman Call

So far, we've explored broad aspects of the watchman calling, beginning with the revelation that God Himself is the Watchman we are coming alongside. He is the greatest mentor to help you grow in your call. So, put on your Holy Spirit Secret Service cap, and let's investigate five dimensions of the watchman calling that are vital for you to cultivate in your daily life.

Prayer for Governmental Leaders

Perhaps the most basic responsibility is also the most vital. That is praying for your governmental leaders. Paul compelled Timothy to teach all under his apostolic leadership to devote themselves to this.

> *First of all, then, I urge that entreaties and prayers, petitions and thanksgivings, be made on behalf of all men, for kings and all who are in authority, so that we may lead a tranquil and quiet life in all godliness and dignity. This is good and acceptable in the sight of God our Savior* (1 Timothy 2:1–3).

Paul tells Timothy the result of this prayer effort will be a tranquil life for believers, where godliness and dignity are upheld as God's shalom prevails.

Say what?

That's crazy talk when you consider Paul was tortured and imprisoned by many of the very leaders he was compelling his protégé to pray for. The apostolic father saw the intercession of the saints—our intercession—as a catalyst to mitigate or even overthrow suppression and abuse within government. When we pray for governmental leaders, we are actually invoking the government of God to prevail.

You may be weary of praying for our leaders. Please don't quit. Don't give up! Destinies are literally in the balance. As Vice President Pence admonished, our leaders need your intercession far more than you could possibly imagine. And their gratitude for your prayers is constant—it is never taken for granted.

Protecting and Defending

As with Secret Service agents in the natural, you are called to protect and defend your sphere of authority, ideally stopping incidents before they occur. Note to self—if it makes the headlines, it's almost too late.

Your *shamar* or guardianship is accomplished primarily through prayer and spiritual warfare. Noting this, the apostle Paul then emphasized the need to move by the Spirit to secure God's protection.

> *For our struggle is not against flesh and blood, but against rulers, against the powers, against the world forces of darkness, against the spiritual forces of wickedness in heavenly places.... With all prayer and petition pray at all times in the Spirit, and with this in view, be on the alert with all perseverance and petition for all the saints* (Ephesians 6:12, 18).

Guarding, protecting, and defending can only be accomplished through the power of Holy Spirit. The best way to keep watch over your sphere is to heed this admonition. Pray in the Spirit. Keep watch!

Receiving Prophetic Direction

Again, our first watch must be before the throne—worshiping Jesus, exploring with Him, feeding on His Word, waiting on Him for revelation to be released. The resolve of Habakkuk as a throne room watchman best embodies this aspect of your calling. He said, *"I will stand on my guard post and station myself on the rampart; and I will keep watch to see what He will speak to me"* (2:1).

As noted before, hindsight is always 20/20. But in this season, God wants to give His people 20/20 foresight. To direct our course through current challenges, we and our governmental leaders genuinely need real-time prophetic revelation from the Lord Jesus Christ.

Imagine the treasures that could be discovered, the destinies secured! And also the pitfalls which could be avoided.

Governing in Prayer

Like Elijah, you are called to align your sphere of authority with God's Kingdom. An extraordinary seat has been provided for you at His table, a seat before His throne.

The Lord longs to relate to you in intimate fellowship, but also out of this seat tied to your sphere of authority. Consider yourself a member of His cabinet. You are positioned to pray into your sphere in a way that manifests Heaven on Earth!

This dimension of prayer also includes accessing the Court of Heaven to release God's redemptive verdicts into situations, knowing that the throne of God's beauty is also the Court of His justice.

Delivering Prophetic Direction

Of all the facts of prophetic ministry, delivering real-time revelatory insights to governmental leaders is perhaps the most consistently documented in the entire Bible. From Enoch to Elijah to Daniel, from Isaiah to Hosea to Jeremiah to Jonah, from John the Baptist to Paul the apostle to John the Revelator, all biblical prophets were given this sacred task. Hard words were often delivered by the prophets, but they also surrounded godly leaders with encouraging direction.

Haggai and Zechariah encompassed Zerubbabel as he rebuilt the walls of Jerusalem and finished the Temple, again by Cyrus's decree. Amos through tears then prophesied its destruction once again. John the Baptist thundered the word of the Lord to Herod, calling him out for adultery with his brother's wife. He lost his head for it. But he forever gained God's crown.

Prophesying to the President—A Missed Opportunity

Throughout this book, we've shared stories conveying how prophetic revelation has shaped the course of government. Here's an opportunity from my own life that was actually missed.

I met President Bill Clinton in a bar called the Hot Tin Roof on the island of Martha's Vineyard. The year was 1997. As a staff photojournalist for the *Cape Cod Times*, I was assigned to cover the First Family's secluded vacation, featuring a lot of private beach time, stops in town for ice cream or souvenirs, and exclusive parties we were not invited to attend. Perhaps this was why President Clinton was kind enough to host a party just for the press to close out his island time.

Entertainment was provided by the legendary Carly Simon, who also happened to own the Hot Tin Roof. She eased her way into a familiar melody. And the jaded hearts of a hundred journalists melted, including mine. My attention thus diverted, it was actually a little startling when the president of the United States suddenly closed the distance on his way to the stage. "Hi, I'm Bill Clinton," he said with a large smile, his outstretched hand grabbing mine. "Who are you?"

Fortunately, intercession had been mobilized for this very moment. I had requested prayer for the Clintons while they were on vacation, and also for me. It was highly unlikely that a window would open to talk personally with the president. But, just in case, I had prayed and had requested prayer for the Lord to give me a prophetic word.

I prayed, and the individuals I had asked to pray did as well. And, soon, a concise message came to me and repeated over and over within my spirit, "Cover him. He is like King David in My eyes."

My friends must have been tremendous intercessors because, when the moment came, there was no striving for the opportunity. It just sort of happened. President Clinton actually sought me out!

"My name is Jon Hamill, sir," I nervously replied to the president's query. "I'm with the *Cape Cod Times*. It's an honor to cover you. I'm also a man of prayer. And the Lord spoke to me that you, sir, are like King David in His eyes."

Well, that's at least what I meant to say. But the prophetic impression seemed so superficial with no supernatural knowledge of dates or details, nor any high-level governmental directive upon which the fate of nations hung. The message was, in short, without substance.

Or so I thought.

Standing before President Clinton, his hand grasping mine, I decided not to give the word. "My name is Jon Hamill, sir, a photographer with the *Cape Cod Times*," I replied. "Mr. President, it's an honor to cover you."

Hindsight being 2020, I soon realized just how substantive the prophetic word deleted from my conversation actually was. To me, it seemed like an overblown compliment. But to President Clinton, the phrase would have conveyed a hidden, detailed warning that only Clinton, God, and one other person would have known.

You, sir, are like King David in God's eyes. At that very time Bill Clinton was carrying on an illicit sexual relationship with a White House intern. His was a hauntingly similar scenario to a certain biblical king's most infamous transgression.

God was seeking to convey 2020 foresight to a king of our time. What if the true warning had been given, just as it was given to me from the Lord? What if it had actually been received by the president?

As it was, a year later his abusive affair was exposed. It almost led to his impeachment. I so wish I knew then what I know now. This lesson learned made for a rough start to my training as a White House watchman.

Obedience is not an option but a mandate. Trust the word that God has given to you. Remember that accuracy begins with honesty. Give the word the way Jesus gave it to you, without presumption.

It is likely more meaningful than you know.

For Review

Please take a moment to reflect on what you've just read. We suggest taking notes as you answer questions below.

1. Do you pray regularly for the president? For the vice president? The administration?

2. What does shamar mean? What did you learn about God as a watchman? How has He guarded your life?

3. Do you feel you have a calling to be a watchman? A White House watchman? Describe the sphere or spheres you feel the Lord is assigning to you to pray over.

CHAPTER 8

SECURING YOUR
PERIMETER

WHEN Secret Service agents are deployed, their most important job is to secure the perimeter for the president. Doors, elevators, windows, walls, garages, kitchens, bathrooms, closets, ventilation shafts, floors above and below, airspace—every point of potential access must be evaluated and guarded, including sightlines. To protect from snipers, all points of access by which an accurate shot could be fired must be considered, even from a mile away.

Then there are the crowds. Establishing gates for entering and exiting are essential. So are metal detectors at these gates.

But this task of stopping perpetrators has been made even more difficult in the age of the coronavirus pandemic, when a simple handshake could prove as lethal as a weapon. In March 2020, one Denver councilwoman actually retweeted a vow to weaponize the disease to infect Trump supporters. "For the record, if I do get the coronavirus, I'm attending every MAGA rally I can!"[67]

It is terrifying that an elected official is publicly promoting bioterrorism attacks, even if only sarcastically. Meanwhile, teams from rogue nations have already attempted to strike against us on our soil.

Securing a perimeter is an essential first step for securing the president's safety. It is essential for the nation's safety, as noted by the president. And it's essential for yours. Further, whether keeping watch for a government leader or for your pastor or your family, securing a perimeter in the spirit realm is as essential as the work of Secret Service agents in the natural. At times, it may seem almost as challenging.

That said, learning to establish boundaries through prayer is one of the most important aspects of your calling to *shamar*. And it's as old as the garden of Eden.

Watchmen in the Garden

As representatives of humankind, Adam and Eve were given stewardship of the earth. When Adam was placed by God in the midst of Eden, he was given two primary commissions. God told Adam to *"tend the garden and keep it"* (Gen. 2:15 NKJV). The word *keep* is actually the first biblical reference where the Hebrew word *shamar* is used. As noted in the last chapter, *shamar* means to keep watch.

Then from the very beginning of mankind, *keeping watch* has been part of God's call for all of us.

If this is true, then keeping watch is still a vital part of the stewardship of your spheres. Let me go further. Keeping watch *to secure your boundaries*, Adam's original commission, is a vital part of this stewardship. Yet precious little is ever taught about how to actually accomplish the task.

You would think that, with Eden being a paradise created by God, the garden would automatically be free from any threats. But the Bible makes clear it was otherwise. God told Adam and Eve to *shamar*. So, when a snake showed up, it should have been forcefully removed immediately, especially when it started talking with them.

Watchman principle number one: Remove the talking snake! Especially if rebellion against God is on its tongue.

The occult realm overtook the natural world to form this talking snake. When Adam and Eve refused to kick it out of the garden God assigned them to *shamar*, they both soon succumbed to its seduction. All humanity fell as a result. For this reason, they became the ones escorted out of the garden.

And from that time on, a curse took root in all creation.

Thank God, through the cross, Jesus took the curse for us so that we can be redeemed! We can begin even now to see the light of His resurrection power bring life. The garden can be restored.

Like your garden, Eden existed in many realms at once. It was a place where God directly encountered His creation. Not only was His heart joined to His creation, but the throne of His rulership was joined there. Therefore, the spiritual realm interfaced with the natural world in a way that brought harmony and life to God's creation. To Adam and Eve, there was no dichotomy between the realms of God's glory and the natural realm. Heaven had literally come to Earth.

The biblical narrative hints that things were vastly different outside the realm of the garden. God told Adam and Eve to be fruitful, multiply, and replenish the earth—which implies that prior to their arrival perhaps earlier expressions of creation had largely perished.

So, let's look at the garden of Eden story another way. Eden is a prototype for us, conveying God's desire to establish a beachhead on the earth from which to replenish creation. His glory was present to renew, just as pictured in Genesis 1 where the Spirit of God manifested His brooding presence to shine into darkness and give creation form. The implied picture of Eden is as a secure base from which God, in partnership with Adam and Eve, could extend the boundaries of creation's fullest potential—and drive out the spiritual darkness.

Securing Your Perimeter

This pattern of being placed within a sphere to cultivate it and keep watch over it, protecting and defending God's covenant purposes, is still our primary model of transformation today. It is a primary strategy to secure the harvest Jesus longs to bring. Further, how we steward our assignment, through obedience or disobedience, does not merely affect us. It dramatically affects the garden of our spheres.

What garden has God has assigned to you? What sphere has He placed you in to watch over and cultivate? Maybe it's the executive branch, or the economy, or the tech world, or even the nation as a whole. Answering these questions is important because knowing your sphere is knowing your destiny.

Another question begging an answer is this: How are you dealing with the snake in your garden? In other words, with sin and idolatry? We're going to equip you with a few solid tools to help. But your own will is the first wall of defense.

Generations after Adam, when God commissioned Joshua to take the Promised Land, He made it clear to His young apprentice that, *within the boundaries designated,* His authority would be with him throughout his entire life.

"Every place on which the sole of your foot treads, I have given it to you, just as I spoke to Moses.... No man will be able to stand before you all the days of your life. Just as I have been with Moses, I will be with you; I will not fail you or forsake you" (Joshua 1:3,5).

Notice the promise. No man would be able to stand before him—as long as he functioned within the boundaries assigned to him. Friend, that's a promise for your garden and for the garden of America today.

Dutch Sheets, a longtime watchman for the nation of America, wrote in his book *Intercessory Prayer* the following observation.

> In the nineteenth chapter of Joshua, the word paga (intercession in Hebrew) is used several times. The passage is describing the dimensions or boundaries of each of the tribes of Israel. It is translated several ways in several different translations, including reached to, touched, bordered, boundary....
>
> Does it surprise you that the word used for intercession, paga, is also translated "boundary"? It really shouldn't. It only seems logical to me that the perimeters of protection be linked to

prayer. I want to state emphatically: We CAN build boundaries of protection around ourselves and others through intercession. What a comfort to know that this truth is inherent in the very meaning of the word.[68]

Covenant Unlocks Authority

Here's a tag-on to this excellent insight. In Joshua's case, God had already cut covenant with Himself for the land and the people Israel. That said, boundaries or perimeters can be governed much more effectively through watchman prayer when covenant with God over these spheres is established. It's why it's so important for you to know the sphere the Lord has assigned to you. We will close out the chapter with a prayer for you to enter into covenant with God over your sphere.

But for now, let's make this easy. What geography of the earth do you possess by contract? Maybe you rent or own a home. Maybe you've just secured a hotel room and know it needs to be cleaned out spiritually. Or maybe you've just struck a deal for a conference hall.

Also, what occupation do you hold? In all these spheres, your signature grants you legal right to take authority, including spiritual authority, during the time agreed within the contract. Take out the snake!

Please remember this basic principle. Covenant unlocks governmental authority to secure your perimeters.

Exercising Your Authority

In Luke 10, Jesus is pictured commissioning His disciples to advance the Kingdom. He was sending them into the spheres He had assigned them in preparation for His visitation. And He made a promise that carries over to today, *"Behold, I HAVE GIVEN YOU AUTHORITY to tread on serpents and scorpions, and over all the power of the enemy, and nothing will injure you"* (Luke 10:19 emphasis added).

Jesus' redemption has secured your authority to *shamar* your garden in the spiritual realm as well as the natural. But, like Adam and Eve, you must exercise the authority He has given you to secure your domain.

This is a very important discipline that even watchmen in the natural, such as Secret Service agents or military and intelligence leaders, must gain mastery over to truly protect their spheres.

Here's an example. A friend of mine served in Iraq and was stationed at one of Saddam Hussein's former palaces. The area came under massive shelling. One of these times, my friend was on the phone with his wife when a bomb exploded nearby. Her pleas were met with stunned silence on the other end until a commanding voice nearby declared, "Get under your desk!"

My friend's wife prayed fervently. She awoke with a tremendous sense of urgency in her spirit. On their next call, she shared the instructions the Lord had given her: take communion, bless the land, and pour out a portion of the bread and wine, representing God's covenant with the land.

My friend followed through. He walked the perimeter of the compound, establishing what we now call a *bloodline* by pleading the blood of Jesus step by step and asking God to secure it from shelling. He asked God to forgive all sin which had defiled the land. He decreed Psalm 91, saying, "Lord, we choose to dwell in the secret place of the Most High, and abide under Your shadow. Surely You will deliver us!" After completing the perimeter prayer walk, he sealed the journey with communion. A portion of the bread and wine was carefully placed in the ground as a witness of God's covenant protection over the land. He then blew a shofar, returning afterward to his quarters.

When your compound is being targeted with shelling, how do you gauge when to take your walk? It's a risky venture, night or day. But it was worth the effort of my friend. Shelling continued in the region, but near his compound it immediately stopped.

Another friend served on the Mexican border as a Customs and Border Protection agent. He was high-level, even joining special-ops teams to take down drug cartel leaders. Again and again, the drug lords would elude them, almost as if vanishing into thin air. He discovered later that these cartel leaders were engaging in satanic rituals in which they actually made covenants with death and hell to protect them from being discovered (see Isa. 28:18).

The good news is that, through Jesus Christ, these covenants can be annulled! My friend sought the Lord, pleading the blood of Jesus to annul pacts made to invoke these demonic powers, keeping watch before the throne until he knew breakthrough had been granted. He then took authority over the powers being invoked. Finally, on another raid, the drug lord was captured. And the battle turned.

These are just a few examples among many we could share from the battlefields of foreign lands to the threshing floor of the Oval Office. Re-present Jesus' covenant of redemption. Take authority in the spirit realm over demonic powers whenever needed. Take out the snake!

You will discover amazing results, for when God sets you in a sphere, He grants you the authority to subdue the adversaries assailing it.

When Nations Become Your Garden

The expression of covenant authority was conveyed in garden imagery for one of Israel's greatest watchmen, the prophet Jeremiah. He wrote:

> *Behold, I have put My words in your mouth. See, I have appointed you this day over the nations and over the kingdoms, to pluck up and to break down, to destroy and to overthrow, to build and to plant* (Jeremiah 1:9–10).

His watchman call involved specific spheres he was responsible for. The Lord promised prophetic insight. Just as with Adam and Eve, just as with you and me, Jeremiah was assigned to *shamar* the spheres assigned to him with great care.

From that day forward, Jeremiah's mouth became a sharp threshing instrument to harvest the nations. But I want you to see something. He didn't necessarily have to leave his own nation to steward his call for nations and kingdoms. The Spirit of God moved him to prophesy.

Through his seeding the word of the Lord into the spheres assigned to him, nations and kingdoms shifted.

Some of the greatest watchmen I know rarely leave their own homes. Yet as they lean into the Spirit and invest in prayer for those to whom they are assigned, God breathes secrets into their spirits. What they see and decree comes to pass—even thousands of miles away.

Take my friend Martin Frankena, for example. Martin is a spiritual father to us, a profound teacher gifted to bring healing and restoration. Holy Spirit's gift of discernment works more accurately in his life than anyone I know. And by some miracle of God, he was assigned by the Lord years ago to look after Jolene and me. To keep watch!

One day while I was ministering in Africa, a paralyzing pain shot through my body. There were no warning signs. And there were no nearby medical facilities if things got more serious. I called Martin for prayer, whereupon he told me exactly where I had been and precisely where this attack, sourced in the occult, was coming from.

With so much detailed information, I literally looked behind me, halfway expecting him to be in the next room. *Was not my spirit with you?*

Martin then prayed. He took authority over the occult forces sent to harm me. The oppression left immediately, as did all symptoms. In a hot moment, I was completely fine and completed the ministry tour with no further disruptions.

Now, that's a pretty high standard for keeping watch. But God is limitless in His capacities. The lesson for you is that your intercession can directly and immediately touch those assigned to your care in prayer, whether in Africa or around the corner or at 1600 Pennsylvania Avenue. The key is to step out in your call. Keep watch!

Securing the Perimeter of Your Home

Faithfulness in small things pays great dividends in God's economy. For instance, David as a young Bethlehem shepherd dedicated himself to becoming an incredible watchman, tending the sheep while taking down lions and bears prowling around to snatch them. He harnessed his skills with a slingshot. Faithfulness in seemingly small things prepared him to confront the giant Goliath—and ultimately to care for, protect, and defend the sheep of Israel as their king.

Just as God has given you a garden to tend, so He considers you His garden. He knows the seeds of greatness planted within you. And as a great Father, He is determined not just to watch over and keep this garden of your life, but to cultivate you for His glory. Be faithful on your watch! He will reward you as only He can.

Before even the White House, your house is your first priority for cultivating God's watchman call. It's your greatest training ground. I guarantee you lessons gained while meeting God in the daily life of your own heart, home, and family will carry you through greater challenges when your borders are expanded.

Take, for instance, securing your perimeter. What access points does the enemy have within your home? Your family? Your generational line? And how can you partner with God in watchman prayer to shut these gates of sabotage? Here are seven suggestions to get you going.

Enthroning Jesus

First, Jesus should be enthroned at the center of your garden. Are you cultivating personal time with Him? With His Word? Do you wait on Him until His Spirit authentically connects with you? The transformation of your garden begins with prioritizing this intimate communion. Don't allow distractions to pull you away from the secret place because it's really His presence that transforms!

What Are You Watching

Here's a hard question. When was the last time you took stock of what you're viewing on the internet or on television? By saturating yourself in any media too long, you are ultimately submitting your spirit to its influence. Obviously, some sources are godlier than others. But ungodly worldviews, even embedded in the midst of programs that are clean overall, can ultimately affect you. They can defile or deaden your spirit.

Don't ask me how I know. Just ask the Lord to cleanse you from all defilement. Call your human spirit to the forefront again. And stop meddling!

Familiar Objects

Many people are snagged by souvenirs and mementos that, through ungodly dedications, may have occult power attached to them. Throw them away!

More difficult to extract from your garden are the sentimental gifts that bear human attachments. A married friend of mine was haunted by recurring dreams of a former lover. I asked if he had kept any of her gifts or notes. It turned out he had a secret stash of photos and cards—the ones that pledged undying love—tucked away in a box.

At first, that box wasn't going anywhere. Some access points are honestly hard to let go of. I prayed with my friend, asking the Lord to annul all covenant that had organically formed between him and his former girlfriend through their intimacy and shared pledges. We asked God to sever all spirit ties, soul ties, and body ties between them.

Finally, my friend gained the courage to let the box go. The dreams stopped. His marriage is now stronger than ever. Access removed!

Expressions of Idolatry

Above everything else, your covenant of betrothal needs to be protected. This goes for your relationship with Jesus as well as your relationship with your spouse. God considers idolatry to be exactly the same as sexual immorality. It is a violation of covenant.

To be an effective watchman, do yourself a favor and rid your home of every object that could possibly be tied to idolatry or the occult. This includes crystal balls, and many rock albums and videos featuring the occult. Throw out the physical stuff and erase the digital stuff.

It is amazing to me how many Christians own collections of Harry Potter books, DVDs, and occult paraphernalia when every aspect of their sorcery is expressly forbidden by the Bible. Many even entertain their children with it! And then we naively wonder why, when our kids grow up, they want little to do with God or the Church.

Countless guardians not only failed to protect their children from the snake in the garden, they encouraged the relationship. And a door of access was opened. Take out the snake! God has a strategy to redeem your family, even from what you and I allowed the enemy to influence. The program begins with repentance. Stop tolerating what defiles you and separates you from God.

As a gatekeeper, you cannot defeat what you embrace. And every decision, right or wrong, bears an influence on your offspring.

Family Heirlooms and Generational Curses

All this said, just about every person in the Western world has some tie to the occult, either personally or within their generational line through overt witchcraft or more subtle forms such as Freemasonry, DeMolay, Eastern Star, etc. Ask the Lord to forgive you and your family line for embracing the occult in any form. Plead His blood to annul all covenants with these powers that dedicated your family line to the enemy. Get rid of family heirlooms dealing with the occult, and command the demonic entities attached to them to immediately and permanently leave your presence and your family.

Securing your perimeter ultimately begins with you. I suggest strongly that you work with a competent, proven prayer counselor to pray through generational pacts with darkness made by your forefathers through the occult, unjust bloodshed, sexual immorality, etc. It's time to shut the gates of sabotage. You will be surprised at the new level of freedom you experience!

And every inch of ground gained, every victory won, ultimately carries over as earned authority in securing your sphere. The principles are exactly the same. So are the results.

Tithes and Offerings

Another aspect of securing your perimeter in the spirit realm is to participate in the divine exchange of tithes and offerings. In Malachi 3, God again uses garden language to describe how He will move within your sphere according to your faithfulness, *"Prove me now herewith, saith the Lord of hosts, if I will not open you the windows of heaven, and pour you out a blessing, that there shall not be room enough to receive it"* (v. 10 KJV).

In short, God will be your watchman over your sphere, working with you, and completely apart from you, to tend your garden and keep it!

Jesus' Midnight Watch

It was in a garden, teetering in their responsibilities as watchmen, that Adam and Eve fell—and all humanity with them. In this age especially, we take their sin so lightly. Biblical boundaries crossed in open defiance of God are often celebrated and encouraged by our peers—by our culture—and even by religion. Our corporate conscience has become seared.

Consequences of our sin are now more often medicated than authentically mitigated through repentance. "His watchmen are blind, all of them know nothing," Isaiah proclaimed over his generation and ours.

> *They are shepherds who have no understanding; they have all turned to their own way, each one to his unjust gain, to the last one. "Come," they say, 'let us get wine, and let us drink heavily of strong drink; and tomorrow will be like today, only more so"* (Isaiah 56:10–12).

To the garden of contemporary America, it's just normal life. Who then is truly keeping watch?

The first Adam, watchman over the garden of Eden, failed. The consequences were very high. But a second Adam, again representing all of humanity, was placed by God as a watchman in a garden. This time to redeem you, and through you, the potential of your sphere.

The journey of humanity which began in Eden crescendoed in Gethsemane, where the greatest Watchman the world had ever known— *Shamar Israel* wrapped in flesh and blood—took the strongest measures possible to protect and defend those He loved.

Satan offered Adam and Eve fruit from a forbidden tree, and all humankind fell. God the Father offered Jesus a garden transaction to reverse this curse. The "plague" of the sins of us all was compressed together into a single cup the Father offered Jesus to drink. There was no escape from its infection. By this, He would not just take our sins but would *become sin* for us. And He would suffer the just punishment accordingly. *"God made the only one who did not know sin to become sin for us, so that we who did not know righteousness might become the righteousness of God through our union with him"* (2 Cor. 5:21 TPT).

Earlier, Jesus had compelled His disciples to stay awake and keep watch with Him. Yet in His most desperate hour, struggling to embrace the horror of this unimaginable defilement followed by crucifixion on our behalf, He found His disciples slumbering. In this moment, God Himself kept solitary watch over His only begotten Son. Jesus said, *"Father, if You are willing, remove this cup from Me; yet not My will, but Yours be done"* (Luke 22:42).

An angel was dispatched to intervene. What transpired was one of the most astounding moments in the history of prayer: *"Now an angel from heaven appeared to Him, strengthening Him. And being in agony He was praying very fervently; and His sweat became like drops of blood, falling down upon the ground"* (Luke 22:43–44).

Jesus was strengthened for agony. Most of the time, you and I want angelic intervention to deliver us from agony—like anxiety over finding a parking spot, for instance, or the struggle to forgive the barista who messed up a coffee order.

But Jesus was strengthened so He could endure to prevail in prayer, in an agonizing travail that would ultimately bring you and me to new birth.

Jesus noted that a servant is not greater than His master. In seasons of your watch, you will occasionally experience agony as well, even as you represent the covenant victory Jesus won for us. Sometimes, you will understand the circumstances, sometimes not. Sometimes, travail by the Spirit in prayer will be so all-encompassing that you will feel as if you are literally giving birth. Sometimes, for the benefit of those you love, you may even be required to lay down your life or at least aspects of it.

Strengthened for agony, Jesus prayed more fervently and clung to the Father to see His mission through. We should resolve now to do the same, praying through our travails of justice until His breakthrough authentically comes.

Maybe not coincidentally, the garden marks the first location where Scripture records Jesus' blood fell upon the ground. By His blood, the curse which began in a garden with Adam and Eve would be entirely broken. Communion with God would be restored. The crown of thorns would be transformed into a crown of glory. And you and I would become eternally redeemed.

In the garden, the Lamb assumed the full responsibility for both the gross negligence and the casual, unintentional mistakes that daily fill our lives. He suffered on the cross in our stead. With great power, Jesus was later raised from the dead in a garden tomb and then presented His own body and blood before the throne of His Father for humanity's redemption. Heaven's Court convened to evaluate the purity of this blood. The gavel fell. Request granted. Covenant with death and hell annulled!

And a new covenant was released to Heaven and Earth that forever secures our redemption.

Here's a thought. Jesus didn't just die for sinners on broad terms. He died for the sins of the watchmen. But more than even that, He lived, died, and rose again as a watchman to redeem the watchman's call. Through Jesus' mighty redemption, the watchman call itself was restored from garden to garden—for all humankind to enter into once again.

Covenant Over Your Sphere

And it is this sacred covenant you bear witness to in consecrating your sphere to the Father and consecrating yourself as a watchman over your sphere.

The final principle I want to explore in this chapter is vital for your success, especially when it comes to securing answers to prayer that transform your spheres long term. Amazingly, it is one of the least taught principles of prayer. Yet it essentially governs both the spiritual and the natural realms.

We've mentioned it before. Covenants establish thrones of governance.

In a way we can barely fathom, Jesus secured His assigned sphere of authority through covenant with His Father. The cost was unimaginable. But the rewards catalyze the redemption of His love through all time.

Here are seven benefits of covenant we have covered so far in this book.

1. Covenant unlocks intimacy with God.

2. Covenant unlocks forgiveness and healing.

3. Covenant unlocks authority to protect and defend your sphere.

4. Covenant unlocks provision.

5. Covenant unlocks the genuine prophetic.

6. Covenant unlocks transformation.

7. Covenant unlocks God's glory.

Throughout the past seven years, we have been graced by God to experience turnarounds in our national governance of an unprecedented magnitude. Further, the Lord has consistently given us insight and courage to prophesy these turnarounds before they ever materialized.

Is God just in a mood to show off? Are the turnarounds granted simply to prove the prowess of our prophetic words?

By no means. Again, our nation was established in covenant with the Lord Jesus Christ. This means that the thrones of our national governance belong to Him by covenant. And as we come into alignment with His covenant, we can serve as watchmen to unleash His purposes. Establishing covenant with Christ divorced from "the snake," in other words from historic idolatry, is key to unlocking His transformation within our spheres.

Years ago, at Jesus' direction, we came into covenant with Him over the White House and executive branch of our government as part of our overarching covenant for our nation and for Israel. We've found it to be true that covenant unlocks the fullest measure of intimacy, authority, and provision necessary to release His Kingdom within our respective spheres.

That's why David had to restore the ark of the covenant before even pitching his tent for 24/7 worship. He first had to realign his nation with the foundations of God's covenant.

Centuries later, Isaiah the prophet referenced David's move of restoration when he declared, *"For Zion's sake I will not keep silent, and for Jerusalem's sake I will not keep quiet, until her righteousness goes forth like brightness, and her salvation like a torch that is burning"* (v. 1). Isaiah went on to share how desolation would break when Israel's sons and daughters came into covenant with Him for the land.

> *It will no longer be said to you, "Forsaken," nor to your land will it any longer be said, "Desolate"; but you will be called, "My delight is in her," and your land, "Married"; for the Lord delights in you, and to Him your land will be married. For as a young man marries a virgin, so your sons will marry you; and as the bridegroom rejoices over the bride, so your God will rejoice over you on your walls, O Jerusalem, I have appointed watchmen. All day and all night they will never keep silent* (Isaiah 62:4–6).

In other words, God has set watchmen on our walls in covenant with Him to release His redemption over their respective spheres. Here is the ultimate secret to watchman prayer that transforms the inheritance the Lord assigns to you.

With this, let's now come into covenant with God just as Isaiah described. The prayer below serves as a good guideline. Consider receiving communion as you pray.

> *Father God, I desire to relate to You and serve You as a White House watchman. Please direct me. Show me the sphere which You're calling me to keep watch over, and how to release Your Kingdom transformation within it. Lord, please keep watch with me and through me. Right now, I come into covenant with You*

for this sphere. I dedicate my sphere to You, and calling within this sphere to You, in Jesus' name.

Thank You that You have seated me with Christ in heavenly places. I receive my throne of authority before Your throne! Help me to access this seat continually. Relate to me out of Your affection, and also over the sphere You've called me to. Grant me an excellent spirit to steward responsibilities well and achieve my full potential for You. Be enthroned over my spheres of authority as I commit them to You!

Please help me to secure the boundaries of my spheres and establish them as places of safety—where You are free to dwell. Expose all hidden points of access to the enemy. I plead the blood of Jesus over the sins which opened this access and ask that You remit the sins that have taken place previously within my sphere.

Lord, in Your presence, before Your throne, I lean into You now. Synergize me with Your heartbeat. Synergize me with Your throne and the activities of Your throne. Synergize me with the move of Your Spirit from Your throne to my sphere. Synergize me with Your angelic hosts. Release Your angels to have charge over me, to watch over and keep me in all my ways—to watch over, protect, defend, and prosper my spheres as well!

As I seal this covenant now, please grant me Your Spirit of wisdom and revelation to unlock the fullness of Your Kingdom within my sphere, in Jesus' name, Amen.

CHAPTER 9

DANIEL'S SECRETS

JOLENE here. We are excited you are choosing to become a watchman over your sphere! Let's now look at ways your call can be fulfilled in your life and career. The prophet Daniel is a profound model for White House watchmen, and Jon and I and are excited to share with you a few secrets we have learned. Me first! Jon will share in the second half of the chapter.

Like a good workout, rehearsing these principles will help you grow in hearing God, praying more effectively, and even becoming more successful in your workplace.

As Jon mentioned earlier, during New Year's 2019, we were staying at a house owned by a man named Gabriel Speaks. I've always known Jesus to be extremely funny as He relates to me. And He never passes up an opportunity to display His hilarity! We had been praying intensely for fresh revelation. And by bringing us to Gabriel Speaks' home, He was definitely making a point: "Your prayers have been heard, and they're being answered!"

Really, we had no idea how profound the answer that night would turn out to be. God showed us Daniel 10. We also discovered a blood moon would rise over DC that would signal the third year of rulership for America's Cyrus.

Spirit to Understand

As Jon told you earlier, the moment I sat down in the home of Gabriel Speaks, my eyes fell on the book of Daniel—specifically Daniel 9:22, where the angel Gabriel came to Daniel, bringing an anointing and ability to understand. In other words, Gabriel speaks! It was like that was the anointing in the room.

I've read the Bible through many times, but that day, the book of Daniel opened up to me, and revelation flowed, giving me a supernatural ability to understand Scripture more clearly than I had ever understood:

> *While I was still speaking in prayer, then the man Gabriel, whom I had seen in the vision previously, came to me in my extreme weariness about the time of the evening offering. He gave me instruction and talked with me and said, "O Daniel, I have now come forth to give you INSIGHT WITH UNDERSTANDING. At the beginning of your supplications the command was issued, and I have come to tell you, for you are highly esteemed; so give heed to the message and gain understanding of the vision"* (Daniel 9:21–23 emphasis added).

As previous generations used to say, sometimes more is caught than taught. I felt the Lord imparted a spirit to understand that day—what the apostle Paul called *"a spirit of wisdom and revelation in the knowledge of Him"* (Eph. 1:17). And He gave me an ability not just to discover revelation myself, but to impart the anointing for revelation to others—not just keys in head knowledge, but *the anointing to understand.*

Certainly, as a White House watchman, what's most important is for you to grow in this aspect of your relationship with God. You need clarity of revelation like Daniel, not just for those you pray for, but also to prepare the Body of Christ for what's ahead.

From that day forward, I have experienced a greater ability to gain revelation personally and through God's Word. I am able to better discern how Holy Spirit is moving, as well as understand angelic activity and interaction with us.

> *So, Father, just as the Scripture says in Daniel 9:22 that You granted a supernatural ability to understand, I ask that You grant Your Spirit of wisdom and revelation in the knowledge of Jesus to all reading this who hunger and thirst to know You more. Thank You for the season that we're in and for the increased angelic help assigned for the season that we're in. I thank You that You are imparting to my friends a spirit to understand—a spirit of guidance and knowledge, and an ability to discern and act upon things previously not known to them. Thank You for a fullness of revelation of who You are and how You feel about us.*

You are Cherished by God!

Gabriel came to Daniel and said, *"And I have come to tell you, for you are highly esteemed"* (Dan. 9:23). And this was one of the most important aspects of the revelation Daniel gained.

These same words are for you too. Please let this go deep in your heart. Know that you are qualified to receive revelation and answers to prayer simply because God esteems you! He loves you and appreciates all that you do for Him.

Since coming to Jesus, I have always known that He delights in me because He shows how He cherishes me in big ways and in small. One key of intimacy with the Lord is to recognize all the little ways in which He sends love our way. Understanding and experiencing His delight for us is what makes us want to be excellent for Him.

An Excellent Spirit

Daniel was described over and over as having an excellent spirit—a spirit of excellence:

Then this Daniel began to distinguish himself among the commissioners and satraps, because he possessed an excellent spirit, and the king planned to appoint him over the entire kingdom (Daniel 6:3).

Part of the understanding imparted at the home of Gabriel Speaks was how to carry a spirit of excellence.

First, I want to describe what an excellent spirit is not. It's not striving for religious perfection. It's not about being without weakness. In many ways, it's the opposite of that. An excellent spirit means embracing your weaknesses and asking God to be strong through you. An excellent spirit mandates honesty. You can no longer run from your personal challenges in denial. Instead, you need to confess your faults and sins, and invite God to work on overcoming them together with you.

Let me give an example. If fear is one of your weaknesses, *"perfect love casts out fear"* (1 John 4:18). But the perfection has to be on God's side, not yours. It's His perfect love that casts out your fear, not your perfection in walking in love. Lean into Jesus for assistance and deliverance, and you will gain ground you only dreamed of!

An excellent spirit is not perfection; it is keeping your faults before the throne. As Scripture points out, it's the Lord who keeps us from stumbling. It's He who presents us without fault. And the most important part is that He presents us before His glory with exceeding joy (see Jude 1:24). When our focus is on Him, we carry joy. When our focus is on ourselves and our faults, we carry condemnation.

It's the enemy who keeps you focused on where you've fallen down. If you keep your eyes on the Lord, He will keep your feet from stumbling. Our weakness in and of itself does not disqualify us. What we do with our weakness could.

Faithfulness to God During Persecution

The Lord gave me understanding of many things through the book of Daniel during our time at the Gabriel Speaks house. I want to share on one other aspect. It hopefully shows why God is calling you closer to Him, as well as how to embrace a watchman's call as Daniel did.

Daniel was first a watchman of God's covenant with his extended family, the Jewish people, and then with us as well. Within Daniel's message, there is a warning for God's people about times of increased persecution. What we could eventually come up against today became clearer. It is obviously occurring throughout the world, but it could soon happen even in America if we do not engage now to preserve religious freedom.

Previous administrations already began to implement programs targeting Christians for persecution. Thank God, President Trump rolled them back! But an American Cyrus is needed as president right now for this very reason.

And it gives a great perspective on why God is asking you, like Daniel, to keep watch.

Daniel's Integrity

While serving as the king's primary counselor, Daniel was faced with imminent death. The deep state of his day plotted to take him down through the one aspect that defined his life more than anything else—his unwavering devotion to God.

Other advisors within the administration became jealous of Daniel's favor with the king. So, they plotted to bring him down.

> *Then the commissioners and satraps began trying to find a ground of accusation against Daniel in regard to government affairs; but THEY COULD FIND NO GROUND of accusation or evidence of corruption, inasmuch as HE WAS FAITHFUL, and no negligence or corruption was to be found in him* (Daniel 6:4 emphasis added).

This passage speaks volumes about Daniel's character. Why was Daniel so esteemed before God and successive kings?

He had yielded to God's excellence through consistently practicing faithfulness and integrity. He refused to compromise this standard.

Daniel's greatness came from the inside out. Faithfulness and service were the genuine hallmarks of this prophet's legacy. Kings trusted him to rule their kingdom. They not only sought his counsel, but also his companionship because he exercised a high level of discretion that consistently protected those he served.

Daniel conveyed hard messages, never manipulating facts for personal preservation or advancement. I'm not saying that Daniel was not ambitious. He wanted to get ahead. That's why the Bible describes him as "distinguishing himself" among his peers. And he distinguished himself to others by consistently offering two precious commodities—integrity and solutions. The practical innovations he offered were always on point and often came from the very counsel of God.

Daniel fulfilled what he said. He completed his work. No negligence or corruption was found in him! Let the same be said about you. Your conduct before people is a reflection of your devotion to God.

When Government Becomes God

With no basis to accuse Daniel and topple him, the other counselors finally conceived a plot to either compromise him completely or bring him to death. They said, *"We will not find any ground of accusation against this Daniel unless we find it against him with regard to the law of his God"* (Dan. 6:5).

So, the counselors created a law magnifying the king as God. Anyone who prayed to any other god than the king would be put to death—the lion's den!

Government as god is the private dream of many rulers and many systems of dictatorship, including the "theocracies" of socialism and communism. The deep state of Daniel's day conspired to shift the government fully into this role—and conveniently, take down the one man who would stand in their way.

The Lord showed me clearly that a time was coming when many of us would be faced with similar situations. And Daniel's response to that was not only to defy the ruling but actually to do the opposite. He refused to worship other gods. And he refused to worship the God of Israel in secret. Instead of hiding his love for the Lord, he opened up the windows of his upper room and *prayed out loud!*

> *Now when Daniel knew that the document was signed, he entered into his house (now in his roof chamber he had windows opened toward Jerusalem); and he continued kneeling on his knees three times a day, praying and giving thanks before his God, as he had been doing previously* (Daniel 6:10).

Do Not Bow the Knee

Daniel could have made many excuses that would have validated compromise. He was in a very important position of influence with the king, and that influence was needed to protect his fellow Jews. His death would have probably meant only more persecution for them.

But if he had compromised in idolatry, he would have compromised his relationship with God. He would have broken covenant with God. And he would have compromised his seat of authority before God as a watchman for his people.

Remember how Jesus was tempted by satan, *"All these things I will give You, if You fall down and worship me"* (Matt. 4:9). Extreme traps featuring this same temptation are being set to ensnare both Daniels and Cyrus leaders today. Know that the fallen do not just compromise themselves. They compromise their seats of authority, neutralizing God's influence and opening up the influence of demonic powers to rule over their throne.

So, whether it is outright coercion or the seductive promise of a brighter future, you and I must resolve now to recognize this test—and pass it when it comes. Don't bow the knee! As Jesus declared, *"Go, Satan! For it is written, 'You shall worship the Lord your God, and serve Him only'"* (Matt. 4:10).

Daniel—The Turnaround Prophet

Jon here. Jolene's insights on the prophet Daniel have been life changing. At least for me! I hope you received deeply from God's Spirit of understanding. Let's pick up right where Jolene left off.

Daniel was called to heal the history of his people—repairing the past to redeem the present and restore God's dream for the future. Many communities in America are in dire need of the same process, including Washington DC!

Before we explore the process of repairing history, let's look at Daniel's results. One word describes it—turnaround. Like King David before him, Daniel was consumed from his youth with a singular passion that directed the entire course of his life. Brought to Babylon as a captive, Daniel devoted himself to preparing the way for the Jews to return to their Promised Land.

To accomplish this, history had to be healed. A stockpile of generational sins, which defrauded God's people of their legitimacy before Heaven's Court and denied them access to their land of promise, had to be dealt with. Daniel's intercession propelled him before Heaven's Court on their behalf. In time, not only were the Jews restored from exile, but King Cyrus even funded their journey home! As you know, he even provided for the restoration of their Temple.

Now that, my friends, is a turnaround!

Ponder this. Through Daniel's intercession, you and I have been pushed toward freedom as well—because Daniel repaired history in a way that not only redeemed the potential of his generation, but helped to restore God's dream for our own generation.

Discerning Breaches

To repair history, it's important to discern where breaches against God's covenant with His people have brought them into captivity. The void of clear freedom or promise in an area of life is the clearest indicator there's a problem. And usually, the agony we suffer because of this void is what drives us to solutions. We often want to put a Band-Aid on a problem.

But God always desires to fix things at a foundational level. As John the Baptist famously observed, the axe must be laid at the root of the tree (see Matt. 3:10).

And this is so important to remember when looking for a reprieve from an agonizing situation. Sure, Band-Aids and painkillers all help, but what's beneath the surface? Do you discern a cyclical pattern of the same problems from previous generations?

History on repeat, that's how it was in Daniel's day. For his people to be restored from captivity, their own history had to be repaired.

Babylon Idol

Daniel lived in exile, in a kingdom called Babylon, with boundaries encompassing much of what is now Iraq and Iran. His people were under severe discipline from the Lord. Instead of worshiping the God of Israel alone, they had given themselves to idols, embracing immorality and even bringing Baal worship into God's very Temple.

And after centuries of contending, God withdrew His glory. The Jews were sent into exile as captives, *into the very land of the gods they had chosen.*

You can imagine the agony.

But there's a principle to discover. God's discipline many times comes simply by handing us over to our own misguided choices and their consequences. But because He loves us, it's most often His last resort after striving hard with us to change.

Daniel made this "reverse exodus" as a youth. He was born into royalty, and from his childhood possessed great intelligence, humility, and discretion. Above all, from his childhood Daniel devoted himself to the God of Israel with all of his heart.

Recognizing and harnessing human potential was a skill that Babylon was famous for. In fact, they were renowned innovators in governance, military prowess, mathematics, science and technology, shipping and trading. They became a regional superpower and a global influencer. To keep their cutting edge, the human resources wing of the Babylonian government relied heavily on capable recruiters to discover the next bright star. Sort of the Medo-Persian version of American Idol. Let's call it *Babylon Idol*.

Anyway, when the recruiters evaluated this new crop of immigrant talent that had just landed on their doorsteps, Daniel caught their eye. Not only did he make the cut, he immediately became captain of the team. And he remained so throughout his life, serving as the top advisor to at least six successive kings.

Invitation Declined

As Jolene mentioned, Daniel refused to bow to the idols of Babylon—even at the cost of his own life.

This refusal to compromise is perhaps the primary key to Daniel's extraordinary success in Babylon and his God-given authority to shape history. Yet it is probably the most ignored aspect of his legacy, probably because it seems so foreign to our own experience.

I mean, it's not like our kings and rulers set up a gigantic idol in the center of Washington DC, and make innovators and legislators bow down to it in order for their leadership skills to be accepted and put to use. Do they?

Daniel's mandate to bow the knee would have been his initiation into what we call today a *secret society* or a *fraternal order*. Those who bowed the knee were accepted and promoted within the ranks. Those who refused remained mandatory outsiders. Secret societies were the standard entryways into all powerhouse governments in the region, from the Pharaohs in Egypt to the rulers of Greece, Rome, and Babylon. And it's still true in many cases today, even in the Western world.

Further, it's not a coincidence that today's secret societies take most of their rituals directly from the "ancient mystery religions" of Greece, Babylon, and Egypt.

As Jolene mentioned, in the spirit realm, bowing your knee to an idol brings you into covenant with the idol. And that's a primary way in which the enemy establishes inroads into our government and culture—what we like to call "the thrones behind the thrones."

Earned Authority

Why was Daniel's intercession so successful—simply because he fasted and prayed?

No way. Daniel was so successful in his prayer projects because of the *earned authority* or legitimacy he had gained before the throne by refusing to compromise with Babylon's idolatry.

This decision was very costly, even unto death. But because *Daniel conquered the very temptation which had brought his people into exile,* the Court of Heaven deemed him legally justified to serve as a lawyer for their restoration back to Israel. When Daniel cried out, Heaven heard—and responded.

Daniel's Prayer Team

One of the greatest accelerators of Daniel's success also helped him sustain his success and favor long term. Over the entirety of his life, Daniel was sought after by successive kings, including Cyrus, for his wise counsel. It was sourced in a lifetime of prayer.

But Daniel also cultivated a core team of covenant friends, leaders in their own right, to pray with him and for him. They walked together throughout Daniel's life. No doubt they gave him wise counsel.

Jolene and I felt strongly to follow this pattern to build the foundation of our ministry. You've already read about our friends Martin and Cindy Frankena. If you've been on our weekly prayer calls, you have been introduced to Bill and Marlene Brubaker, whom we affectionately call "Dad and Mom" to the Lamplighter family. Longtime house church leaders and counselors, their intercession and care for us have propelled us forward beyond our wildest dreams.

Many times, we have become an answer to prayer for them as well. Living in Washington State, their lifelong heartbeat has been to see Washington DC revitalized, and a collaborative prayer movement arise to impact the highest halls of government. Their prayers have gone so much farther than their feet could ever take them. We in turn have become torchbearers of their legacy.

Russ and Julie have likewise been like the angels of the Lord to Jolene and me, invisible to most, yet helping us far more than we could have ever imagined. In the midst of a personal housing crisis in Washington DC, Julie saw in a vision the new home the Lord had prepared for us. Intercession was being held from the top floor of a watchman's perch with the Pentagon on the left side and all of Washington DC on the right. She even saw a fountain in the middle of a circular driveway. She saw every major detail of a watchman's perch neither of us knew existed. That perch has now become our home.

Another point of connectivity is our Gideon Group, a close-knit group of high-level leaders and intercessors who pray for each other, process revelation together, and above all keep watch together. We bonded initially over a common call to protect President Trump in prayer. The Lord breathed life.

On a broader level, our nationwide Lamplighter family has been birthed out of these core relationships. We are authentically together on this journey. Regular postings provide prophetic perspectives and updates for concentrated prayer. Our weekly conference calls provide a forum for sharing and carrying out the prayer assignments the Lord calls us to together. But the highest priority is connecting in relationship to forge the future together.

That said, the value of collaborative community cannot be overstated. Interdependence must replace independence for you to overcome the magnitude of challenges, especially spiritually, that will be coming your way. And if these challenges are not there, you're probably not yet much of a threat. Plan to be, though.

We recommend that you begin with a group of core friends who will surround you with prayer and wise counsel. Resolve to walk together long term, but don't weigh the relationships down by formalizing them or attaching obligatory tasks. Be relational. Let the relationships form organically.

Daniel succeeded because of it. And as Daniel succeeded, Cyrus then succeeded, and so will you!

Repairing History

Daniel discovered a lost treasure—a prophetic word given a generation before by the prophet Jeremiah. This word is actually a verdict from Heaven's Court, defining the sentence imposed to discipline God's people.

> *In the first year of his reign, I, Daniel, observed in the books the number of the years which was revealed as the word of the Lord to Jeremiah the prophet for the completion of the desolations of Jerusalem, namely, seventy years. So I gave my attention to the Lord God to seek Him by prayer and supplications, with fasting, sackcloth and ashes* (Daniel 9:2–3).

For seventy years, the people of Israel would remain in servitude in Babylon while their capital Jerusalem was to remain desolate, bereft of people, promise, or glory.

The good news is that those seventy years were up! By this scroll of Jeremiah, Daniel perceived God's "now" timing for His people to be released from subjugation and returned to their freedom land. Daniel had literally interceded all his life for this very moment.

If you were Daniel, how would you react? Swing open the doors and throw a party? Get on the circuit and tell everybody they're free? Write a book about it—like the one you're holding in your hand?

That's why Daniel's response doesn't make so much sense—at first. Instead of feasting, he's fasting. Instead of raucous worship, he's pictured in sackcloth and ashes.

As a man of revelation, Daniel bore witness that the time for the Jews' return was at hand. But he also knew in his spirit that a breach remained in their bridge to freedom. The road was still blocked. And to connect this bridge between their past and future, to prepare the way of the Lord, more repair work needed to be done.

Daniel's Day in Court

So, Daniel prepared his case and went before the Court of Heaven, just as he had seen in his visions. His intercession on Earth was actually a legal petition before God's throne. You might want to review the case, recorded in Daniel 9, before we continue. Let's learn some keys from his appeal.

> *I prayed to the Lord my God and confessed and said, "Alas, O Lord, the great and awesome God, who keeps His covenant and lovingkindness for those who love Him and keep His commandments. We have sinned, committed iniquity, acted wickedly and rebelled, even turning aside from your commandments and ordinances"* (vv. 4–5).

In both the Old and New Testaments, a primary key to receiving clemency from Heaven's Court is to take responsibility for your sins and openly confess them to God, holding nothing back while asking for forgiveness.

But Daniel also realized that the sins of his generation were not the primary reason they were in captivity. Again, the misguided choices of previous generations actually brought his generation into captivity. He clearly saw the cycles—*"visiting the iniquity of the fathers on the children, and on the third and fourth generations"* (Deut. 5:9).

In Daniel's appeal, not only does he confess his sins, but he confesses the sins of his people, including his forefathers, almost as if they were his own. God is a God of covenant and of mercy or lovingkindness. Daniel was imploring Him according to this covenant mercy to blot out the iniquities of his forefathers, to remove the reproach they still carried before His Court.

Another way of putting it is that Daniel was asking God to justify His people before Heaven's Court as an act of mercy, to remove the enemy's legal right to hold them in captivity, *even through previous generations.*

Did God answer?

Yes! In fact, that became the very time when the Lord sent an angel in response. The angel Gabriel spoke.

> *While I was speaking in prayer, then the man Gabriel, whom I had seen in the vision previously, came to me in my extreme weariness about the time of the evening offering. He gave me instruction*

and talked with me and said, "O Daniel, I have now come forth to give you insight with understanding" (Daniel 9:21–22).

The Ancient of Days and the Scrolls

One of the most important visions Daniel experienced was his introduction to the Court of Heaven.

> *I kept looking until thrones were set up, and the Ancient of Days took His seat.... Thousands upon thousands were attending Him, and myriads upon myriads were standing before Him. The court sat, and the books were opened* (Daniel 7:9–10).

Note that God's throne is where He holds court. Myriads of angelic hosts and redeemed human beings are pictured worshiping Him and attending to the governance of His throne. As we first mentioned in our book *Crown & Throne*, it's vitally important to understand that *the throne of His beauty is also the court of His justice.*

When Daniel saw the Court of Heaven, the "Supreme Judge" who presided over everything was the Ancient of Days. This title isn't just given to impress you with God's ancient-ness. You know, He's really old, and He's still alive, so He must be pretty righteous.

As the Ancient of Days, Daniel's Judge and yours knew firsthand about every sin of his forefathers. He saw the entry point where these sins introduced bondages into the generational line. Sexual immorality, covenant breaking, unjust bloodshed, theft and perjury, abuse, the list goes on.

After the Ancient of Days took His seat, Daniel 7:10 conveys how *"the court sat, and the books were opened."* Daniel saw how these sins were carefully recorded as part of Heaven's legal records for every life.

Heaven documents our sins as well as our right choices—over our entire generational line. This may at first seem intimidating, especially if you're not right with Him. But as a lawyer in Heaven's Court, you can actually ask the Ancient of Days to open the scrolls of your generational line and review its contents. You like Daniel can confess your sins and the iniquities of your fathers. You can ask Him to blot out these sins and iniquities through the body and blood of Jesus Christ!

You obviously don't know about every blockage or reproach in your generational line. But as the Ancient of Days, He does. Recorded in these scrolls is every instance where your ancestors made pacts with demonic idols to gain something they didn't feel God would grant. Also recorded are legal claims by these powers that have held your generational line in captivity from that time forward.

And the good news is that you can ask God to open the books, review your case, and annul every legal covenant or pact with hell that your forefathers made—that now claims your generational line (see Isa. 28:18). Before Heaven's Court you can commit your bloodline to Him, and ask Him to cleanse, restore, and redeem!

What's more, you today have more of a legal precedent to receive forgiveness—for your sins and the sins of your forefathers—than even Daniel.

Through visions of the Court of Heaven, Daniel saw the scrolls of God's justice opened. He saw the Son of Man present His own body and blood as the evidence for the forgiveness of sins and iniquities, or generational bondages. He saw how judgment was rendered in favor of the saints. And quite literally, He petitioned the Lord to receive this same verdict of favor in his Old Testament world.

But if Daniel could access God's grace to repair history even before His covenant was fully sealed, how much more can you access His covenant mercy and forgiveness now that Christ's blood has been shed for you?

When the Sentence Lifts

In Daniel's time, Heaven's records bore witness to how these sins accumulated over time, unleashing greater and greater consequences to ensuing generations—until hardly a man or woman in Israel, His covenant land, even truly knew His heart or ways. They had chosen captivity, and into captivity they went.

Aren't you glad the story doesn't end there?

The same God who brought discipline for sin also had a timing and plan for their restoration. The same principles that apply to nations and peoples apply to each of us as individuals today.

As watchmen for churches, regions, or nations, we must understand this aspect of God's judgment. Like Daniel, we need to seek God for where the spheres of responsibility are experiencing His judgment or discipline. And equally as importantly, we must hear from Heaven when it's time for His sentence to lift!

Sure, the consequences of our stubborn choices remain with us for a while. And it's agonizing! But by God's mercy, a time can come when the sentence is commuted, and your captivity can turn. You cannot escape your past, but you can repair it. You can repair your past to redeem your present and secure a better future. And like Daniel, it all begins with confessing your sin, *"Repent and return, so that your sins are washed away, in order that times of refreshing may come from the presence of the Lord"* (Acts 3:19).

In each of our lives, God has a strategy to restore His glory where we've been compromised. For all of us, there's probably much repair work to be done, especially within our generational line. God will lead you each step of the way. And I guarantee, the results will be worth it!

Daniel Watch—Twelve Priorities—Daily Checkup

1. **Pray daily.** Three times a day is ideal. Worship, read the Word, and focus simply on dwelling in God's presence before you begin interceding. We also suggest receiving communion before bed.

2. **Forgive, and seek forgiveness quickly!** Hold short accounts.

3. **Keep watch.** Stay alert in the midst of your day. If Holy Spirit quickens you to pray for someone or something, pray immediately, even if just a "flash prayer." Pray in the Spirit!

4. **Receive and document prophetic revelation.** Be sensitive to Holy Spirit, and write or record what He gives you.

5. **Pray daily for those the Lord assigns to you.** As a White House watchman, begin with the president, and then pray for those around him! Pray for Israel and America, and then other nations as led. Pray over the justice issue which drives your heart.

6. **Embrace a fasted lifestyle.** Daniel kept a disciplined life as a foundation which he could then shift as the Lord required.

7. **Cultivate a prayer team to surround you.** Just as Daniel prayed for Cyrus, so he also cultivated a prayer team to surround him that was made up of long-term, covenant friends. I cannot emphasize enough the importance of this.

8. **Embrace excellence in serving others.** Whatever you do, do with all your heart as unto the Lord. Let the signature on your work be that it was done with consistent excellence.

9. **Embrace integrity, including relational integrity.** Keep your promises. Pay your bills. Be on time. Don't make commitments "by faith," which you may not be able to fulfill. And if you do—fulfill them.

10. **Embrace rest.** Rest daily and rest weekly. Daniel took time to recover after stressful events and intense spiritual warfare. So should you! Keep shabbat. Enjoy life and have fun!

11. **Guard your personal gateways—your eyes, your ears, and your heart.** Idolatry and sexual immorality in all forms are always defiling. Keep watch over your conduct!

12. **Keep your life vision before you at all times.** Rehearse the assignment God has given you. Define it. Prioritize it. Relate to the Lord continually over it in prayer. Pursue until you fulfill!

CHAPTER 10

COVENANT RESET

WHILE circling the White House on a prayer assignment, the Spirit of God spoke to me. What He said came to define our project. He said, "The circle of My covenant trumps, triumphs over, and prevails against the circle of Baal meant to confine you, and even define you."

A few intercessors had committed to daily walks after members of our home group sensed strong turmoil spiritually within the administration—even more than usual! Espionage and sabotage. Baseless accusations. Leaks and betrayals. Deep state sinkholes from a swamp in process of being drained. Threats from wayward dictators. Storms and more storms. A veritable crossfire hurricane.

The principality of Baal was identified as a force needing to be restrained as we prayed. We're going to explore this ahead. But essentially Baal means master, taskmaster, or slave master. And it's not a coincidence that whenever you see the influence of the Baal principality, you find slavery.

Surprisingly, another definition of Baal simply means husband. It's probably not a coincidence that Jezebel, whose name literally means married to Baal, sought to overtake the covenant land of Israel with Baal worship through subjugation, sexual immorality, and occult practices. All the while, she systematically targeted the true prophets of God.

The Bible identifies this global principality as a driving force behind slavery and covenant breaking, personally and nationally. The good news is that Jesus still holds the trump card—His unbreakable covenant with us, sealed with His own blood.

> *The covenant that I have made with you, you shall not forget, nor shall you fear other gods. But the Lord your God you shall fear, and He shall deliver you from the hand of ALL YOUR ENEMIES* (2 Kings 17:38–39 emphasis added).

As you stand on His covenant, God promises to deliver you from every adversary! For this reason, the circle of God's covenant trumps, triumphs over, and prevails against the circle of Baal meant to confine you and even define you.

And the Lord is decreeing, *"Let My people go!"*

Condition of the Covenant

The first planning meeting for the One Voice Prayer Movement, founded by Paula White Cain, was held on August 20 in a cramped meeting room near the Capitol. Prayer leaders from across the Body of Christ convened. Given the One Voice mandate of strength through diversity, I was grateful that the room was accentuated with many shades of color. Worship and prayer simply overtook us. A sense of urgency and expectancy became palpable.

The last action of the meeting was a special commissioning. Todd Lamphere, chief of staff to Paula White, summoned leaders to surround a black pastor named Joseph Green. He is an inspiring figure. But tears soon overtook us all when his mission became clear.

Joseph had been appointed by both President Trump and Congress to oversee the commemoration of the four-hundredth anniversary of slavery in America. The first slaves came ashore in what is now the Hampton Roads area, across the James River from Virginia Beach. Events were just days away. Joseph mentioned how, after four hundred years of bondage, God moved to free Israel from Egypt. All I could think of was the freedom movement God had promised "we the people" together.

Amazingly, history records August 20 as the actual date the twenty shackled prisoners actually came ashore, which meant that the birth of the One Voice Prayer Movement, culminating with Joseph's commissioning, occurred on the actual four-hundredth anniversary of their arrival. How appropriate that on this date a turnaround for our time became the first prayer project the new group engaged in, with a literal Joseph reconciling his brothers.

You cannot erase history. But, as we explored in the previous chapter, you can repair it. This is vital to understand as a watchman called into the continuing process of repairing our nation's covenant with God, as well as aligning your own spheres in covenant with God.

Last chapter, we highlighted many secrets to Daniel's success as a watchman. The Jewish people had succumbed to idolatry and had been sent into exile. Daniel's personal repudiation of idolatry, even at the cost of his life, proved vital in gaining the earned authority to intercede for their restoration. It is amazing how Cyrus soon came into rulership and mandated that Daniel's prayers of restoration essentially become government policy!

We are seeing a lot of this even today.

In this chapter, you're going to gain understanding on how to repair covenant with God in your sphere in a way that heals history from the reproaches of idolatry. Further, you will learn to receive this dimension of covenant restoration as a verdict from Heaven's Court. Your world is about to change!

As you know from the introduction, my own forefathers crossed the Atlantic on a small cramped boat called the *Mayflower*. Their voyage was brutal. But, when the Pilgrims waded ashore and consecrated the land to Christ four hundred years ago this November 2020, they knew at least they had come for freedom.

The covenantal legacy of my forefathers is at the core of my watchman call today. But I knew little about the group of English sojourners who, with a passion similar to the Pilgrims, established the Virginia Company in 1607. So, I was grateful when my good friend Chris Mitchell Jr. took me to school. As a black pastor and gatekeeper for Virginia Beach, he soon convinced me I had a lot to learn.

Standing at a seven-foot wooden cross commemorating the original planted by the Virginia Company upon arrival, Chris explained how chaplain Robert Hunt committed the land to Jesus Christ for the propagation of the gospel throughout the continent and world. Their aspirations were not impractical. At the time, the colony known as Virginia stretched from the East Coast to what is now known as California.

Chris recited Chaplain Hunt's words of consecration virtually by heart. Probably because he has embraced their covenantal legacy as his own.

> We do hereby Dedicate this Land, and ourselves, to reach the People within these shores with the Gospel of Jesus Christ, and to raise up Godly generations after us, and with these generations take the Kingdom of God to all the earth. May this Covenant of Dedication remain to all generations, as long as the earth remains, and may this Land, along with England, be Evangelist to the World. May all who see this Cross remember what we have done here, and may those who come here to inhabit join us in this covenant....[69]

The founders of Virginia established their sphere in covenant with Jesus Christ, an astounding beginning blessed by God. The Virginia Company soon began to flourish.

Twelve years later, the first slaves arrived. Like my forefathers, they crossed the waters in a cramped ship, this one originating from Angola, West Africa. Whereas my forefathers aspired to freedom, these Africans were brought ashore in chains. In the promised land of the New World, they became property. Worse, these slaves were welcomed by the very founders who established Virginia in covenant with God.

Thus, slavery was validated by the original gatekeepers of our nation—first, by the Body of Christ and, second, by the formal government which they had established. This decision set a precedent for more than 250 years of horrific injustice through slavery in America, followed by enduring struggles with prejudice until this very day.

We've come a long way. But prejudice and racial inequity still mar the landscape of this freedom experiment meant by God to fulfill the founders' declaration that all men are created equal. Division still haunts even the Body of Christ. Meanwhile human trafficking in our nation, which should be unimaginable in our day, is actually reaching an all-time high.

Dream—Slavery a Covenant with Death and Hell

Jolene and I traveled to Virginia Beach to take part in a few of the meetings. During this time the Lord gave me a dream. I literally saw how covenants with hell were formed by the validation of slavery by the Body of Christ and government. The Lord showed me that this entry of slavery in the land was not merely a breach of His covenant with the land. Instead, it was considered by Heaven a covenant with death and hell. In other words, it was sourced by hell itself!

I also saw that through the validation of institutional slavery by both governmental authorities in Virginia and the Body of Christ, not only was the Hunt covenant defiled, but it compromised every other foundational covenant with Christ built upon it, including the Declaration of Independence, the US Constitution, and even the Pilgrim covenant made by my forefathers just a year after the slaves arrived.

Verdict: Covenant Repaired

In this dream, the Lord showed me that, after four hundred years, God was willing to grant an annulment of this covenant with death by verdict from Heaven's Court just as He had decreed in the days of Isaiah, *"Your covenant with death shall be annulled, and your agreement with Sheol will not stand"* (Isa. 28:18).

Again, the Lord made it clear that this verdict was similar in magnitude to the days recorded in Exodus. After four hundred years, the covenant with death and hell made through the validation of institutionalized slavery by both the Body of Christ and civil government was annulled by Heaven's Court. A dark thread which tied government to slavery was removed. Even abortion, founded by the prejudice of eugenics, was impacted.

Legal authority was finally granted for the principality over the covenant with death and hell to be restrained and removed. The primary obstacles holding back God's freedom movement were thus restrained. And America's covenant with God was finally repaired, as validated by Heaven's Court. A future forged by His freedom movement has thus been secured.

After four hundred years, *"Let My people go!"*

After an early conversation with Chris Mitchell Jr. on Sunday morning, we ministered together and prophesied the word of the Lord over this covenant issue. That afternoon, Joseph Green took the podium to address the ceremony Trump and Congress had appointed him to moderate. The healing and restoration brought covenantal alignment not only to Virginia, but to the highest governmental seats in our land.

> "We acknowledge that slavery was a horrible and inexcusable institution that was perpetrated on people of color," Dr. Green solemnly proclaimed. "We also acknowledge that after slavery was abolished there were years of discriminatory laws that also targeted people of color. Families were destroyed, communities devastated, and people were mistreated because of the color of their skin. These atrocities were perpetrated with the protection of laws and institutions and allowed to exist through the inactions of others.
>
> "However, in this season we choose to forgive...."[70]

Covenant Reset—My Journey

My personal journey to repair America's covenant with God began on May 7, 1998. Cindy Jacobs had asked me represent Massachusetts for her national network, with an immediate assignment to hold a solemn assembly and repent for the root sins of the state.

From the Pilgrims' landing to the First Great Awakening, to Paul Revere and the birth of the American Revolution, many of the covenant roots of our nation were seeded into this soil. Small wonder even the license plate declares Massachusetts as "the spirit of America." The challenge was that, along with the magnificent roots, there came extraordinary evil ones as well. By dealing with the unholy roots while empowering the holy roots, I knew we could shift the spirit of America.

Historic Faneuil Hall in Boston, Massachusetts, known as the womb of the American Revolution, was chosen as the location for the regional solemn assembly. It was the first ministry gathering ever hosted by Lamplighter Ministries.

I knew then that Paul Revere and other early firebrands had mobilized Boston from this hall to engage in the Revolution and that our quest today was similar to theirs. I never would have imagined I would rent the hall for at least six more successive gatherings throughout the ensuing twenty-two years. Or that the whole time, God had been summoning us to "Face of God Hall"—before His face—to change the course of history.

But it was at this hall that those of us assembled consecrated ourselves to God for the restoration of His covenant with our land. David as a youth pledged the same thing. If you read Psalm 132, you'll discover this covenant set the course for the rest of his life. We knew that, to bring genuine reformation in our world, the same resolve would be required.

Divorcing Baal

What was not known was the rest of the equation. Realigning with our covenant with God was only half of what was required for this work to be validated by Heaven's Court. The other half was to gain a divorcement from our historic idolatry.

The Call Nashville, on 07/07/07, introduced the world to the movement to divorce Baal. Dutch Sheets shared a series of prophetic experiences where he was shown that the principality Baal was the primary strongman over the nation. To defeat this principality, America needed to return to covenant with Christ. Seven is the Hebrew number for covenant. In Hebrew language, on 07/07/07 we were called to "seven ourselves" to the Lord.

Led by visionary Lou Engle, with Dutch Sheets, James Goll, and Mike Bickle assisting, a packed stadium worshiped, repented, prayed, declared our divorcement from Baal, and sought God in covenant renewal.

Critics later mocked the gathering because no major blessing seemed to immediately materialize, even though it had been prophesied. In fact, things got worse. The truth is we are only now in this hour receiving what we thought we would immediately receive then.

From my perspective, the Call Nashville was somewhat like a marriage proposal. We became engaged. But for Heaven's Court to actually be satisfied in covenant renewal, more work needed to be accomplished, especially regarding the issue of idolatry.

We needed a true divorce. And for that we needed to face the Judge.

Your understanding of this facet is essential. Just as we as human beings exist in the spiritual and natural realms at the same time, so your covenants exist in both the spiritual and natural realms at the same time. And these covenants become gateways which invoke the spirit realm to influence the earth.

Hosea's Watchman Call

Hosea was a watchman over God's covenant. The Lord mandated that he marry a prostitute. First to bear witness to all Israel that God considered His covenant nation a wayward bride. Secondly, and virtually as important, Hosea was called to enter into the very suffering and heartbreak God was experiencing through the unfaithfulness of the people He cherished.

Here's a point. As preparation for your calling, oftentimes your life's journey will be orchestrated by God to bring you into a wholehearted identification with His heart, His feelings over people and situations. I promise that, by relating to Jesus' joy and suffering in your own journey, your life will begin to make much more sense. Thus, David the shepherd became king. Jesus the carpenter was nailed to a cross to rebuild humankind. And a brokenhearted Hosea made a new covenant to redeem his bride.

So, you're called as a White House watchman. What has your preparation been?

Hosea introduced to the world the original call to divorce Baal and reset covenant with the Bridegroom. He prophesied:

> *"It will come about in that day," declares the Lord, "that you will call Me Ishi and will no longer call Me Baali. For I will remove the names of the Baals from her mouth, so that they will be mentioned by their names no more"* (Hosea 2:16–17).

For the record, *"the names of the Baals on her mouth"* represent the worship of her covenantal betrothal to them. Their removal represents her divorce from them.

Divorcing Baal—Completing the Work

And in 2009, the Lord made clear that for America to receive a divorce from Baal as validated by Heaven's Court, the same repudiation required of Hosea's bride must take place by believers in Christ in our land.

After the global call went forth, apostle John Benefiel of Oklahoma City picked up the mantle and spearheaded the movement to divorce Baal. To obtain the verdict the Lord had offered our nation, the mandate was given to pray on-site at every known altar of idolatry in all fifty states—including Masonic lodges, abortion clinics, and more—seeking the Lord on-site to grant an annulment of the covenants which had been made. Native American apostle Jay Swallow had received guidelines from the Lord in a vision on restraining the principality of Baal through Heaven's Court. Dr. Jerry Mash, a respected Oklahoma lawyer, brought procedural clarity and legal verbiage to fashion a literal divorce decree from Baal. John and Jay mobilized teams to pray through the divorce decree from Baal throughout Oklahoma.

After a few short years, they saw dramatic turnarounds. Droughts broke. A desolate economy began to flourish. The power of debt became broken. And multitudes came to Jesus.

It was then that apostle John's Heartland Apostolic Prayer Network was tasked with Heaven's charge to divorce Baal nationally. Cindy Jacobs' Reformation Prayer Network partnered alongside. Together, we prayed on-site at more than ten thousand altars of historic idolatry in every state of the nation, seeking a verdict of divorce from Baal and a reconstitution of covenant with Jesus Christ.

The endeavor to divorce Baal soon became the largest and most comprehensive repudiation of idolatry in American history.

By 2011, thanks to the sacrificial efforts of hundreds of watchmen, this extraordinary work had been largely accomplished. On July 4, 2011, Jolene and I hosted apostle John Benefiel and a gathering of apostolic leaders including Negiel Bigpond, Abby Abildness, Tom Schlueter, and many others at the Lincoln Memorial. On the anniversary of the signing of the Declaration of Independence, we approached the Court and presented the project the Lord had mandated we fulfill. We then presented a petition called the *Declaration of Covenant*, seeking the reconstitution of the covenant our forefathers had made. I was privileged to write this proposal, seeking God's hand in marriage to our land once again.

We boldly asked for a sign that God had approved this covenant restoration. Prophet Rick Ridings had seen a vision of a nutcracker which cracked a hard shell of demonic resistance over Washington DC. Our request was framed accordingly, "Lord, grant the fullness of this divorcement from Baal. Grant a restoration of covenant with You. And as a sign that You have heard us, crack the hard shell of resistance!"

Fifty days later to the day, our request was answered. On August 23, an unprecedented earthquake measuring 5.8 on the Richter scale shook Washington DC. Gargoyles toppled from the National Cathedral. The altar of a prominent temple to Baal was damaged. Even the Washington Monument cracked in the earthquake![71]

It was as if Heaven's gavel fell and all of Washington shook in response.

I keep saying it, but it bears repeating: You can't make this stuff up. The covenant with Christ was restored!

The four-hundredth anniversary of slavery showed that, even with this significant restoration, our covenant with Christ still was in need of further repair. As a watchman, you must remain continually alert for God's leadings.

But the largest and most comprehensive repudiation of idolatry soon became the legal foundation for the largest and most comprehensive governmental turnaround in modern history. We'll explore this more in the next chapter.

For now, just know that covenant with God, divorced from historic idolatry, secures His Kingdom influence within your sphere to catalyze transformation and turnaround. The success of your watch depends on it.

Covenant with Death Annulled

So far, we've given you some basic training in understanding the significance of covenants in the spiritual and natural realms. You've gained core principles to realign your sphere in covenant with Christ. Now here is some special ops training—forerunner training. You may or may not be ready for it.

Just understand two things. First, the men and women in the special ops world can often accomplish in small teams what entire armies were once hired to do. Often with better results. Secondly, special ops teams are trained to deal with life and death situations of a magnitude few even know exist. If you're okay with that, read on. But, once you gain this understanding, there's no turning back. You will never look at your world the same again.

Remember when Jesus was led into the wilderness to be tempted by the devil? The final temptation He overcame was perhaps the evilest that satan had devised. And it was also the most overarching in its consequences.

The Word of God is the primary framework by which satan understood Messiah's role in the earth. It's why he recognized Jesus from birth—and sought to kill Him. And it's also why he later tempted Jesus primarily as a political ruler. In a way only kings and presidents may truly understand, the fate of the world was literally at stake.

> *And he led Him up and showed Him all the kingdoms of the world in a moment of time. And the devil said to Him, "I will give You all this domain and its glory; for it has been handed over to me, and I give it to whomever I wish. Therefore if You worship before me, it shall all be Yours." Jesus answered him, "It is written, 'You shall worship the Lord your God and serve Him only'"* (Luke 4:5–8).

"Here's a shortcut to obtain Your goals, Jesus. You can rule the world. It's all been given into my domain. I own the nations as the ruler behind their thrones. They come into covenant with me when they bow their knee. Take it; You can have it. Only bow Your knee and all this can be Yours."

Bow Your knee, and all this can be Yours. That's how satan tempted Jesus. And it's how he still tempts every governmental leader today. Through this contract, he seeks to gain legal right to spiritually rule the seat of authority that is occupied by the initiate. What we like to call *the throne behind the throne.*

Jesus' reply dismissed the devil. And it secured both your salvation and your dominion in Him. *"You shall worship the Lord, and serve Him alone!"* Aren't you glad Jesus chose the valley rather than the mountaintop?

But that said, our nation is rife with corrupted seats of authority due to covenants with idolatry. Whether seats within family lines or seats within business or seats within government, presently or generationally, they are legally claimed by the enemy, that is, until these covenants with death and hell are annulled.

Note the divorce decree from Baal conveys the annulment of a covenant with death within the sphere applied, that every initiation rite through Freemasonry, every pledge of loyalty to occult powers, is essentially a covenant with death.

> *Therefore, hear the word of the Lord, O scoffers, who rule this people who are in Jerusalem. Because you have said, "We have made a covenant with death, and with Sheol we have made a pact, the overwhelming scourge will not reach us when it passes by, for we have made falsehood our refuge and we have concealed ourselves with deception." Therefore thus says the Lord God, "Behold, I am laying in Zion a stone, a tested stone, a costly cornerstone for the foundation, firmly placed. He who believes in it will not be disturbed. I will make justice the measuring line and righteousness the level; then hail will sweep away the refuge of lies and the waters will overflow the secret place. Your covenant with death will be canceled [annulled], and your pact with Sheol will not stand; when the overwhelming scourge passes through, then you become its trampling place"* (Isaiah 28:14–18).

Let's review a few points here.

1. **Who? Government leaders.** Isaiah is addressing the political world of his day, which ruled the capital city of Jerusalem and ruled the nation from the capital city.

2. **What? Pharaoh covenant.** These political rulers entered into covenant with demonic powers in rites of initiation patterned after those of ancient pharaohs to establish what the Bible terms a "covenant with death, a pact with Sheol" or the underworld. The initiation rites of Freemasonry, as well as other occult orders, are directly sourced from these mystery religions. They often include the unjust shedding of blood to attain greater power in the occult realm.[72]

3. **Covering corruption.** These covenants were purposefully made to invoke demonic powers to establish their rulership and shield them supernaturally so their evil deeds of corruption, deception, and abuse could remain undetected.

4. **Unjust bloodshed.** By inference in this passage, unjust bloodshed is perceived merely as a commodity by many rulers, a means to an end utilized to gain and retain more power and better cover over their deeds. The unjust bloodshed of abortion must be considered in this light!

5. **Covenant with death annulled!** When God declares that a covenant with death and hell is annulled, He is granting a ruling, releasing legal authority from Heaven's Court to remove the occult empowerment and covering of these rulers.

6. **Exposing evil deeds.** By this verdict their evil deeds can now become exposed. The evasion of justice ceases.

7. **Freedom movement.** The "exodus" of this hour is just as the first Exodus. God has declared the annulment of covenants with death and Sheol. He is bringing freedom from the gods of Egypt and those who have sold themselves into alignment with them. "Let My people go! Let my government go!"

How do you annul covenants with death and hell over seats of authority?

Good question. Remember thrones are established by covenant. And because the Lord granted the restoration of our nation's original covenant with Jesus Christ, at God's leading and our request, every other covenant must then come into alignment with the original.

From 2012–2016, this quest became our primary assignment in Washington DC. We prayed over every seat of authority in the US government from the Presidency to the House and Senate to the Supreme Court, seeking God for a divorcement from Baal and restoration of covenant with Jesus Christ alone. We then went to the Pentagon, the State Department, the intelligence communities, and every other known department, again claiming these seats of authority for Christ.

What transpired was nothing less than a spiritual revolution. With the Trump administration, virtually every seat of leadership became filled by an adherent of Christ. Spiritually, it became perhaps the most comprehensive overhaul of government in our nation's history.

That said, if it will work for Washington DC, it will work for your sphere. This is actually part of establishing your perimeter. Here are seven steps to annulling covenants with death and hell.

1. **Prepare your case.** Exercise due diligence in defining what you desire Jesus to accomplish. Find out what you can about whatever legal claims the enemy may have. Seek the Lord to annul them according to the legal precedent set by Isaiah 28.

2. **Approach the bench.** Daniel saw the thrones cast down, and the Ancient of Days take His seat as Judge. Take time to worship and interact with the Lord. Ask Him for an audience with the Court of Heaven over which He presides. Court of Heaven be convened!

3. **Make your appeal.** Remember the body and blood of Jesus Christ alone grants us the requested verdict that these covenants with death and hell be rendered annulled.

4. **Ask God to review the scrolls.** Each seat has a history. As the Ancient of Days, God ultimately knows everything that has transpired. Ask Him to open the scrolls of history over the seat, and annul every covenant of idolatry, both known to you and not known to you, over the seat since it was established. Ask Him to forgive and remit every other sin, including unjust bloodshed, coercion, corruption, abuse, financial indiscretions, sexual immorality. Be led by Holy Spirit in your interactions.

5. **Divorce Baal.** Pray through the decree of divorce with this specific seat or sphere at heart. Declare His judgment—all covenants with death and hell annulled! Cut the ties in the spiritual realm to every leader that has claimed the throne. Shut the door to every principality and power in every realm and dimension.

6. **Covenant reset.** Consecrate the seat to the Lord Jesus Christ. As covenants establish thrones of governance, ask Him to be enthroned on this seat in the spiritual realm.

7. **Summon the Eliakims and Esthers.** Pray for God to choose
   and summon the ruler He desires to steward the seat of authority. Forbid the wrong leaders to occupy the seat. Open the door
   to the Eliakims and Esthers who will uphold and perpetuate
   His covenant blessing in their governance!

The Code of Covenant

As White House watchmen, Jolene and I are among many in covenant
with God for the restoration and destiny of our nation's highest office.
This sphere was assigned to us as part of our overarching assignment
for the United States, aligning the thrones of government with His covenant. When we moved to Washington DC in January 2012, it seemed
like there was no way possible to fulfill the assignment. Through decisions made, we had slipped too far into the abyss.

But God gave us His 20/20 vision. Despite crazy setbacks, He has
remained faithful to the covenant. And the turnarounds set in motion
have now changed a nation. As I've shared before, our highest privilege is
simply to bear witness to what the Lord has done!

Millions, of course, have prayed, including you. The keys I have
shared with you here are actually vital to unlocking the fulfillment of
your prayers and ours combined. By resetting covenant with the Lord,
you are unlocking the flood tide of intercession, even through the ages,
that has been dammed up until this covenant alignment is met with
Heaven's approval.

To understand this better, let's return to basic training. Have you ever
had to reset your email account?

It's never easy. And the need to reset always seems to come just when
you're expecting the most important email of your life. If you're like me,
you try everything you know to get the flow back without calling the
email host, because you just don't want to spend hours on the phone
troubleshooting your account.

But here's the point. Until you enter the right code for the server, the
emails you are expecting will never get downloaded. It's not that the

emails don't exist—they do. But they will never reach your inbox until your account is reset with the right code.

It's the same with prayer. Covenant with God, divorced from historic and present idolatry, is the code which connects Heaven and Earth to secure the perpetual download of answered prayer. This is true whether it be for a family, a sphere, a city, or a nation. In the spirit realm, covenant reset *is that code*.

And now you have the key.

For Review

Please take a moment to reflect on what you've just read. We suggest taking notes as you answer questions below.

1. What does it mean for you to enter into covenant with God?

2. Have you ever experienced a betrayal of covenant? How did it make you feel? Describe the process of healing. How does the pain you experienced relate to Jesus?

3. In your own words, what does it mean for Jesus to be a watchman over His covenant? What does it mean for you to keep watch with Him?

4. Pray through the divorce decree from Baal. We suggest first making it personal for you and your family. Ask the Lord to disengage you from all generational bondages tied to historic idolatry in your family. Then pray this over the spheres of authority the Lord has assigned to you. Note: the revised divorce decree from Baal, the declaration of covenant, and many other verdicts from Heaven's Court are included in the Appendix. Please pray through them personally and for your sphere!

5. Recommended resources to broaden your understanding include apostle John Benefiel's book *Binding the Strongman* as well as our books *Crown & Throne* and *Midnight Cry*.

CHAPTER 11

THE TURNAROUND
VERDICT

IT was late fall 2016. The "locker room" tapes defaming presidential candidate Donald J. Trump had just been released. News from a hostile press flooded the airwaves. Stunned supporters began to bail. Campaign staff and volunteers quit. With the election just weeks away, it seemed there was no way the famed businessman could survive.

Atara, a friend on the campaign staff, called us for urgent watchman prayer. Atara means crowned. Six months beforehand, the Lord showed me a vision of our crowned friend walking down a path into the White House. We had no idea she had taken it to heart, pursuing a job with the Trump campaign in DC. They soon promoted her to the headquarters in New York City.

And when the crisis broke, Atara insisted we come pray on-site.

Jolene and I made our way to New York City. And in a very surreal moment, we were escorted through the double doors of the Trump Towers, through the gilded elevator doors made famous by everyone from Kanye West to Jared and Ivanka Kushner to Henry Kissinger. We ascended to campaign headquarters on the fourteenth floor.

It was surreal. Giving credit where credit was due, maybe I should mention the guitarist who contributed to the otherworldly feeling we experienced. Wearing only a cowboy hat, cowboy boots, and underwear that said, "Trump," he serenaded us as we walked into the Towers. He was proof that Trump's fans truly cross many cultural spectrums.

Just a few days before our New York City visit, I had been privileged to be a guest on a special conference call with Pam Pryor, who was serving as the evangelical coordinator for the Trump campaign. She briefed people on the call. She then asked for feedback and prayer. What I shared with Pam and her group formed the basis of what Jolene and I would later pray at the Trump Towers.

Given the circumstances, what I sensed from the Lord did not make much sense. But God was going to bring a turnaround. The Scripture He had given me was Daniel 7:22, judgment in favor of the saints, restraining the enemy and releasing the saints to possess the Kingdom. This turnaround was not just on behalf of Trump, but on behalf of the believers nationwide who believed the Lord had chosen Trump to "Make America Great Again." I also encouraged her that the American people would see right through the last-minute attempt to sabotage the campaign and, in the end, remain resolute.

For Jolene and me, this was more than a spontaneous prophetic perception. It was a word upon which we staked our lives and ministry. We were on the final leg of a fifty-state tour at the time, mostly by train, prophesying this Daniel 7:22 Turnaround Verdict to every state in our nation.

From the beginning, we saw the restoration of God's glory in our land as the key "engine" that must drive this train. Form following function, we named the 2016 journey the "Glory Train— Turnaround Tour."

A little lightweight, I know. But it described our assignment. Our battle cry—"All aboard—The Glory Train is rollin'!"

And on October 20, the Glory Train found its station at Trump campaign headquarters on the fourteenth floor of the legendary Towers, at the request of our friend Atara.

For about forty-five minutes, a small conference room became a hallowed prayer chamber. Small talk with Atara quickly led to intercession, and together we literally threw ourselves on the mercy of Heaven's Court. We prayed through the Turnaround Verdict as well as other decrees, including the divorce decree from Baal. After lingering awhile longer, covering issues and people in prayer as the Holy Spirit directed, we felt a release that the Lord had heard and would soon respond.

"Would you like a tour?" Atara asked.

"Absolutely," we replied.

She showed us the "command center" and introduced us to a few staff members. On the way out, a train poster caught my eye. The similarity to our Glory Train graphics was unmistakable. The same steam engine, at even the same angle! And under the photo was just a slight variation of our own war cry. "All aboard the Trump Train!" We took it as a true sign.

Exactly eight days later, our friend Atara called from the Trump Towers. "Did you see the breaking news?" She exclaimed. "We got our turnaround!"

FBI Director James Comey had just announced his decision to reopen the investigation into Hillary Clinton's emails after discovering more potential security breaches on an assistant's private computer.

Turnaround. Against all odds the election momentum turned on a dime.

Christian leaders on the fence soon got back on the Trump Train, thanks in large part to Pam Pryor's ceaseless efforts. And on Tuesday, November 8, just a short eleven days later, Donald J. Trump won the presidency in one of the most extraordinary election turnarounds in American history. Studies showed that evangelicals had strongly tipped the polls in the new president's favor.

As recounted in the first chapter, President Trump's election has in turn catalyzed perhaps the largest and most comprehensive governmental turnaround in modern American history. Economic resurgence. Judicial reform. Innovative solutions in diplomacy. Global conflicts averted.

Religious freedom replacing governmental persecution. A return to honoring our Judeo-Christian foundations. A turnaround for *life*!

The magnitude of these shifts can only barely be perceived right now. But, to put it simply, America has gotten back on track—in a way that benefits every US citizen.

After the Election

Our friend Atara actually gained a position at the White House, just as prophesied. She served as Deputy Chief of Staff for the National Security Council and is now working as a consultant.

Other friends were promoted into various positions across the administration, including the Department of Health and Human Services and the US Department of State. Small teams that helped in intercession organically adopted different departments in prayer. We fell in love with the mission and people. In turn, we have seen some of the most dramatic answers to prayer in our entire lives.

Here's just a few examples. On 7/22/2018, a small team of leaders joined for Daniel 7:22 prayer on behalf of the State Department's first-ever Global Ministerial to Advance Religious Freedom. We were also asked to pray for freedom for Pastor Andrew Brunson, who was imprisoned by the government of Turkey. How appropriate to ask for judgment in favor of the saints, literally releasing Andrew to possess the Kingdom! God met the accumulated prayers of many intercessors over many years with an immediate turnaround. Two days after the prayer time, Pastor Brunson was released into house arrest. Within two months, he was completely free.

Andrew's sudden release was announced in real-time at the State Department gathering by Sam Brownback, the US Ambassador at large for Religious Freedom. In many ways, Andrew Brunson became a symbol of the very quest that representatives from around the world had gathered to attain.[73]

And as mentioned, religious freedom has unexpectedly become a pillar of the Trump administration.

That said, the grace of God that we've come to know as the Turnaround Verdict is still very much in play. Your watchman intercession is needed to secure these victories for future generations. It is vital for America to complete the turnaround.

From the White House to your house, the principles I am sharing with you will greatly accelerate your effectiveness in seeing God's turnaround secured within your sphere. Maybe it's not surprising that we are turning again to the words of our mentor, the prophet Daniel, to guide us through the next watchman lesson.

Daniel—Watchman of Heaven's Court

Remember that, as a White House watchman, you are first called to be a throne room watchman. In other words, a watchman over the government of God and how His government desires to influence the earth. Your most precious commodity remains counsel from Heaven's council.

Isaiah 33:22 declares that the Lord is our Judge, our Lawgiver, and our King. Note that even before our founders, the Bible clearly defined what would become our three branches of government.

In context with this expression of His governance, the biblical pledge is given that *"He will save us!"*

More than any other prophet, Daniel became a watchman of Heaven's Court. Daniel 7 records his encounter in full. The thrones were cast down, and the Ancient of Days was seated. The Court sat. The books or scrolls were opened. Ultimately, what we call the Turnaround Verdict was unveiled. And as mentioned, Daniel kept watch.

> *I kept looking, and that horn was waging war with the saints and overpowering them until the Ancient of Days came and judgment was passed in favor of the saints of the Highest One, and the time arrived when the saints took possession of the kingdom* (Daniel 7:21–22).

Until this verdict was released, the Bible says that the saints of God were being overpowered by a demonic horn, symbol of an antichrist spirit.

Theologians have long debated whether this antichrist horn represents a spiritual entity, a human being, or both. I personally believe both. Scripturally, the antichrist horn is a human being who, like Pharaoh of old, is empowered in life and governance by a high-level demonic power. They're united together in covenant for evil.

The Bible implies that, at the time of this decision, the saints were doing everything they knew to do—worshiping, fasting, praying, tithing, assembling together, living righteous lives in their professions and at home. They were mobilizing to affect the seven mountains of society for God.

Yet instead of victory, they were losing ground at every turn. They were isolated, divided, marginalized, impoverished, defrauded of covenant promises, many even making the ultimate sacrifice, the flame of their very lives extinguished for their faith.

That's when the Court of Heaven intervenes and rules in their favor. The beast that opposed them is immediately restrained. And in every dimension of life and the spirit where the saints were opposed, *they suddenly win.* These same war-weary believers are immediately released to possess the Kingdom!

Please note that a courtroom verdict accomplishes for the saints what their own spiritual warfare and cultural engagement could not alone attain. All are needed. But verdicts from Heaven's Court often bring the alignment that secures greater victory in our engagement.

Revelation 19:11 describes how the Lord judges, or renders a verdict, and then wages war to establish this verdict in the earth. The Lord Himself honors, upholds, and defends every verdict that He legitimately renders. This is vitally important to understand, because the process of seeing judgment rendered by the Lord by no means negates spiritual warfare, as some have implied.

Instead, the same Judge who renders the verdict then makes war, and the saints are pictured with Him in the movement.

Short conclusion—verdicts from Heaven's Court do not replace spiritual warfare. They empower it!

This should explain for you why we actually refer to this Daniel 7:22 judgment as the Daniel 7:22 Turnaround Verdict. Over many years, like the saints in this passage, we ourselves have consistently witnessed impossible situations turn on a dime while standing on this ancient courtroom decision.

The Turnaround Verdict

Daniel lived some 2,600 years ago. And from his time forward, billions of legal decisions have since been issued. Most of them are now dust. What makes this verdict so different?

The key to the power of this verdict rests within its origination. It's not a byproduct of man's discernment, logic, or will. Instead, the words recorded by Daniel convey a decision by the Court of Heaven, presided over by One who identifies Himself as the Judge of the entire earth.

Ponder the implications. That such a Court even exists, let alone that its judgments can affect the thrones of earth, is staggering. In reality all nations, governments, and people have already been greatly impacted and will soon be impacted again.

Daniel 7 provides the clearest chapter in the Bible on the Court of Heaven. I encourage you to read through the entire chapter and make it a steady companion to your training as a White House watchman. Throughout this visionary encounter, the prophet Daniel served as sort of a court reporter, documenting the greatest cases in all recorded history.

Consider this, for instance. The Turnaround Verdict, recorded in Daniel 7:22, is so extraordinary that it ultimately catalyzes the return of Jesus Christ. God's response to the grave injustice faced by the saints at the very end of the age directly correlates to Revelation 19:11 as a parallel passage.

> *And I saw heaven opened, and behold, a white horse, and He who sat on it is called Faithful and True, and in righteousness He judges and wages war.... And the armies which are in heaven, clothed in fine linen, white and clean, were following Him on white horses* (Revelation 19:11, 14).

Jesus renders judgment and makes war. And He is pictured in a great procession with His saints, bridging the gap between Heaven and Earth to wage war in the ultimate battle for all humanity.

Esther's Verdict

That said, throughout the world, we've been asked one consistent question as we've ministered on this message: Daniel's verdict, does it apply to his generation or to the saints in the time of the antichrist, or to us?

The answer is—yes! Biblical records actually convey how the Turnaround Verdict was first applied only a generation after Daniel lived, a generation that consumed much of his own intercession.

Queen Esther ascended to power. A watchman named Mordecai, who raised the legendary beauty queen, passed on terrifying intelligence. A holocaust was being planned against the Jewish people throughout the Persian Empire. Esther stood before her king in the natural as well as the Ancient of Days in the spirit realm. Judgment was rendered in her favor. The beast of the day was restrained. The Jews were miraculously preserved. Further, they literally were released to possess the kingdom—returning to the covenant land in fulfillment of Cyrus's decree (see Ezra 4–5).

Now that's what I call turnaround! It's precisely according to the vision Daniel prophesied. The Jews still celebrate this victory today with a holiday called Purim.

But as much as this verdict was meant for Daniel's generation or ours, it will find ultimate fulfillment with a future generation of saints marked to live in the final moments of what the Bible calls *the end times*—when an antichrist spirit openly defies constitutional governance, betrays covenant, changes times and law, rules through deceit and retribution, persecutes the saints and unleashes immorality and evil on a level never before experienced.

The nations then clash at Armageddon—ultimately in a war against God Himself, as He makes war according to the judgment rendered. The dramatic conflict will be followed by the promised earthly reign of our Messiah from His covenant land of Israel.

Perhaps this is our generation, perhaps not. But we're already gaining some experience in dealing with the tumult.

To those living right now through extreme resistance from the enemy, Jolene and I wrote this for you. Though we may not know you by name, we have been praying for you. The enemy has tried to mark you for subjugation. But the Lord has marked you for victory! It is our genuine hope you will find clarity, courage, guidance, and resolve that will equip you to advance, including benefitting from the strength of Daniel-Cyrus partnerships.

And as with saints of old, may you find within this ancient verdict a key that unlocks your turnaround.

In the Appendix, you will find the expression of the Turnaround Verdict which we received at Faneuil Hall. Looking back, it marked the start of a revolution.

For Review

Please take a moment to reflect on what you've just read. We suggest taking notes as you answer questions below.

1. What turnarounds to you want God to bring into your life? Into your sphere? What do you believe is holding them back?

2. Have you, like Daniel, ever experienced an interaction with God before Heaven's Court? Describe your experience.

3. How have you been growing in your watchman call through this book? List the revelations which have impacted you.

4. What are your perceptions about America's political climate? How is it affecting you? Your family?

SECURING

YOUR FUTURE

CHAPTER 12

DRAIN THE SWAMP, SECURE THE HARVEST!

THE view from Armageddon is literally breathtaking. Known in Hebrew as *Tel Megiddo* or *Har Megiddo*, the prophesied overwatch of humanity's final battle is actually a small mountain overlooking the fertile Jezreel Valley. *Jezreel* means "God's sows." It's not a coincidence that much of Israel's history has been harvested from the soil of this valley. According to Bible prophecy, much of her future will spring forth from there as well.

Right now, the mountain serves primarily as a tourist attraction. Archeological digs are ongoing, and the park museum showcases recent discoveries. The buffet lunch at Armageddon is distinctively Israeli, with an American hamburger as an option. The souvenir shop is endearing. That said, beware in your purchasing because there are only so many places you can wear an Armageddon baseball cap without arousing suspicion.

Don't ask how I know this.

For thousands of years, Har Megiddo or Mount Megiddo served as a fortified watchman's perch, guarding the valley and especially its western gateway leading to Israel's coastal plains. It cannot be emphasized enough that the end-time battle prophesied in Revelation is not named for a battlefield. It is named for the fortified mountain where a battlefield watch was kept over thousands of years. According to the book of Revelation, it will be kept there again.

Har Megiddo, "mount of invasion" in Hebrew, is aptly named. From ancient times all the way through World War I, the Jezreel Valley below served as a blood-stained Super Bowl for clashing empires. Abraham, Isaac, and Jacob all traversed the valley. Deborah and Barak defeated Sisera there. Gideon routed the Midianites. Saul lost his life to the Philistine army. Solomon and Josiah both fought their respective Pharaohs. Saladin defeated the Crusaders in this valley, then marched to claim Jerusalem.

While fighting the Ottomans, Napoleon Bonaparte famously called Armageddon "the most natural battleground of the whole earth."[74]

In addition to clashing armies, the Bible records an endless parade of farmers and tradesmen, merchants and vagabonds, prostitutes and prophets, whose sojourn ushered them through the gates of Armageddon. Hosea's bride was restored there. Ezekiel prophesied to dry bones there. Elijah kept watch nearby. Jezebel was cast down from her tower there.

Even the Savior of the world made his way through these gates— many times, actually, beginning while He was still in His mother's womb as Joseph and Mary (or Miriam) made their way from Nazareth to Bethlehem to register with the census.

Later in Nazareth, Jesus grew up overlooking the Jezreel Valley and learned to commune with His Father there, which means He literally grew up watching and praying over Armageddon.[75] What are the implications that the King of the nations was conceived, matured into manhood, and learned the power of watchman prayer by the very valley that will host the end-time battle for all humankind?

Armageddon Dream—Securing Inheritance and Harvest

Oddly enough, Armageddon invaded my dream-life when President Trump was first elected. And the primary emphasis of the dream was about securing our inheritance.

On Wednesday, April 12, 2017, the third day of Passover, I dreamed I was on a high hill overlooking the Promised Land. I saw both our view of Washington DC and a view of Israel's Jezreel Valley from Tel Megiddo.

Yes, in the dream Washington DC was superimposed on Armageddon.

Honestly, that's kind of unsettling. Though a clear warning was conveyed in the dream, the Spirit's primary emphasis was actually good news. It was time to secure the harvest! God was summoning us to begin taking His Promised Land.

Before we go there, let's focus more specifically on the view. From our own watchman's perch, Jolene and I overlook the seats of authority for all three branches of our government—the White House, Capitol, and Supreme Court. If we stand on a stepstool, we can also see the Pentagon. So, on our prayer calls, your declarations are resounding to these highest seats of power. No king but Jesus!

In the dream, the Jezreel Valley was juxtaposed with this view of Washington DC from our perch.

As noted, Revelation bears witness that Har Megiddo or Armageddon will be the site of the ultimate, cataclysmic battle between good and evil, marking the end of days. That said, war was not the primary emphasis of the Spirit in this dream. It was harvest.

Note that for the first time in centuries, the previously uninhabited land known as the Jezreel Valley now produces the vast majority of the produce for Israel. Jezreel has become Israel's breadbasket—just as the biblical prophets foresaw. More on this in a moment.

Call to Take the Promised Land

In the dream, a group of us were strategizing on the next steps to take the Promised Land. The view from the hilltop was so expansive—as if we could see from one end to the other.

I knew the "land" we were overlooking represented promises from God to us personally as well as to nations. Harvest, blessing, promotion, increase. We saw the ground we are called to take in this Crown & Throne movement, including the restoration of His glory across the land.

And—this is so important—the glory of the Lord is now leading us as a movement. God's angelic armies are going before us to prepare the way. All that said, Heaven and Earth are now resourcing us all to take the land. You must understand that is what this dream is conveying.

"Their Defense Is Removed from Over Them"

A key issue is whether or not we are willing to obey God by engaging in supernatural conflict to secure our Promised Land. Joshua admonished, *"Only do not rebel against the Lord. And do not fear the people of the land, for they are bread for us. Their protection is removed from them, and the Lord is with us; do not fear them"* (Num. 14:9 ESV).

Did you catch that? When God opens the window to possess your portion, the defense is removed from *over* your enemies. You will still have to engage. But the demonic realm will be fully restrained!

It cannot be emphasized enough. This Crown & Throne movement is a *freedom movement*. The Lord promised to marry the miracles of Exodus with the miracles of Acts. And His eyes are absolutely on the multitudes still in subjugation to the enemy. They are our harvest. *"Let My people go!"*

Here's a personal question. What specific promise is the Lord making alive for you in this season? The opportunity and anointing will be there for you. Shift your mindset. Take time now to receive God's direction. And then let's take the land!

What Do You See?

In the dream, I could see both opportunities and obstacles that were both near and far. In other prophetic experiences, my vision was limited to what I was shown. But in this prophetic experience, it was as though my vision was only limited by what I chose to focus on!

I looked. I saw.

In this season of training as a watchman, God is giving you fresh vision. Some of what you receive will be by God's sovereign choice. But some of what you see by His Spirit will actually be determined by what you choose to focus on. *"Watchman, what do YOU see?"*

Jezebel

Here's what I saw in my dream as our primary obstacle. A woman in a loose-fitting robe was resting on a rock in the exact geographic center of the field. She smiled at me, waved, and leaned forward, showing her cleavage. Jolene was by my side, and I turned to her and said, "That is witchcraft!"

Here's a clear warning to us all. The primary risk to the advancement of God's movement in the earth is still covenant breaking and idolatry. We must pray even for our government leaders in this. *"Lead us not into temptation, but deliver us from evil!"*

Keep in mind again that Jezebel was thrust from her tower in Jezreel. Because this was the primary enemy identified in the dream, I believe the Lord desires for this spiritual stronghold to fully come down in this hour. This means the defenses of this principality are being disempowered in a way they have not been in decades.

Let's take this ground.

I will also say now that the covenant right of Israel to possess her land will be called into question these next seven years. This promise not only prophesies the end-time prayer movement we are all in, but it promises the restoration of the Jewish people from captivity as well. Their vineyards will be restored. They will be planted in their land, *"AND THEY WILL NOT AGAIN BE ROOTED OUT from their land which I have given them,' says the Lord your God"* (Amos 9:15 emphasis added).

Jezreel

Okay. All this to get to here. Let's revisit Tel Megiddo for a moment. It was actually one of our wildest sites on our recent Crown & Throne Tour through Israel. We climbed ancient stones which bore witness to the conflicts and glory that birthed the Western world. These stones again will witness a "conflict of thrones" by which this entire age will culminate.

And if you know our friends James Nesbit, Ed Watts, and Jamie Fitt, they were determined that these same rocks be loaded with Heaven's sound for the hour, resounding the scrolls of Heaven!

Our team ascended the summit. As we prepared to worship, our pioneering Israeli tour guide Eran Salamon gave us a history lesson. Note that *Eran* literally means "watchful or vigilant" in Hebrew. Watchful, otherwise known as Vigilant, was teaching us from the summit of Armageddon. Just can't make this stuff up!

Eran informed us that the Jezreel Valley was primarily swampland when the Jewish settlers returned to Israel for its rebirth. Swampland. For endless centuries it was uninhabited, because mosquitoes bearing malaria kept anyone from cultivating the fields.

The settlers knew their Bible. *Jezreel* means "God sows." They knew the scrolls of their forefathers had prophesied the Jezreel Valley would one day become a premier region of harvest in the land. Hosea 2 even declares that not only will corn, wine, and oil respond to Jezreel, but Heaven and Earth will as well!

So, to take the land and possess it, one thing was necessary. They needed to *drain the swamp*!

When our guide uttered these words, our team drew a collective gasp. The shofar sounded. A new song began to be formed. And from Armageddon to Jezreel to Washington DC, we all began to sing a holy declaration, "Drain the swamp!"

Drain the Swamp, Secure the Harvest

Friend, you must understand this. Draining the swamp was the primary catalyst to unlocking the harvest God had promised. This process secured the harvest promised to Jezreel in God's own Word. And it will for you as well.

Why in my dream did God juxtapose a view of Jezreel from Tel Megiddo with a view of Washington DC? God has a plan to unlock the harvest of precious seeds—of our nation, Israel, and the nations. Despite much opposition, these freedom seeds have been sown purposefully and relentlessly over many generations. You've sown them as well.

God is showing us Washington DC and the nation as our primary Jezreel. And completing the turnaround requires that we continue to drain the swamp! The mosquitoes that drain the nation of its lifeblood, that spread the sickness and disease of iniquity, idolatry, compromise and corruption, need to go.

Of course this is already happening. But now is not the time to stop! You must see this is how we complete the turnaround the Lord has called us to stand for. It's how we take the ground. Drain the swamp!

Remember that Jezreel means God sows, and unless a seed falls into the ground and dies, it abides alone (see John 12:24). But if it dies, it will produce a great, global harvest.

God sows. Jesus is our ultimate Seed, the harvest of the nations our ultimate Jezreel. Let's again resound the resolve thundered by the Moravians—that the slain Lamb, the Lion of the tribe of Judah, receive the full reward of His suffering, here and in the nations of the earth.

Prophetic Word

While writing this chapter, the Holy Spirit spoke to me:

> I have made Armageddon a reference point for securing America's inheritance. Further, I am establishing many fortified watchman perches throughout Israel, America, and the nations to keep watch and govern over emerging spiritual battles and even conflicts of thrones in the natural.
>
> These watchtowers shall be angelic command posts, fortified with My holy weapons of war. And they will serve as strategic reference points and gateways for My covenant people to possess their portion in this freedom movement.

In summation—the Lord wants you to have a fortified watchman's perch over your battlefields. Together with Him, you will gain vision and revelation for victory!

Overthrowing Jezebel, Securing Inheritance

In my dream, the primary resistance set by the enemy to keep God's covenant people from possessing their portion was not a vast army equipped with fighter jets, tanks, or nuclear bombs. It wasn't a terrorist organization.

Instead, the totality of advancement by the Body of Christ was checked by a seductive woman representing a Jezebel spirit.

Strong women leaders are often given the horrific label of being a "Jezebel," especially within the Body of Christ. They're not. They are simply strong women leaders. God is raising up women and men together to lead His transformation army for the hour. Remember, God made both man and woman in His own image. And without this covenantal expression within His leadership, the totality of God's heart and counsel would be sorrowfully incomplete.

Here are a few facts about Jezebel, sourced from the Bible.

Jezebel was the daughter of Ithobaal, King of Sidon. Historically, this king was a strong conqueror who expanded his rule throughout ancient Phoenicia. His daughter Jezebel was given to Ahab, king of Israel, with the intention of forging an alliance which would essentially expand the kingdom to overtake God's covenant land.

The name *Ithobaal* or *Ethbaal* literally means "with Baal." In other words, the king of Phoenicia established his rulership in covenant with the ancient god of Phoenicia, the principality Baal. Ithobaal worshipped Baal. And spiritually, the offspring of his relationship with Baal was his daughter Ishi-baal or Jezebel, whom he named, of course, for Baal. Kind of like in a marriage, the last name carried over.

Maybe it's not a coincidence that *Ishi-baal* or *Jezebel* can literally be translated as "Baal is my husband." Jezebel is actually a feminine face of the Baal principality. In Elijah's day, she openly defied the prophets while laboring without rest to infuse Baal worship into the core of Israelite society, including sexual immorality as the norm as acts of obeisance to Baal. She was seeking above all to separate God's covenant land and people from genuine covenant with God.

By contrast, Ahab's name is far less interesting. *Ahab* or *Ahav* means "brother of father or uncle." You might think that Uncle Ahab, the king of God's covenant land of Israel, would shy away from a woman whose name means "Baal is my husband," like run from the room screaming. But, instead, like many who are naive about the detrimental effects of idolatry and the occult, he yielded to her seduction. He decided to marry her, thereby plunging all Israel into a horrific era of idolatry, covenant-breaking, sexual immorality, and finally severe discipline from the Lord.

Jezebel became queen. Notably, when "Baal is my husband" married Uncle Ahab, they decided to settle in the Jezreel Valley under the shadow of Har Megiddo. It is a variant of Israel often used by prophets to symbolize the nation of Israel itself. And what would soon transpire would come to even foreshadow the great end-time battle which will take place in this valley under the shadow of the watchtower Har Megiddo.

But on a shorter, more parabolic note, a clear lesson can be gleaned that all of us can benefit from. Marry Jezebel, and you will get Armageddon. This word is true.

Again, Jezebel worked with her husband Ahab to transform Israel from a nation whose identity was forged in covenant with God into a globalist empire sourced in Baal, embracing the very covenant-breaking which caused God's glory to lift from the land. There are vast parallels to this hour.

Elijah—Watchman of Israel

And that's where a watchman of Israel named Elijah entered into the narrative.

The name *Elijah* means "the Lord is God." Elijah was raised up by the Lord to steward the rulership of Israel according to His covenant with the land and people. Elijah was tasked with the sacred purpose of restoring the nation to alignment to their God and its covenantal heritage once again.

As noted in the previous chapter, Elijah gained a throne over the covenant land which no man could obtain, nor could any man take it away. He was leveraged by nobody. Instead, his throne of rulership was established by God alone. From our first book, *Crown & Throne*:

> In this respect, Elijah's calling was similar to Jeremiah. "I have appointed you this day over the nations and over the kingdoms,

to pluck up and to break down, to destroy and to overthrow, to build and to plant" (Jer. 1:9–10).

God still establishes His seats of governance over nations and kingdoms, or spheres of society. He still grants covenantal authority to root out, tear down, throw down, destroy, build, and plant. The prophet Isaiah conveyed this process another way:

"I have put My words in your mouth and have covered you with the shadow of My hand, to establish the heavens, to found the earth, and to say to Zion, 'You are My people'" (Isa. 51:16). Note that these seats of rulership are meant to bring the governance of God into every facet of community. They are ultimately meant to bring government in alignment with God's covenant.[76]

Thank God for Elijah in his day, who confronted this force head-on by the Spirit of God. Thank God for the Elijahs, the burning and shining lamps of our day as well! Most likely you are among them. In your potential at least. It's time for you to shine!

Securing the Vineyard of Prophetic Destiny

Most Christians rightly associate Jezebel with sexual immorality and idolatry. But what you probably don't know about Jezebel is far more important right now than what you believe you know. Jezebel also creates and perpetuates slanderous lies to take down God's covenant people. First Kings 21 exposes the manufacturing of her "fake news," and even her use of the media toward this end. I will summarize the passage for you.

A farmer named Naboth owned a vineyard right next to the land where Ahab and Jezebel erected a military palace. Naboth was the steward, or watchman, appointed over the vineyard. This vineyard was passed down from his forefathers as a family inheritance. Hear me in this—the vineyard was his by covenant. Not coincidentally, both the vineyard and the palace were located across the Jezreel Valley from Har Megiddo or Armageddon, in a town called Jezreel.

It's interesting that *Naboth* comes from the same root word as *nabi* or *prophet*. In fact, in Hebrew the name *Naboth* means prophetic words! And his inheritance was literally "the vineyard of prophetic destiny."

So Prophetic Words owned a vineyard in Jezreel, right next to Jezebel's stronghold. The harvest of Prophetic Words was incredible. And, of course, the corrupt "deep state" political leaders of the day wanted to overtake this vineyard to use it for their own purposes.

Ahab sought to purchase the vineyard from Naboth. I will summarize the story for you, with a focus on Naboth's response, because for us to succeed it must become our own.

Naboth refused the offer—vehemently. "God forbid that I should give you the inheritance of my forefathers!"

Jezebel, chief witch of Israel, began to target Naboth three ways. First, with the occult power from which she derived her rulership. Second, with fake news she made up and distributed to the nation's most influential leaders in order to disqualify Naboth from owning his vineyard. Third, by recruiting despicable men to give fake news, otherwise known as false testimony.

Beloved, your testimony is a reflection of your integrity. The Bible describes as "despicable" those willing to compromise their sworn testimony to appease Jezebel by ruining reputations through deceit.

Here's an alert for you. A fuller translation of *despicable men* means "sons of Belial or sons of Baal." Jezebel was essentially head over their secret society. And together they plotted in secret to disenfranchise Naboth to steal his wealth. Many legal processes today have been compromised by similar secret alliances.

Jezebel's ploy seemed to have been working. The false testimony of the sons of Belial prevailed. Naboth was convicted of dishonoring God and king, and was stoned to death. Jezebel summoned Ahab to take possession of the vineyard.

And as he walked through this newly acquired vineyard of prophetic destiny, he was met by the prophet Elijah. The prophet had been summoned into Heaven's Court to deliver God's verdict on the matter. And His verdict was a death sentence for both Ahab and Jezebel.

Amazingly, Ahab repented. Jezebel did not. History records that she was cast down from the tower of her great fortress, right next to Naboth's vineyard.

So, let's review. Jezebel used three means of power to take Naboth down. First, occult targeting. Second, fake news in the court of public opinion. Third, fake news in the court of law.

Sound familiar? I submit to you the process is very similar to today's intentional targeting of President Trump and his administration, which essentially began election day. First, with occult targeting, as we have documented previously. You have to wonder why occultists nationally and globally are so united in cursing this man—one reason again why we need the night-and-day vigilance of White House watchmen.

Second, Jezebel has been targeting the administration by generating fake news to influence the court of public opinion.

Third, Jezebel has been creating fake news in the court of law to discredit a Naboth of this hour, take him down, and thereby steal his vineyard.

Jesus Is Our Naboth!

Jezebel took Naboth down. Though Elijah's verdict may have restored justice, it never brought back Naboth from the dead. My cry is that God intervenes to expose and restrain Jezebel before she is able to take down the Naboths of this hour!

This decision is ultimately also secured by Heaven's Court alone. The good news is we have great verdicts as precedent, including the divorcement from Baal, covenant restoration with Jesus, and more. But let's take a moment to see how the greatest verdict granted by Heaven's Court plays into this.

Naboth was slain as a victim of false accusation. This man whose name means "prophetic words or prophetic destiny" was seeded into the soil of his own vineyard in Jezreel—God sows.

Naboth's plight gives you a foretaste of another prophet from the region who grew up praying over the Jezreel Valley. Described in parables as a vineyard owner himself, this man's life was bartered away by a very close friend so that the title deed of his inheritance could finally be disenfranchised from him. His reputation thus ruined, he was judged by a fake court on false charges and swung up between Heaven and the harvest fields of Earth to die on a cross.

What looked to be satan's greatest victory became his greatest defeat. By atoning for our sins, the title deed for all humanity was actually redeemed and transferred from satan's hideous grasp. It has been restored to you and me.

Here's a verse that must terrify the enemy to this day. In foretelling His death, Jesus exclaimed that unless a seed falls to the ground and dies, it abides alone. Jesus became that Seed. He died and rose again to secure for you your inheritance—eternally and here on Earth. Now where there was one Naboth, there are now billions of Naboths in the earth—appointed as stewards or watchmen over their respective vineyards of prophetic destiny.

The verdict, my friend, has been rendered on your behalf ultimately through the broken body and shed blood of Jesus Christ. He has granted us to be joint heirs with Him. In redeeming us, He also redeemed your inheritance. And it's now time for the saints to possess the Kingdom!

Naboth's Resolve—The Inheritance of Our Forefathers

The fact that Jesus died and rose again to redeem our inheritance makes gaining Naboth's resolve all the more important. "God forbid that I should give you, Ahab and Jezebel, the inheritance of our forefathers!"

Naboth's battle speaks to our hour with great clarity. The harvest is what was at stake then, and that is what is at stake in this hour of history as a totalitarian machine built by Jezebel has sought to perpetually invalidate the leaders the Lord has set over this vineyard.

God forbid that we should yield it. Let's all gain this same resolve because there's more at stake than what any of us know. Again, the ultimate battle being waged by this manifestation of the Baal principality is over America's inheritance and Israel's inheritance, both secured by covenant. You must drain the swamp to secure the harvest!

Jezebel's war to take over Naboth's vineyard gives us just a foretaste of the ultimate war for all humanity, which Scripture says will be fought on that very farmland in the Valley of Jezreel.

Let's remember again that the Jezreel Valley was protected and defended from a watchman's perch called Armageddon. The epic battle prophesied in Revelation will ultimately be fought over the harvest field of prophetic destiny. The war will be engaged between people in covenant with dark powers and those in covenant with Jesus Christ, deemed by God as the lawful inheritors of the harvest fields.

As it is in the final battle of the end times, so it will be in the epic Armageddons in your life and world. Because Jezebel always seeks to overtake the vineyards of prophetic destiny. To win, you must embrace Naboth's resolve. Set a watch! Gain a perspective for breakthrough that secures your victory.

Let me share with you prophetically where we are in real time. In this Armageddon battle over Washington DC, we are now moving beyond Jezebel's blockade. By verdict of Heaven's Court, this principality has been restrained to the extent that we can now begin to secure our inheritance, our covenant destiny, in a way previously unimaginable.

For Review

Please take a moment to reflect on what you've just read. We suggest taking notes as you answer questions below.

1. Take a moment to personalize the dream we shared on overlooking the Promised Land. What promises from the Lord are you keeping watch to see fulfilled? List them. What is your harvest? What is your swamp? Ask the Lord to give you clarity on the obstacles and how to remove them. Seek Him for victory!

2. The enemy is after your covenant inheritance. Many times, he seeks to marginalize you in the very areas where you are called

to flourish. Have you experienced this? Have you received prayer to counter the accusations? Time to approach Heaven's Court over your promise!

3. On a national level, how do you perceive Jezebel has attacked the Trump presidency? What do you perceive is the inheritance the forces of darkness are trying to take over?

4. How would you apply Naboth's resolve regarding your life? Regarding your nation? What tangible actions will you take?

CHAPTER 13

DETHRONING JEZEBEL!
THE CONFLICT OF QUEENS

AS noted before, Yom Kippur is the holiest day on the Jewish calendar, the day of national atonement. To spend the first evening of Yom Kippur 2018 at the White House was a high honor—but it was more than coincidence, especially when hours earlier the Lord had given a startling prophetic perception that could only be described as a verdict from Heaven's Court.

The verdict? Jezebel down. The Oval Office and West Wing of the White House became the first place where this verdict was governmentally released, while presenting the body and blood of Jesus for the atonement of our sins. It was done privately, of course.

But when a word comes from the throne of God, even whispered prayer can reverberate like thunder in the Spirit.

Here Comes the Judge

Keep in mind that during the time surrounding Yom Kippur 2018, the battle to seat Justice Brett Kavanaugh on the Supreme Court was at its most intense. President Trump had nominated Justice Kavanaugh to fill a vacancy on the Supreme Court after Justice Anthony Kennedy retired. Kavanaugh was serving as a US Circuit Court of Appeals Judge for the District of Columbia and was very well respected within the legal community of Washington DC.

Further, he had earned high marks on both sides of the political aisle. Until his nomination, that is. Then came an American Armageddon—with Jezebel on overdrive. Complete with manufactured false accusations, including charges of rape during his college years. In the end, an FBI investigation proved the lies against Kavanaugh to have been completely fabricated.[77] The story of this battle is worth sharing. Then we are going to explore another dimension of Kingdom advancement that has been released in context with Jezebel's defeat.

Why did Kavanaugh's nomination stir such a fight? Very simply, with Kavanaugh the door finally would open to overthrow government-funded abortion. It was the kind of opportunity that comes once in a lifetime. And both sides knew it.

All rise. Here comes the Judge!

Given what was at stake, receiving the Yom Kippur verdict for our nation and then releasing it at the gates of the Oval Office was a feat only God could pull off.

The Lord backed up His verdict with power. And His judgment had everything to do with overthrowing the immediate assault against Justice Kavanaugh as well as President Trump. In due course, watchman prayer over this war took us from the White House to Rome, Italy, all the way to Jezreel, Israel, ancient host to both Jezebel's stronghold and Naboth's vineyard—and on the very day of Justice Kavanaugh's final hearing.

Rome to Jerusalem—Watchman Prayer for Kavanaugh

God's timing never ceases to amaze. Because the day after visiting the White House on Yom Kippur, we flew out on a Crown & Throne Tour planned for almost a year beforehand, with the twofold focus of restoring God's lampstand from Rome to Jerusalem and cutting ancient ties empowering abortion from Rome to Washington DC (and state capitals nationwide). But by God's orchestration, He intended the tour to seal a governmental turnaround for a judge whom we did not even know existed when the journey was planned. Complete with a West Wing visit.

Like all our Crown & Throne journeys, the Rome to Jerusalem tour was headed up by a joint team consisting of apostolic and prophetic leaders Jamie Fitt, James Nesbit, Ed Watts, and me. Of course, whenever you get my direction, you get Jolene's prophetic leadership as well. And when Queen Jolene hears from God, you supernaturally have no choice but to follow—whether into Costco, Chuys, the prayer chamber, or the battlefronts of humanity.

When she quickens the pace, we quicken. When she slows the pace, we hit the brakes. Over the years, I've come to discover that resistance is simply futile in the most positive way—like the time on the Rome to Jerusalem tour when we toured the Vatican.

The Voice of the Victims—Vatican Encounter

I was walking a few steps ahead of Jolene as we toured the Vatican Museum, the Sistine Chapel, and St. Peter's Basilica. She lagged farther and farther behind. When I looked back, she was hardly moving. A fountain of tears was gushing from her eyes. She could barely even talk.

"As we've been walking, Holy Spirit opened my ears," she stammered. "And I heard the screams of the children who were abused by priests. They are echoing through these halls. I cannot get away from them!"

For more than an hour, walking through the halls of the Vatican, Jolene had entered into full-blown travailing prayer for these children. She heard their cries. She could feel their fear and pain, even children through previous ages who had suffered abuse.

The rest of the group had to stop and wait. For good reason. Really, Holy Spirit had taken the lead.

Again and again, I sent friends to walk alongside Jolene to speed her progress. And again and again, Holy Spirit came upon each one with a solemn, overwhelming travail so heavy that they themselves would nearly collapse. None of them were seeking it. Obviously, it was not protocol. And yet it was happening.

In the Sistine Chapel, the intensity of their intercession had dissipated, and my eyes were free to take in the priceless paintings adorning the ceilings and walls.

But when we entered St. Peter's Basilica, the travail began again with great intensity. A few nuns gathered at a distance, watching. The Vatican police were not far behind. I decided a conversation was in order.

"This woman, she is your wife?" asked a cloistered nun in broken English.

I nodded.

"What then is wrong with your wife. Is she okay?"

"She is having an experience with God," I replied, my mind racing to find common ground. "Kind of like the mystics, the contemplatives who had visitations of Him."

A visitation at the St. Peter's Basilica, that they could understand—and even appreciate. Their countenances brightened.

"Ah, this is like St. Catherine of Sienna, yes? Or St. Theresa of Avila?"

"Perhaps, Sister. Jolene is often prone to visionary experiences like them. But probably not like this. While we were walking, the Lord Jesus opened her ears, and she began to hear the cries of children who have been abused by priests. She heard their pleas for help. Nothing like this has ever happened to her."

The two nuns stared back at me, wide-eyed. "I don't know if this makes any sense."

The Sisters generously suggested we let Jolene and the other women alone until the experience with God subsided. Then it would be time to leave.

About five months later, Pope Francis made a very courageous statement during a Vatican summit to counter child abuse: "Our work has made us realize once again that the gravity of the scourge of the sexual abuse of minors is, and historically has been, a widespread phenomenon in all cultures and societies," he said. "I am reminded of the cruel religious practice, once widespread in certain cultures, of sacrificing human beings—frequently children—in pagan rites."

What he shared next brought tears.

"The echo of the silent cry of the little ones who, instead of finding in them fathers and spiritual guides encountered tormentors, will shake hearts dulled by hypocrisy and by power," Pope Francis exclaimed. "It is our duty to pay close heed to this silent, choked cry!"

Perhaps Pope Francis had heard of Jolene's Basilica encounter, but I would find that hard to imagine. Her prayers sure made a way though. Sometimes, more is caught than taught. Your prayers make a way!

Anyway, we are grateful to Pope Francis for his profound, humble words—and even more, his very courageous stand.

We all must be humbled by the fact that the cries of the victims are still resounding before Heaven's Court. Whether the courts of Earth ever hold the perpetrators accountable or not, there is one Judge they will stand before, whose verdict they will by no means be able to evade. Not after death, and not even in this life.

In fact, Exodus 3:7 conveys how God convened a special hearing to hear the cries of His afflicted. He rendered judgment against both the demonic principalities and the governmental authorities who abused His covenant people.

The Ancient of Days *"heard their cry"* and remembered His covenant. The word *heard* is actually *shema*, a word conveying a courtroom hearing. He held court and brought the cries and groanings of His people into the hearing. He reviewed each case with great focus, and great intentionality.

What should terrify us the most is that the Lord hears the cries of all victims of abuse, even those in the womb. And in the rendering of God's verdict, *their voice prevails.*

Overcoming Abortion

Amazingly, our team's most comprehensive assignment in Rome was also alluded to in the statement made by Pope Francis. Long before the Catholic Church existed, Rome had become a prototype for the capitals of nations throughout the world. Capitol Hill, for instance, was patterned after Capitoline Hill in Rome, once the epicenter for global governance in the known world.

And Capitoline Hill was built upon an ancient altar of child sacrifice.[78]

While praying into the tour, Ed Watts and I began to see a correlation between Capitoline Hill and Capitol Hill. Ed in particular perceived how, for the Senators and House members to be free to reverse the scourge of abortion in America, the ungodly ties in the spirit which connected Rome and Washington had to be severed.

We also realized that, with Rome as a prototype for every other government center in the earth, these ungodly ties needed to be severed between Capitoline Hill and other capitals as well, especially our state capitals.

So, on Thursday, September 27, during the start of the Feast of Tabernacles, our team prayed on-site at Capitoline Hill as prayer leaders on Capitol Hill and in each state capital sought God together to sever all ungodly ties which had empowered abortion from Rome.

Perhaps not coincidentally, on the very same date, Justice Brett Kavanaugh endured his first Senate hearing for the Supreme Court. The opposition, primarily abortion advocates, sought to prevent him from being seated by any means necessary. In the pattern of Jezebel, extraordinary lies were manufactured against him. And with his wife in attendance during this hearing, Brett Kavanaugh was excoriated for rape and other crimes he simply did not commit.

Our nation's top leaders, even including Senator Diane Feinstein, perpetuated the deception. I have personally admired Senator Feinstein's balanced stewardship of the Senate Intelligence Committee over many years previously. That said, to present false claims as actionable intelligence was absolutely inexcusable. In a way that no words can convey. The uproar was instantaneous.[79]

And the toll these manufactured lies took on the Kavanaugh family was crushing. To protect his family, the battered judge came perilously close to withdrawing from being considered.

But a week later, the FBI investigation proved the lies against Kavanaugh to have been completely fabricated.

Always remember—"Armageddon" is fought by Jezebel to disenfranchise you from your vineyard of prophetic destiny. The great news is that Jesus is ready to render judgment on your behalf and set the record straight.

Speaking of which, by God's orchestration alone, we and our Rome to Jerusalem team were visiting Tel Jezreel on the very day of Kavanaugh's hearings. Remember the itinerary for this tour had been planned many months in advance. There was no way we could have known then that Brett Kavanaugh would take the stand on the same day we worshiped at Tel Jezreel.

Archeological ruins of both a military palace and a wine vat where grapes were once crushed attest to the validity of the biblical description. Jezebel and Ahab owned a palace there. Naboth owned a vineyard there.

And from the very place where the gavel of God's justice put an end to Jezebel's lies, we decreed God's verdict for this hour for Brett Kavanaugh. Here comes the Judge! Redemptive exposure and deliverance from occult power and deception. Jezebel down! Justice Kavanaugh must be seated over his vineyard, the sphere assigned to him by God.

About five hours later, Justice Kavanaugh was confirmed. And the prospect of overcoming the scourge of abortion in America suddenly became real. Jezebel dethroned. We are moving from abortion to awakening!

The verdict released first at the White House, then at Capitoline Hill, and finally at Tel Jezreel, is featured in the appendix.

Now that this verdict has been rendered, let's look at one aspect of the freedom movement being birthed.

Conflict of Queens—by Jolene

We have been in a midnight hour. With the turnaround of breakthrough against Jezebel, Jon and I believe it's now time for a midnight awakening, as pictured in Matthew 25. Let's remember that the context of the passage is a wedding. And it was the bridal party, maybe including God's end-time reserve of women warriors, that is awakened. It's time for Esther to arise!

Have you ever noticed the parallels between Jezebel and Esther? They are striking. Both were queens in a foreign land. Jezebel, from the region of Babylon, served as queen of Israel. Esther, from Israel, served as queen of Babylon—or Medo-Persia as the Persian empire had conquered Babylon by this time. Both were given rulership by their husbands, the kings. Both altered the course of their nation through their covenant loyalties in the spirit.

But that's really where the similarities end.

Jezebel served the vicious principality known as Baal. Through her governmental influence, she seduced God's chosen people into sexual immorality and idolatry, breaking covenant with the God of Israel. She continually used those under her governmental reign for her own purposes. As you have just read, Jezebel sought to possess Jezreel—a symbol of all Israel—through deceit and murder. God judged her, and she was thrust out of her tower. Jezebel was thrown down in a very dramatic picture story!

Esther, on the other hand, was a Jewish refugee exiled in Babylon approximately one generation after Daniel. Driven by her loyalty to God and her people, she preserved her people from a holocaust. She understood in a profound way that it might even require her life, which I believe is something we are all coming face to face within this season. Revelation 12:11 puts it this way—overcoming by the blood of the Lamb, the word of our testimony, and not loving our lives unto death.

In Esther's scenario, this risk was first because she had kept her Jewish identity hidden from the king throughout their marriage. The revelation that Esther was Jewish essentially meant that the king had chosen as his beauty queen an orphaned slave. To make matters worse, there was the Haman plot, very similar to what transpired under Hitler years later, that was being secretly unfolded behind the scenes.

It is important to note here that the plot being planned was the mastermind of Haman's wife Zeresh. She planned to bring down Mordecai and make sure it was as public as possible in the town square. Again, the storyline of an evil woman behind the scenes plotting and scheming to annihilate the Jews and without even knowing the extent of the plot bring down the queen at the same time. As we all know, in one dramatic moment worthy of the greatest love stories, Esther's king favored her by extending the scepter to her. Haman ends up publicly hanging on his own noose, and the people were preserved. And Esther was given governmental authority to rule half the kingdom (see Esther 9:29). She received authority to possess!

As we progress into what the Bible refers to as the end times, both the contrast and conflict between the Esthers of God and the Jezebels of the antichrist are prophesied to crescendo. There has been much written about the Jezebel spirit and the political spirit in today's Christian writing. I believe we have to raise our vision higher and see what is empowering this battle in the heavenlies. Maybe you will be shocked by my answer, but I believe that this end-game conflict of crowns is actually a battle between the queens.

For many years, we have been teaching and celebrating our position as the king. We have matured to see how the priestly ministry needed to embrace the kingly dimension in both identity and calling. I believe that there is one step further we have to go. A hidden truth shown throughout the Bible is that the queen has a very distinct calling. Many know the story of queen Esther, but how many understand the battle strategy that the Lord is raising up in this hour? The strategy is this—dethrone the false queen with the true queen of the Kingdom.

What is the false queen—and how does she operate? For years, I have known that I have a queenly calling on my life. Many in our home group hilariously call my chair the "throne of the queen." When Jon and I are away ministering, our home group tradition is they send us pictures with them seated in the chair. It is a fun thing we all tease about, but there is a measure of truth to it.

You see, for years when I first got saved, I went through a process with the Lord where the Lord trained me and treated me as royalty to Him. I learned not just about how special I was to Him, but an authority came with the understanding of His love for me. I always knew that He had my back in all situations. He went out of His way to show His love for me, and in many ways, I was spoiled by Him. When I was going through deliverance ministry in the beginning, my mentors would oftentimes comment about how unique my experiences with Jesus seemed to be. He responded to me unlike any other of their ministry appointments.

Let me say at this point I believe this "beauty preparation" was a forerunner calling to train me in the queenly anointing that would be most important for many in the Body of Christ in this end-game, end-time battle. There is nothing more special about me. I have an assignment in the battle of the queens, and knowing how beloved I am is one of the first things He cultivated in me. To be honest, when the season to actually battle came to pass, I struggled with "the honeymoon phase" dwindling. The season of special love was a preparatory season meant to engrain that truth in my spirit, and it would not necessarily carry through so intensively in later years. But I must say that, in preparing to battle with the false queen, intimacy with our Savior is the most important battle gear we can gain. Not many would call it a weapon of war, but I understand in the depths of my being that it is the greatest strategy of all. Our intimacy with Him is where He truly covers us. There is also a joy and fun aspect of serving the Lord that many are missing when they don't understand this key.

Beauty Treatments—Come to Him, Come Out of Her!

The story of Esther is the first example. We all are taught from the first part of the story where the false queen is deposed due to her disrespect for the king, and another is chosen in her place. This transition in leadership is echoed throughout the book of Revelation. *"Those who overcome"* are granted to sit with Jesus at His right hand and rule with Him.

Jesus said, *"Behold, I stand at the door and knock; if anyone hears My voice and opens the door, I will come in to him and will dine with him, and he with Me"* (Rev. 3:20). And Revelation 18:4–5 reads,

I heard another voice from heaven, saying, "Come out of her, my people, so that you will not participate in her sins and receive of her plagues; for her sins have piled up as high as heaven, and God has remembered her iniquities."

Dream—An Esther Movement

I hope you see the pattern. As we gain freedom from the influence of Jezebel and Babylon, we gain authority to rule with our King. To the one who overcomes, Jesus will grant!

Now, let's look at the Esther movement God is birthing. Many precious seeds have been sown into the ground. A harvest of Esthers is appearing in the earth. Below is a very impacting dream I had recently that relates to Esther's story.

In the dream, I was given the task of inviting a group of women together who were highly adorned and prepared for a very important assignment. I saw a picture frame with all of them together similar to the screen on a Zoom call. I was telling them about a very special invitation that was coming to each one of them. It was so special that we would need to find a formal dress from our closets to wear for the event. The two dresses I was impressed to find were my formal gown that I wore to President Trump's inaugural ball, and my wedding dress that I purchased under very specific instruction from the Lord. It had to be ivory with gold beading down the front.

The frame of the dream shifted, and a very prominent woman prophet was in a dressing room near a bathroom with one of the women I did not immediately recognize. The woman was grieving because she no longer fit into her gown because years had long passed since she had worn it. The woman prophet was giving her a plush velvet dressing gown to put on instead. The dream ended.

As you've probably experienced, in dreams there are just senses that you have as you wake up that are key to their interpretation. This is what the Lord highlighted to me. As I prayed into the dream, I felt that I was calling together a group of women that would collaborate together as a "corporate Esther" for the moment. I also knew that we were getting together to call a banquet that was designed to invite Haman to the feast of his own defeat—just like in Esther 5.

The banquet was entirely about exposing Haman for his heinous plot to annihilate the Jewish people of the time. The plot is similar today just with different characters. We as a collective group were being called to take down the Haman structure publicly, the same way Haman was trying to take down the entire nation publicly.

And the action of putting on garments of royalty was very intrinsic for the plot to unfold. For me, this was both my bridal adornments, representing covenant intimacy, and specifically chosen by me to represent the wedding dress in Psalm 45 and the gown for the inaugural ball which represents the "royal robes" of rulership. Both were key to interpreting the dream.

> *Now it happened on the third day that Esther put on her royal robes and stood in the inner court of the king's palace, across from the king's house, while the king sat on his royal throne in the royal house, facing the entrance of the house* (Esther 5:1 NKJV).

The Inaugural Ball

The other aspect of the dream that was important was the symbolism of the gown from the inauguration party in Washington DC. Previous chapters show the importance of the forty-fifth president of the United States being prophetically tied to Isaiah 45 and King Cyrus. I believe prophetically that the Lord is specifically highlighting the time of the rise of the women, also highlighting Psalm 45.

> *Listen, O daughter, consider and incline your ear; forget your own people also, and your father's house; so the King will greatly desire your beauty; because He is your Lord, worship Him.... The royal daughter is all glorious within the palace; her clothing is woven with gold. She shall be brought to the King...*(vv. 10–14 NKJV).

Do you see that it is all about the Bride? As a matter of fact, its title in my Bible is "The Glories of the Messiah and His Bride—A Song of Love."

As with Esther, Psalm 45 is also a story about a king, a scepter, and a beautiful bride. You cannot escape the beauty within the symbolism of this story of Esther and her king. It is as though this passage interprets my dream of the two dresses.

Verse 9 talks about the King's daughters being among my honorable women, the beautiful "Esther friends" the Lord wants to be invited into intercession in this hour. I hope your response is like what I saw in the dream because the Esthers of today are not passive. They are full of excitement, bursting in joy to meet the Bridegroom—and rule with Him.

> *She shall be brought to the King in robes of many colors; the virgins, her companions who follow her, shall be brought to You. With gladness and rejoicing they shall be brought; they shall enter the King's palace* (Psalm 45:14–15 NKJV).

The Women's Movement

There is a women's movement that is being raised up in this hour. Our task is to confront the false queen that stands behind the false king as they attempt to overthrow King Jesus! The movement will be about joy and beauty—beauty cultivated by extended time with our King! Something I believe this pandemic season is all about. A quiet confidence rising up that will make us roar!

> *For thus says the Lord God, the Holy One of Israel: "In returning and rest you shall be saved; in quietness and confidence shall be your strength"* (Isaiah 30:15 NKJV).

We will have gone through the Esther beauty treatments and will be beautiful inside and out. With joy and in rest, we will undertake our tasks, and the enemy will not know what's coming. The world, and the Pharaohs of the world, have so underestimated us and tried to keep us in our places of isolation and servitude. But the Word says in Genesis 3:15 that, in the battle between the woman and the serpent, we are going to bruise its head. The same battle we started with in the garden of Eden culminates in the dramatic battle of Revelation 18.

For Review

Please take a moment to reflect on what you've just read. We suggest taking notes as you answer questions below.

1. What parallels do you perceive between the assault on Naboth and Justice Kavanaugh?

2. Many of the breakthroughs in this chapter came with on-site prayer. Have you ever been led to pray on-site? What results have you experienced?

3. In Jolene's dream, a prophet tried to force a woman into a dress that she could not fit into. What does this mean to you?

4. The "beauty treatment" process was preparatory for Esther's rulership. How has the Lord worked with you to prepare you for your destiny?

CHAPTER 14

AUTHORIZED TO POSSESS

"YOU know, Jon, there are ISIS snipers right across the border here."

Not what I wanted to hear. On March 24, 2017, Jolene and I somehow found ourselves on the border with Syria in Israel's Golan Heights. With live worship from our team resounding off the hills. Our tour guide Eran motioned to the other side of an open field with large metal fences, marking the border. "I bet they can even hear us. Any suggestions?"

Strategically, the Golan Heights is one of Israel's most vulnerable points along her northern border. When our Crown & Throne Israel tour journeyed to the demilitarized zone for a live worship set in March 2017, we may have stirred things up a bit. Unintentionally, of course. Sort of. It's just that amplified spontaneous worship attracts attention—especially when led by the relentless Jamie Fitt, accentuated by vocals from Heaven's greatest rock star James Nesbit.

I probably shouldn't mention this. But when I shared Eran's warning with our team, somehow the decibels increased. We sang salvation songs over the Golan and prayed for God's shalom. Then in agreement with countless thousands who have also prayed on-site, we claimed this vulnerable outpost of land for Israel.

By 2019, ISIS had been largely driven out, which was good news. Unfortunately, Iran's Revolutionary Guard had taken up the very positions ISIS once occupied. The initiative was led by none other than General Qasem Soleimani, the Iranian mastermind who lived to remove the Jewish people from Israel. As you know, Soleimani was killed in a US drone strike. But for months beforehand, the Iranian general had been attempting to launch armed drone strikes against Israel from across the Golan. Thank God, all attacks were foiled.

Then, on March 21, 2019, at the White House, Purim 2019 arrived precisely three months after the blood moon appeared at midnight over the White House, signaling the third year of rule by America's Cyrus. Ministry leader Mario Bramnick had invited Jolene and me to the White House EEOB complex for a series of meetings. And they were running late.

Our team was escorted to a well-appointed room overlooking the White House to wait on staff for a briefing. No time was wasted. We immediately engaged in Purim prayer with whispered tongues of fire. We covered President Trump and America. We covered Prime Minister Netanyahu and Israel. We prayed for powerful deliverance from the Haman forces seeking to attack both nations in this hour. Deep state exposed. Terror plots foiled. Esther prevails!

And as with the biblical narrative, we declared it was time for Esther and her people not just to be preserved from Haman's noose, but rule in the midst of her enemies. A few hours later our team met at our place to debrief. A tweet by President Trump interrupted our conversation—and rocked the order of global diplomacy. Keep in mind it was Purim.

"After 52 years it is time for the United States to fully recognize Israel's Sovereignty over the Golan Heights, which is of critical strategic and security importance to the State of Israel and Regional Stability," Trump declared into his twitter feed.

As it turned out, the spontaneous decision to rescue the Golan and secure Israel's northern perimeter was made while we were on-site praying. By God's orchestration, we were privileged to bear witness.

And as America honored the covenant boundaries of Israel, I believe the guardianship of America's boundaries is now being strengthened by God's hand in a new way, because He blesses those who bless Israel. In early December 2019, the Lord spoke prophetically this very blessing. For defining your future, this is probably the most important directive of the book:

"Heaven's gavel has fallen, even over the cornerstone of national governance. In this season a mantle is being transferred. I am imparting to My covenant people an anointing to possess. And even as your president authorized the possession by Israel of the land and promise I have allotted for her, I am now authorizing you to possess the land and promise of America according to her longstanding covenant with Me.

"Through this year, I have given you many markers to define the year 2020 and the new decade you are entering," says the Lord. "As I brought Jacob before My face at Phanuel to become Israel, so I have brought you before My face at Faneuil Hall, to become a covenant nation. Jacob crossed over as Israel into Israel. So I have brought you into the baptism waters to confirm My work, from Georgia through New England and even to Washington DC.

"Watch now the movement of My glory for your future. For mercy has indeed secured your covenant with Me. I have sevened Myself to you! And in redeeming you, O Jacob, I have redeemed both your legitimacy and your authorization to now possess your inheritance as Israel. The pey [mouth] year and decade will now be marked by My anointing to possess. For I am crossing My people over to possess the inheritance I have ordained for them, which I promised to their forefathers.

"Watch how I manifest My glory to you even during Revolution. For I will visit My people with a crossover moment. I will bring them before My face into the summation of My work this year to release America into your inheritance. It will be widely known as a defining moment for My glory. From this time My ark will both secure your way and secure your possession of My dwelling for your future.

"See and observe My progression with Jacob. With Joshua. With Elijah and Elisha. With John the Baptist. Believe me for a 'Face of God moment' which defines the future for My people. Legitimized, authorized, and anointed to possess!

"You are now coming to this threshold. Therefore in this 21-day season of preparation allow Me to strip off of you the final wilderness garments still confining you from perceiving and advancing. I speak shalom. Let go of old limitations. Let go of the old to embrace the new. I will mantle you even as you continue to wait and watch with Me.

"And I say watch! Watch for I will visit you on your watch, even as I visited My servants of old. Watch even for a new wineskin to form that will cover My remnant people. Suddenly it will appear!

"Watch even as the scrolls of My inheritance now appear for distribution. For as Israel has now been blessed, so my body will now be blessed and released into a greater expression of covenantal inheritance.

"As with Moses so will I be with you," says the Lord. "I will never leave you or forsake you. I say, watch, abide and prepare! 'Be strong and courageous, for you shall give this people possession of the land which I swore to their fathers to give them'" (Joshua 1:6).[80]

This is a defining word for America. Weeks after the Lord spoke it, the promise of God's glory manifesting during Revolution dramatically came to pass. I believe the rest of the word will do so as well.

Remember that the Lord always speaks the end from the beginning. Vision for the Promised Land anchors us through the testings, the trials, the wars that form in our path. Perhaps for this reason, in the Hebrew calendar, evening always marks the new day. You may be moving through a dark night right now. But brightness is just ahead.

Please don't just review the prophetic word but rehearse it. By verdict from Heaven's Court, things are about to change. As a believer in Christ you are now authorized to possess your inheritance.

Jezebel Restrained—The Breaker Breaks Open

Because of the weight of importance I sense over this word, the rest of the chapter will be shortened a bit. But it's important to show you where we stand in God's timetable. Jezebel has been defeated. Therefore, the primary resistance keeping God's people from securing our inheritance has been restrained.

Remember the dream in which Washington DC was superimposed on the Jezreel Valley. Jolene and I were among a group of leaders convened at Har Megiddo to strategize on possessing the Promised Land. Only one force of resistance was identified by the Lord—a representation of the Jezebel spirit. God forbid that we should give Ahab and Jezebel the inheritance of our forefathers!

That said, the closest representation to a Jezebel spirit I have ever known came before me in a dream recently. In the dream, this woman served essentially as a legal representative for the Baal principality. To my amazement, she signed over the title deed to a vast inheritance legally owed to me, which she had previously refused to release. In this inheritance were cars, keys to each of the cars, and a stack of papers representing lands, estates, inheritances, and even bank accounts which Heaven's Court had ruled were mine.

The Court had ruled. But securing the settlement had been a long time coming. It was clear this force had finally been restrained to the extent that she and her minions had no option but to become compliant with the Court's orders.

Extremely puzzled by her actions, I asked why the sudden change. She looked at me in sullen defeat and simply replied, "The Breaker breaks open." Then she turned away.

The Breaker breaks open! I awoke to Holy Spirit literally flooding my being with the Micah 2 Scripture on the Breaker, *"The breaker goes up before them; they break out, pass through the gate and go out by it. So their king goes on before them, and the Lord at their head"* (v. 13).

Friends, the Breaker breaks open! On God's timetable, we have now moved beyond the constraints of Jezebel's occult forces. The Lord has sent His angel of breakthrough to lead the procession out of the wilderness and into possession of our covenantal heritage. The Lord is commanding restoration and replevin for all that these forces have occupied in open defiance of the Lord. You are now authorized by Heaven to possess your inheritance!

Two Confirmations

After ministering on this subject recently, ministry leader Vanessa Battle came to us, a look of astonishment energizing her beautiful face. She held her phone up to my eyes. "Read this text!"

During our message, she received a text notification that a title deed to land long promised to her had finally been released. In real time.

Then came news from our friend Lynnie Harlow. Lynnie's family once owned large tracts of land in Texas. From a young age, she had been assured of generational prosperity. But the inheritance from her grandfather became squandered by siblings. By the time she was supposed to receive the promised inheritance, only large tracts of debt remained.

Or so she thought.

As revelation came about possessing the promise given to our forefathers, Lynnie began to approach Heaven's Court over her portion. Through many tears, she petitioned the Lord for replevin. According to the *Merriam-Webster Dictionary*, replevin is: "An action originating in common law and now largely codified by which a plaintiff having a right in personal property which is claimed to be wrongfully taken or detained by the defendant seeks to recover possession of the property and sometimes to obtain damages for the wrongful detention."

Replevin. The thief only came to steal, kill, and destroy. Jesus came that we might have life, and life more abundantly (see John 10:10). Restoration and reconstitution by Heaven's verdict. Replevin. Man's ways are limited, but God's ways are endless to secure the inheritance He has ordained for you!

We prayed in agreement with Lynnie for this miracle. Within a week, we got a call. Through many tears, Lynnie called us with big news. Out of the blue, an energy company from Texas had called her. Oil had been discovered on a tract of land she owned. Court documents indicated it had been passed down to her by her grandfather.

Though Lynnie lives in Virginia, there's a part of Texas in her that never backs down from a fight. And these were fighting words. With great fierceness, Lynnie argued with the kind energy representative, telling him how wrong he was and then telling him off for bringing up this painful subject in the first place. The hapless recipient of her aggression simply suggested that she check with the courts herself.

Lynnie and her husband, Tom, hired a representative to check on the story. And against all odds, it proved to be true. Her grandfather had tucked away land in her name separate from the other inheritances, without telling anybody. Probably out of fear for the squandering that would soon come to pass.

There's now a functioning oil well on Lynnie Harlow's family acreage, which she had no idea she had the title deed to.

Replevin. Can't make this up.

Just as the righteous Judge answered Lynnie's plea, so He can bring restitution to your home and family for what was stolen. These testimonies will multiply exponentially in the season ahead. And on a broader level, we as believers in the Lord can take back the land that has been stolen from us.

Judgment has been rendered in favor of the saints, restraining the enemy and releasing the saints to possess the Kingdom.

2020 Vision—Redeeming Your Scrolls of Destiny

The final prophetic revelation we want to share right now is both sobering and encouraging. Recently the Lord gave me a visionary experience. In the vision, I was ascending through the sea of glass before God's throne. As described in Revelation 15, it was mingled with fire.

I thrust my head above the waters and saw Him! Interestingly, I immediately ducked back under the water. My intuitive reaction was actually holy fear and awe, both to see and be seen. While praying into the vision, I sensed the Lord is wanting us all to experience both profound cleansing and renewed vision of His holiness and majesty.

When I looked again in the vision, I immediately found myself on the other side of a large table being used by Jesus as a desk. He had regathered a large stack of crumpled paper which had obviously been thrown away. One by one, Jesus took the crumpled balls of paper and placed them with care into the sea of glass. I kept watching as each scroll unfolded in the waters. Faded, smudged ink was restored to precision. The messages of these scrolls were literally being reconstituted before my eyes and then released through the sea to the earth.

Jesus baptizing scrolls? This may seem strange until you realize that He considers your life to be a scroll. And in your baptism is reconstitution!

> *YOU are our letter* [scroll], *written in our hearts, known and read by all men; being manifested that you are a letter of Christ, cared for by us, written not with ink but with the Spirit of the living God, not on tablets of stone but on tablets of human hearts* (2 Corinthians 3:2–3 emphasis added).

I also sensed the scrolls being reconstituted represent invitations and commissions from Jesus which had been thrown away. Some had been trashed intentionally, simply rejected by those who received them. Some had been trashed by people in authority over the ones who were supposed to receive them. Some were clearly sabotaged by the enemy. Some ended up in the trash bin simply out of neglect, unbelief, and disobedience.

Some, like Jeremiah's title deed, were sown as seeds to establish God's legal precedent through the future.

And some scrolls represented portions of Scripture which were rejected because they were either offensive or beyond the revelatory paradigm of those who read them.

Whatever the case, know that the Lord is re-releasing many scrolls to the earth that had been crumpled up and rejected. Many revelations, commissions, and invitations are being re-released as the Ancient of Days redeems the time on your behalf. Watch how many missed opportunities come full circle in this hour. Your reconstituted scroll is the title deed to many re-constituted windows of opportunity!

Again, the comprehensiveness of our salvation in Israel's Messiah is simply astonishing. In light of current circumstances, I hope this speaks deeply to you. God can redeem the time. You have been granted an inheritance. And as of Passover 2020, the time has come to possess this resurrected deed.

For Review

Please take a moment to reflect on what you've just read. We suggest taking notes as you answer questions below.

1. You are authorized to possess your inheritance! What aspects of your inheritance are you focusing on, for you and your offspring?

2. What legacy do you desire to leave your children? Your grandchildren?

3. What aspects of America's legacy would you like to see perpetuated to your children? What aspects do you feel are threatened right now?

4. In a vision, the Lord showed Jon crumpled up paper, representing invitations, commissions, and inheritances rejected by His people. God was re-releasing these opportunities. What opportunities have you rejected? What promises would you like to see reconstituted? Seek Him for this!

CHAPTER 15

AMERICAN PASSOVER

SLEEP has proven scarce due to continual prayer against what we perceived to be an imminent terrorist threat. Telltale signs abounded. Roads were patrolled nonstop by either police cars or the ever-mysterious black SUVs. Low-flying helicopters moved throughout the entire metro region.

Most importantly, the urgency in my spirit has remained unabated. *"Watchman, what of the night?"*

Jews worldwide have called the coronavirus pandemic "the eleventh plague of Passover." For Passover 2020, this term seems entirely appropriate. It is the first time in history where the entire globe remains sheltered in place, just like our Jewish forefathers. Tonight, we are again placing the blood of the Lamb on the thresholds of our homes. And we are seeking together for the death angel to pass over.

Looking out over the White House and Washington DC, a clouded dawn is now emerging. The roads are virtually empty, save for a lone red ambulance making its way across the river. The solitude of my prayer time was broken by its siren.

He is risen! He is risen indeed. Texts have already begun to flood my iPhone with images of lilies, the empty tomb, and Christ's outstretched hand. A news report interrupts the greetings. After a vicious bout with the coronavirus, British Prime Minister Boris Johnson has been released from the hospital. He mentioned his gratitude for all who prayed. A full recovery is expected.

Make America Great Again

Resurrection Day 2020 marks a tremendous shift for our nation. An American Passover. A covenant reset. Though the vigil continues, it feels in the Spirit that a turnaround is finally gaining momentum. It's time to recover. To rebuild. To make America genuinely great again.

During the 2016 elections, then-candidate Donald Trump used the phrase to convey his vision to restore the economy, move jobs back home, secure America's borders, and stem the tide of globalism in favor of national sovereignty. Unexpectedly, it soon became a wedge of division. But in light of challenges we now face, the mandate to make America great again has proven hauntingly prophetic. And it conveys the highest aspirations of us all.

In a time of rebuilding, let's seek the Lord. Let's dream. And let's return to the values, passion, and discipline that made us great in the first place. Let's return to covenant. And like Nehemiah, with a brick in one hand and a sword in another, let's remain vigilant on our watch.

The Conflict of Crowns

Our freedom remains vulnerable. One of the most significant words the Lord has given through this "conflict of crowns" is that a globalist agenda has been waiting in the wings, seeking to exploit the pandemic for a push toward global governance. It's the word of the Lord. Thank God, Trump has perceived it!

The agenda in the shadows actually clarifies the opposition Trump has faced all along. What if Hillary Clinton had won the 2016 election instead of President Trump? The globalist agenda would have most likely been accelerated greatly by the coronavirus. Building on the groundwork laid as past presidents broke down national borders, denied our covenantal foundations, empowered abortion, and enacted policies directly targeting believers for persecution, nobody thought we would see that day in America. But it happened. And the legacy was almost perpetuated.

Against all odds, New York businessman Donald J. Trump prevailed to win the 2016 election—and God upended the agenda. Instead, the "Trump turnaround" was set in motion, just as prophesied.

As we have documented, opposition came in unceasing waves from election night on. But the freedom movement continues. God is now declaring an American Passover with deliverance from the gods of Egypt and the government tied to the gods of Egypt. *"Let My people go! Let My babies go! Let My government go!"*

A prophetic word from Jerusalem prayer leader Rick Ridings in 2012 makes this clear. Rick and Patricia were ministering in Washington DC, when Rick essentially prophesied a Passover for our city. And in the same word, he prophesied the Crown & Throne movement.

I will judge the gods of Egypt in this city. As thrones have been set in the gates in the north, and the south, and the east, and the west of the District of Columbia, those thrones of the enemy shall crumble in this season. And I am raising those up in the north, and the south, and the east and the west who shall act as arms to lift up, as pillars lifting up my Throne, and My throne shall rest upon this city in a way that it has not been in the past....

We previously thought a few believers would somehow change everything. But you don't change everything unless the foundations, and systems, and demonic structures are changed. And I believe the Lord is saying this is a season where I am judging demonic structures and demonic systems in government....

In the book of Revelation when you see the elders of God, they have harps and bowls. And the Lord says I have been restoring the harp and the bowl in the last 10 years in a very special way throughout the earth ...But the Lord would say there's two more things that those elders have. They not only have a harp, they not only have a bowl, they each have a throne and they each have a crown. And in these next ten years, as I have restored the harp and the bowl, I am

> going to further restore now the walking with the throne and the crown. I'm going to restore to My people walking in governmental intercessory, kingly authority.
>
> That what you proclaim on earth shall be that which you have already heard proclaimed in heaven! Governing, legislative authority in prayer to shift and change foundations, and structures, and systems.

The Threshold Covenant

White House watchmen, you have been trained and equipped. You have been authorized to possess your inheritance. And you are now being summoned to your posts. Let's return to Passover for a final lesson on covenant to equip you for the season ahead.

The book of Exodus shows how, in an unprecedented display of power, a subjugated people experienced God's hand of deliverance from Egypt. The Red Sea parted. They crossed the threshold and escaped four hundred years of slavery and death. The sea then flooded the pathway again to provide a barrier between Israel and her enemies—and a point of no return for the Jewish people.

Then during a dramatic Passover exactly forty years later, a threshold opened up again. This time the waters of the Jordan parted. Joshua, or Yeshua in Hebrew, led His covenant people across to the Promised Land. Note that from the time the Jews were sheltered in place, and the blood of the Lamb was placed on the thresholds of their homes, every other threshold they encountered gave way to them.

Some fourteen hundred years later a second Yeshua, Jesus of Nazareth, was baptized in the waters of the Jordan. There's no way to prove this, but I bet He chose Passover, the date His forefathers crossed the river, as the date of His immersion. Whether or not this is true, Jesus' crossover moment marked the activation of His calling to redeem humanity as the Passover Lamb. From that time forward, especially, He lived to die.

Because of His great sacrifice, whoever embraces Jesus' body and blood is now immediately pulled from the threshold of death into eternal life. And through His blood covenant, every other threshold must give way!

Most of us have wrongly learned one of the most important aspects of Passover. Since we were kids, we've been taught that the blood of the Lamb was applied to protect homes and families *from the Lord* as He entered the land of Egypt. Our expectations have therefore been programmed to apply the blood as a barrier which ultimately protects us from God.

Actually, the truth is quite the opposite. The Jews were invited to enter into a "threshold covenant" at Passover not to distance themselves from God, but to invite His presence to enter their homes and protect them. An ancient protocol had been followed whereby the invited Guest was actually welcomed across the thresholds of their homes.

Covenant unlocks glory. And from the beginning, the Passover meal was given by God first as a protocol to welcome Him into our homes and spheres.

When the Lord first began to speak to me about the Threshold Covenant and communion, our friend Lori Perz recommended a book. Published in 1896, a neat little book titled *The Threshold Covenant* by Clay Trumbull provides extensive research recording ancient Mideast traditions connected to this ritual. Archeological finds prove that threshold covenants were commonplace long before the Jews were freed from Egypt. In other words, it was already customary, familiar language.

Bridegrooms and brides established threshold covenants, even placing blood on the doorposts of their homes. Sovereigns were welcomed into dwellings with sacrifices for their feast prepared at the gateways of their hosts. Blood from the meat would be applied on the doorposts as a protocol display of invitation and honor. Covenants likewise welcomed gods of their region through the thresholds of their homes and temples.

"In dealing with his chosen people, God did not invent a new rite or ceremonial at every stage of his progressive revelation to them," Trumball writes. "But he took a rite with which they were already familiar, and gave to it a new and deeper significance in its new use and relations." Trumball continues, "And now Jehovah announced that he was to visit Egypt on a designated night, and that those who would welcome him should prepare a threshold covenant, or a pass-over sacrifice, as a proof of that welcome; for where no such welcome was made ready for him by a family, he must count the household as his enemy."[81]

Astonishing, isn't it? Yet isn't it just like God, in His nature and character of love, to provide the very covenant meal by which He is welcomed to enter into our lives.

The blood is applied. The presence is welcomed. The thresholds thus dedicated, your home becomes a throne for His glory. The death angel must pass over. And from this moment of covenant, every other threshold you encounter must give way.

Your Home—God's Refuge

Perhaps recounting the Passover Exodus, Moses described this very sequence when writing Psalm 91.

> *He who dwells in the secret place of the Most High shall abide under the shadow of the Almighty. I will say of the Lord, "He is my refuge and my fortress; my God, in Him I will trust." Surely He shall deliver you from the snare of the fowler and from the perilous pestilence.... Because you have made the Lord, who is my refuge, even the Most High, your dwelling place, no evil shall befall you, nor shall any plague come near your dwelling; for He shall give His angels charge over you, to keep you in all your ways.* (vv. 1–3, 9–11).

Maybe it's not a coincidence that over Passover, as we all sheltered in place, homes across the globe have now become transformed into altars of prayer that welcome His presence. You are now going to see a dramatic shift in the Body of Christ worldwide. God bless the Church. It has such an important role. But, for too long, believers have yielded to the Church their own responsibilities in teaching their families, building community, and enthroning Jesus.

Beloved, communion belongs first in the home. Presence belongs first in the home! And every other threshold we encounter will bow.

Your Watchman Commissioning

Maybe it's not a coincidence that communion was my focus when the angel of the Lord suddenly crossed my threshold to bring a "Joshua" commissioning that transformed our lives. The story of this visitation is recounted in chapter 5. We'd like to extend this commissioning to you as a watchman for your sphere.

Let's briefly review our journey so far. The year 2020 marks a new era for America and the world. Not a coincidence that it also marks the four-hundredth anniversary of America's covenant with God from which our democratic governance was birthed. As with the Exodus from Egypt, a movement is now at hand that is bringing deliverance from bondage tied to idolatry and is realigning our nation covenantally for freedom.

Prominent threats explored in this book still remain, including China's totalitarian surveillance, Iran's pursuit of sparking Armageddon, and a globalist agenda tied to the deep state which seeks to claim the best of America for its dark purpose.

And let's not forget a potential resurgence of the coronavirus or some other weaponized plague.

Despite challenges during the past few years, the Lord has brought dramatic turnarounds within our government. Economic resurgence. Extraordinary judicial reform. The restraining of abortion. The restoration of a godly governmental alliance with Israel. The empowerment of religious freedom. Deep state deliverance.

God did it once. And He will do it again—especially if His watchmen will now take a stand.

And toward this end, we have seen how the Daniel-Cyrus partnership of watchman prayer within government has prepared the way to both empower God's movement and overcome crises in real time.

You have now become part of that watch. You've been compelled to press deeper in your relationship with God, and to gain revelation and training necessary to grow in effectiveness. You've learned how to secure your perimeter. You've aligned your sphere in covenant with Christ. You've grown in proficiency in hearing the prophetic voice of God and carrying through with the directives He gives. Finally, you have seen how Jesus gave His life not only to redeem humanity, but to redeem for all humankind the watchman call over our respective spheres.

In this regard, you are becoming not just a White House watchman, but a throne room watchman. You've gained supernatural insight and learned to relate to Jesus both as an intimate friend and a gatekeeper over your sphere. You have been introduced to realms of His throne where His governance is decided and acted upon, releasing Heaven to Earth!

And finally, you have perceived God's heart to entrust the torch of covenant legacy to you in a way that secures and perpetuates His destiny for our land. To receive this flame, please consider a lifelong dedication as a watchman of His covenant. Power to gain wealth is promised within this alignment, to establish the covenant God swore to our forefathers (Deut. 8:18). Deliverance is also promised—from the hand of every adversary (2 Kings 17:38–39).

Now it's time for your commissioning. Please prepare bread and wine or grape juice for communion. Take a moment to remember Jesus. In other words, to worship Him and take to heart all that He has given you through His body and blood. Seek His forgiveness for any sin. Remind Him of your covenant with Him, already established over the spheres He has shown you. If you haven't fulfilled this yet, go back and follow the directives found in "Chapter 8: Securing Your Perimeter."

Now, in your own words, just ask Jesus to commission you. Take some time with Him over this. Receive communion. And welcome Him across your threshold.

Father God, Jolene and I come before You in Jesus' name on behalf of those who truly desire to receive this commissioning. We validate that they have approached Your throne to see the call You have given them activated for Your glory. According to the authority entrusted to us, in partnership with Your Holy Spirit and the angelic hosts of the Lord Jesus Christ who are sent to minister on their behalf as heirs of salvation, and in the presence of a great cloud of witnesses before Your throne, we commission our friends as covenant watchmen over their spheres. As Joshuas, in Jesus' name. May the rank You deem appropriate now be transferred to them. May Your voice become even clearer. May Your governance over their spheres become transformative. Now may Your very hand synergize with them to impact their world, in Jesus' name. Amen!

CHAPTER 16

THE GOVERNMENTAL GLORY

TWO lamps shone in the steeple of Boston's Old North Church. A midnight rider made his way through the darkened streets, his lamp outstretched, his horse bucking in protest from the unrelenting pace. *Every victim needs a voice,* maybe he thought to himself. *And every revolution a watchman.*

"Wake up!" The message spread through Charlestown and then from village to village all the way to Lexington. "The regulars are coming. The British are coming!"

Paul Revere, quintessential prototype of the American watchman, rode through the midnight hour to rouse the continental army and counter the empire of his watch. Later in the day, the first shots of the Revolution would be fired from Lexington. A British negotiator seeking peace through the continued rule of the Crown would be turned away—according to tradition, with the following words. "Sir, we will have no sovereign but God, and no king but Jesus."

No king but Jesus. This soon became a battle cry of the Revolution. A freedom movement awakened. And a new nation was birthed.

Two decades ago, Cindy Jacobs prophesied that the forerunner announcing the American Revolution would serve as a prototype for the forerunner ministry the Lord has called us to today. Spiritual Paul Reveres, holding out the burning lamp, declaring, "The Lord is coming!" To close her prophecy, Cindy even declared that everywhere we go, revival would break forth.

Now, this new era is being defined by a freedom movement of similar magnitude—a spiritual revolution that restores our covenantal foundations and forges our future in freedom. Revival is definitely key or, more accurately, the restoration of the governmental glory of God.

From the beginning, Jolene and I have taken this call seriously. We even signed our names as a married couple for the first time in the guestbook of Boston's Old North Church, the lampstand of the Revolution. This was actually a measured act of faith, because our wedding was still a month and a half away. Our visit was about to end. So, we decided to redeem the time!

Jolene and I were married on the first day of Hanukkah in 2003. A special menorah from Jerusalem played host to our unity candle. The unity candle ceremony was supposed to be the highlight of our wedding.

Jolene is naturally beautiful. But her stunning elegance as she made her way down the aisle drew a collective gasp. We started our ceremony with worship. And as we were singing, "Glory, glory, send Your glory," the unity candle lit supernaturally—in front of everyone!

Suddenly, we realized the Lord had given us our lamp.

Biblically, burning lamps represent passion. They represent prayer. They represent covenant. They represent the restoration of God's glory.

Long before Paul Revere, spiritual revolutionaries known as Maccabees faced down the strongest army of their era to retake their temple. The lampstand was relit to reconsecrate it to God.

Then there was a revolutionary named Jesus, whose prophetic vision of the forerunner ministry also incorporated a midnight rider—this one announcing His great return. *"And at midnight a cry was heard: 'Behold, the bridegroom is coming; go out to meet him!'"* (Matt. 25:6 NKJV).

And at this forerunner's cry, the bridal party all awakened. They trimmed their lamps to blaze again. And they went out to meet the Bridegroom for a wedding.

Releasing the Midnight Riders

All this to say, we've had some history with the midnight riders, Paul Revere, and the forerunner calling. Our ministry name is even Lamplighter. But when prophetic statesman James Goll began to reference the subject again, this time in context with overcoming a national security crisis that saves our national government, I was deeply perplexed.

James is one of the most unusual leaders we know, both in the magnitude of his high-level prophetic experiences and in the ebullient personality through which these experiences are filtered and delivered. Our time together in August 2019 marked his return to Washington DC after a seven-year absence.

And the first night back, he had a dream.

The Lord showed James a planned attack against our national security somewhere in the Northeast. Two high-level principalities were attempting to push it. James saw how these principalities were collaborating with human agents to extract top secret information and then re-present the information in a way that held America hostage.

The Lord then showed to the prophet His antidote to shift the crisis. In the symbology of Paul Revere, midnight riders appeared in James's dream, horsemen carrying lamps of prayer to illuminate the dark night.

In a surreal moment, I realized that one of the most prolific prophetic voices in our nation was sitting in our living room, prophesying the essence of the "Midnight Cry" to counter a crisis in government, even with midnight riders catalyzing this turnaround to awaken a new day.

Top secret information had indeed been extracted. And it was about to be re-presented. Within a month of James's word, President Trump was accused by Representative Adam Schiff of violating campaign laws during a phone call with the president of the Ukraine. Actions by former Vice President Joe Biden were being questioned by President Trump in context with the call. Not coincidentally, the CIA whistleblower who informed Schiff's staff of his concerns had previously worked for Vice President Biden on the Ukraine.

Word got to Representative Schiff. He moved to impeach. And a national security crisis ensued.

Here's the most important point. In James's dream, a movement from Heaven was released to counter this breach of security. Surprisingly, it did not involve better protocols or firewalls for IT security. Instead, first on God's heart was the release of "midnight riders" to bring the antidote to the crisis. They were holding out burning torches—spiritual Paul Reveres, who were really White House watchmen.

You are inheritors of the burning lamp. You are called by your Creator both to engage in, and to keep watch over, the freedom movement of our time. Please make no mistake—it is a spiritual revolution.

> *For Zion's sake I will not keep silent, and for Jerusalem's sake I will not keep quiet, until her righteousness goes forth like brightness, and her salvation like a torch that is burning.... On your walls, O Jerusalem, I have appointed watchmen; all day and all night they will never keep silent. You who remind the Lord, take no rest for yourselves* (Isaiah 62:1, 6).

The Governmental Glory

Passover 2020 marks the release of God's restoration movement to complete the turnaround and secure our inheritance. I believe Pentecost 2020 marks a fuller release of His governmental glory. Holy fire will be a primary manifestation. We tasted it at Revolution over New Year's Eve. By Pentecost 2021, many will experience the governmental glory from coast to coast, and in Washington DC.

"Revival shaking begins now!" Given all that has transpired since, this word by Chuck Pierce, given at Pentecost 2019 on Independence Mall in Philadelphia, continues to provoke me to trembling. The word continues to manifest.

Philadelphia leader Jamie Fitt was carrying through his vision of worshiping 24/7 through Pentecost in a tent at Independence Mall, where the governmental foundations of our nation were laid. A small crowd ushered in the Jewish feast with awe and celebration. My spirit was on fire for the governmental glory of God to come. During the Saturday evening session, I began sharing prophetically from Isaiah 6. I want to rehearse a few points with you in context. But here's what actually happened.

Keep in mind these were the opening moments of Pentecost—the biblical feast where the glory of God was restored when a fiery whirlwind blew into Jerusalem. I shared from Isaiah 6 how the prophet experienced the throne of God. He had endured a horrific year in which the king he was serving suddenly died. Grief due to death overtook the land. The throne of David was bereft of its leader.

Yet in the midst of this governmental shaking, God opened up the heavens and showed the prophet His unshakable throne.

> *In the year of King Uzziah's death I saw the Lord sitting on a throne, lofty and exalted, with the train of His robe filling the temple. Seraphim stood above Him.... And one cried to another and said: "Holy, Holy, Holy is the Lord of hosts; the whole earth is full of His glory!" And the foundations of the thresholds were shaken by the voice of him who cried, and the house filled with smoke* (Isaiah 6:1–4 NKJV).

Isaiah saw the King, the Lord of hosts. And he was undone. Keep in mind Isaiah was already the foremost prophetic voice in Israel at the time. Yet when the realm of God's holiness encompassed his being, suddenly the deficits of his own heart became clear. *"Woe is me, for I am undone!"* The prophet exclaimed. *"I am a man of unclean lips, and I dwell in the midst of a people of unclean lips; for my eyes have seen the King, the Lord of hosts"* (Isa. 6:5 NKJV).

Through Isaiah's purging, we all saw our own condition. Our lips were unclean. In contemporary America, we were dwelling amidst a people whose lips had become unclean.

Many in the tent began to weep in repentance. Somewhere between "Holy" and "I am undone" virtually all had fallen on their faces before the Lord. Holy Spirit swept in and touched us all.

And He touched our government that night, from the very place it was framed. These foundational thresholds quite literally shook!

Governmental Glory—Israel, the UK, America

Jolene and I had just flown in from a trip to Israel and then London. Over our journey, the Lord began to stir our hearts about a movement of His governmental glory. Isaiah's throne room encounter was highlighted while worshiping at Succat Hallel with our longtime friends Rick and Patricia Ridings. This Jerusalem house of prayer literally overlooks the Temple Mount, the very place where Isaiah saw the Lord enthroned over Israel. The thresholds shook there, and the heavens opened. It seemed the same was occurring once again.

We touched on Isaiah's encounter while ministering at Succat Hallel. A day later, we were in the air, flying to England for the very first time. We visited Bristol, where the Wesleys launched the Methodist movement. We visited Plymouth, where my Pilgrim forefathers launched into the new world.

And we participated in a prophetic roundtable in London, hosted by apostle Betty King. The legendary lioness invited us to minister for her Sunday service. And the Lord breathed into the revelation which began to form at Succat Hallel, overlooking the Temple Mount. A new governmental weight exploded on the revelation of Isaiah 6. It ceased being a message. Instead, it became a gateway to experiencing the majesty of God ourselves.

As part of the message, I prophesied then that, just as in Isaiah's day, within a year God's unshakable throne will be unveiled, and the governmental glory of God will be ushered through the gates. England exemplifies royalty. This nation established by covenant with God was called to display the majesty of the Sovereign King, Jesus Christ. I saw and prophesied how the same glory which framed the nation centuries ago is now being restored to breathe fresh revelation into the soul of the land. Holy, Holy, Holy! The majesty of God will be unveiled. The earth will be filled with His glory. London will be filled with His governmental glory!

A holy awe fell upon us all. Conviction brought many tears. Once again, Jolene and I were trembling, our spirits shaking in His governmental glory. Remember how covenant unlocks glory. During this time, I also saw how alignment among Israel, the United Kingdom, and America is key for this movement.

We saw this manifestation of the Spirit again in Philadelphia. Later on, God moved powerfully during the Glory Train journey.

And when we transitioned from 2019 to 2020 during Revolution at the Trump International Hotel, the governmental glory of God came even more powerfully. As mentioned, we had not experienced such a powerful visitation of Holy Spirit in more than a decade.

Then came the conflict of crowns. Clearly, the shaking the Lord alluded to in Isaiah 6 has now gone global. So will the release of His governmental glory. The majesty of God is about to be unveiled in a way we can now barely appreciate. An anointing of holy conviction will again take hold of the hardest of hearts. Midnight riders are now being summoned to proclaim the awakening of a new day.

And from region to region, even within the halls of government, God is resetting His lampstand and relighting the flame.

Sign of the Lampstand

It was December 31, 2019, in Washington DC. The weight of His presence was heavy in the room. Prophetic leader Briskilla Zananiri was preparing to lead the midnight communion service. Marriage vows would be declared. An altar made up of stones would be built as a memorial to this covenant reset. Communion would follow, sealing the threshold covenant with the Lord.

All of a sudden Briskilla saw a vision. A lampstand appeared to her, gold and silver, almost the height of the room. She described it as the largest menorah she had ever seen. And it was burning.

The prophet Zechariah was keeping watch over the restoration of his people from Babylon when he awakened to a vision of a burning lamp. It was pure gold. Olive trees were providing a perpetual flow of oil, resourcing the lamp so it would continue to blaze. The word of the Lord came to Zechariah that the lamp was a sign to Zerubbabel, the governmental leader presiding over Jerusalem's restoration.

Her broken-down walls had largely been repaired. But due to conflict and crisis, the Temple, ordered restored by Cyrus, remained only half-built. According to Zechariah, the burning lamp was a sign that it was time to finish the work—in our language today, to complete the turnaround. *"'Not by might nor by power, but by My Spirit,' says the Lord of hosts"* (Zech. 4:6).

Note that on the very evening the conflict of crowns first came into view, while we were gathered for a watchman's conference at the Trump International Hotel, the sign of the lampstand was released by God's Spirit. I believe it is a sign to us all. The great restoration which began must now be finished. Grace will be granted, including a perpetual flow of provision from Heaven and Earth. This city on a hill will again become a light to the nations!

And for this to occur, watchmen must be set on her walls. The lampstand is a sign. It is time to complete the turnaround!

COMPILATION OF VERDICTS FROM HEAVEN'S COURT

Revised Divorce Decree from Baal |
Declaration of Covenant | The Turnaround
Verdict | Yom Kippur Verdict—Securing
Vineyard of Prophetic Destiny | Capitol
Turnaround Decree | The Life Decree

DIVORCE DECREE FROM BAAL (REVISED)

The Highest Court in the Kingdom of God

in re the Marriage of:

THE PEOPLE OF GOD versus THE
PRINCIPALITY OF BAAL

Plaintiff, Defendant (Incl. Baal, Queen

of Heaven, Leviathan)

DECREE OF DIVORCE*

This matter comes on for hearing before the Supreme Judge of the Highest Court of the Kingdom of God on the petition of The People of God seeking a Decree of Divorce from the Principality of Baal, the Defendant in this matter (ref: Hosea 2).

The Court finds:

1. The Plaintiff's sins are forgiven. The Court recognizes the Plaintiff's request that this petition be rendered in favor of the people of God based upon this Court's previous precedent granting the remission of all sins through Jesus Christ. The Court recognizes the Plaintiff is an ambassador of Christ, stewarding His gift of righteousness and the ministry of reconciliation, reconciling and restoring the world to favor with God (John 20:23, 2 Cor. 5:18-20, Rom. 5:17).

2. The Plaintiff's assertions are fully substantiated:
    a. That this marriage was entered into by the Plaintiff based on lies and deceit by the Defendant, and
    b. That Plaintiff relied on fraudulent inducements and enticements by the Defendant, which Defendant had

neither the intention or ability to deliver.

3. The Plaintiff renounces any and all right, claim or interest in any possession jointly acquired with the Defendant during this Marriage, and that Plaintiff is entitled to have sole right, claim, and interest, in and to all the gifts, possessions and inheritance from Plaintiff's Father, and the Defendant is to be (now) and forever barred from the title, control, or use of any such gifts, possessions or inheritance.

4. The Plaintiff repudiates any and all joint claims with the Defendant, and requests this court to sever all relationships with the Defendant of any nature, however and whenever such occurred, and seeks enforcement by this Court of Plaintiff's desire to be known by no other name than that given by Plaintiff's Father.

5. All offspring of this marriage are released into the sole jurisdiction of this Court, effective immediately. The Defendant's request for either sole or joint custody is denied. As per the Plaintiff's request, all claims by the Defendant to their lives and bloodlines are rescinded.

6. The Plaintiff also seeks an everlasting restraining order against the Defendant so as to keep the Defendant away from all persons or property belonging to the Plaintiff.

7. The Plaintiff seeks perpetual enforcement of this requested judgement in favor
   of the saints, restraining the enemy
   and releasing the saints to possess the
   Kingdom (Dan. 7:22).

THE JUDGMENT

WHEREFORE, this Court being fully advised in
the evidence does find for the Plaintiff and
against the Defendant in all matters material to
the Plaintiff's Petition of Divorce, and does by
this decree grant the Plaintiff a Divorce and all
requests set forth above. That being the Order
of this Court, from and after this date, so shall
it be.

THE SUPREME JUDGE

* Composed by Dr. Jerry Mash with Apostle John
Benefiel (OAPN, HAPN.US). Revised by Jon Hamill on
4-18-18. Ratified on 4-22-18 at Western Wall. The
gavel of the Ancient of Days fell!

DECLARATION OF COVENANT—JULY 4, 2011

When in the Course of human events, it becomes
necessary for one people to dissolve the political and spiritual bands which have connected
them with another, and to seek and receive from
their Creator both a Pardon and a re-constitution
of Covenant with the Lord Jesus Christ, a decent

respect to the opinions of mankind requires that they should declare the causes which impel them to this dedication.

We hold these truths to be self-evident, that all men are created equal, that they are endowed by their Creator with certain unalienable Rights, that among these are Life, Liberty, and the pursuit of Happiness. And as an Act of Liberty, our Nation was covenanted to Jesus Christ, in the Presence of Holy Spirit, by women and men sent by Him to establish both community and governance for "the glory of God and the advancement of the Christian faith"—

And as successive generations, motivated by greed, compromised these Godly covenants—endorsing the subjugation of their brothers and sisters, both Host People and Immigrants; and embracing various forms of Baal worship, including Freemasonry and the occult—

Thereby yielding in part the corporate will of the people, in community and governance, to the influence of Baal and the consequential denial of justice, even to the unborn—

And whereas stewards of this Nation, rooted in the Land, appointed by God as repairers of the breach, have wholeheartedly repented of these sins, restored covenant, and have labored for a reprieve from the endless reproach these sins have brought upon this land and people—

Having sought and obtained from their Creator a Verdict of divorce from Baal, including the issuance of an everlasting Restraining Order and a Writ of Assistance for the restoration of all the Highest Court has granted as a covenantal right of Possession—and having throughout the year approached this Court with the same intent in every State of the Union, and in towns and cities therein, receiving the same verdict in favor of the saints;

We now, in the Presence of God, present ourselves before the Highest Court of the Kingdom of God, with the intent to re-consecrate this Nation according to the covenants made with Jesus Christ by our forefathers.

And with all solemnity and deference to Your Majesty, request that this Nation, as spoken by Isaiah and Hosea, might again be Married to the Lord, apart from all idols from which You have granted said divorce. And that Your Glory, the Presence and Power of Holy Spirit, might fully return and reside again in this land, releasing awakening, union and reformation. And that by this covenant renewal, as Abraham Lincoln articulated, our Nation, under God, might have a *new birth of freedom.*

For consideration in this Petition, we present to You the Covenantal legacy of the Pilgrims, who on 11-11, 1620 committed the land and government to "the glory of God and the advancement of the Christian faith," according to the Mayflower Compact.

And we present to You the Covenantal legacy of the Huguenots who came to this land with the same intention—whose blood was spilled and mission aborted—whose founder died chanting Psalm 132, begging Your Majesty that this land would be a "dwelling place for the Mighty God of Jacob."

And we present to You the original intent of many Host people of the Land—who agreed from the beginning that both ownership and stewardship belongs to their Creator and Father. Who sought with reverence to honor the Laws of Nature, and Nature's God. To whom You endowed great wisdom, even to convey and implement principles of democratic governance that framed the United States Constitution.

And finally, we present to You the legacy of the Seed of Abraham, by which Your Covenant with Israel and Mankind has been perpetuated. Our gratitude is immeasurable that You have chosen to graft us into this Covenant—even, as Asher Intrater observed, the Pilgrims "saw themselves as a New Israel, a nation wholly covenanted with God." To this end, we fully commit our covenantal stewardship to resource the dream of Your heart for Israel, the Jewish people, and for the nations.

In the Name of God, Amen. Having undertaken, for the glory of God and the advancement of the Christian Faith, the sacred task of repairing our Nation's founding covenants with our Creator; and having diligently and wholeheartedly sought forgiveness for breaches of said covenants, offensive to God and detrimental to mankind; we now solemnly and mutually, in the Presence of God and one another, combine these founding covenants as one Sacred Consecration of this land, the United States of America and all of its territories, to the Lord Jesus Christ.

And to this combined Declaration of Covenant, and all of our founders' intentions in establishing

One Nation under God, with the witness of Heaven and Earth, we do add our agreement that this Land, its people and resources, be entirely consecrated to You. As You have engraved us in the palm of Your hand, we now ask for the Hand of God in marriage, unto whom we promise all submission and due obedience.

In witness whereof we have hereunto subscribed our names in Washington DC this 4th of July, 2011:

We, The Beloved of God, and The Lord of All, do by these present make known that we have on this 4th day of July, 2011, by solemn vow:

Covenanted to be forever bound to one another; I the Lord declare, "You will call me husband" (Hosea 2:16). "I will betroth you to Me forever. I will betroth you in righteousness and justice, in love and compassion. I will betroth you in faithfulness, and you will know the Lord" (Hosea 2:19, 20).

We, The Beloved of God, declare: "We acknowledge you alone" (Hosea 2:20). "You are my God" (Hosea 2:23). It is to you alone that we will be faithful. We will know no other. We, The Beloved of God, do acknowledge and declare: We betroth you in our righteousness and justice, in our love and compassion. It is You, our God, we betroth in faithfulness. We acknowledge You alone as our Bridegroom and our provider (Hosea 2:8). And we will at all times look to You—one with Your heart, in covenant with You for our land. And hereto do we make our sacred promise.

The Church, The Beloved of God
And I do receive it.
The Lord of All

LIFE DECREE:

AMENDMENTS TO DECREE OF DIVORCE FROM BAAL
(January 22, 2013—40th Anniversary Roe v Wade)

THE HIGHEST COURT OF THE KINGDOM OF GOD IN RE
THE MARRIAGE OF:

THE PEOPLE OF GOD, Plaintiff, versus THE
PRINCIPALITY OF BAAL (Incl. Baal, Queen of
Heaven, Leviathan), Defendant,

INASMUCH AS the Court of Heaven has commissioned a hearing to render a verdict on abortion in the United States on the 40th anniversary of its legalization; and having considered the testimony of the Plaintiff as well as the cries even of the unborn; Let the record show that the following Amendments to the Baal Divorce Decree have hereby been rendered by the Supreme Judge regarding the abortion of unborn children:

1. "Your covenant with death shall be annulled, and your pact with Sheol shall not stand" (ref:Isaiah 28:18). The Court finds that, in accordance with the Plaintiff's unwavering plea for the blood of Jesus Christ to cover the sins of this Nation; and in accordance with the

verdicts in both the Decree of Divorce from Baal and the Declaration of Covenant of Marriage to the Lord Jesus Christ; that the covenant with death empowered by nationally legalized abortion is hereby annulled.

2. Whereas the principality of Baal, the Defendant in this matter, demands the systematic sacrifice of innocent blood for the empowerment of his rulership and deception; and whereas this principality has heretofore accessed the unjust bloodshed from abortion for these said means; and whereas the life and blood of each unborn child is claimed by their true Father and purchased with the blood of His Son; therefore the Court finds that all claims by the Defendant to perpetuate this covenant with death through nationally legalized abortion are hereby rescinded.

3. The Court finds that the restraining order previously issued against the Defendant and for the Plaintiff in the Divorce Decree from Baal is extended to include restraining the Defendant's access to all unjust bloodshed from nationally legalized abortion. This restraining order applies to the principality of Baal and all its vast extensions, not limited to but including the Queen of Heaven, Lilith, Leviathan, Set, etc.

4. The Court finds that the unborn are innocent of any sin or crime, and are counted

as martyrs of the Lord Jesus Christ. The Court retains full responsibility to execute judgment to avenge the blood of these martyrs as deemed appropriate by the Supreme Judge. The Court also recognizes that those persuaded to abort their children do so based on varying personal motivations, heavily influenced by lies and deceit by the Defendant; and the Court stands ready to grant full clemency and restoration to all who earnestly seek forgiveness. This Court clarifies its position based on the unanimous request of children once entrusted to their earthly mothers and fathers.

5. After reviewing the founding legal documents of the United States of America, the Court finds that the legalization of abortion (ref:Roe v Wade) is a clear violation of both its laws and National legitimacy. "All men are created equal and have been endowed by their Creator with certain unalienable rights—that among these are Life, Liberty and the pursuit of Happiness." The rights of humans are clearly conferred at creation, not birth. The unborn are thus entitled to the covenantal protection of Life.

6. False weights and dishonest scales are an abomination to the Lord, and the Court finds that lies and deceit are purposefully and consistently employed to deny justice to the unborn. Therefore all judgments recorded in Isaiah 28 pertaining to

covenants with death empowering deception are to be executed against the principality of Baal, its vast extensions, and human principals who remain in covenant with this principality.

7. "Mene, Mene, Tekel, Parsin" (ref:Daniel 5). The Court cites its previous verdict re:Belshazzar, king of Babylon, in the issuance of a restraining order against the human principals who remain aligned with the Defendant and resolved to perpetuate abortion. The name Belshazzar is defined as Baal protecting kingship. "You have been weighed in the scales and found wanting. God has numbered your days of rulership and brought it to an end." This is God's verdict on abortion, and His deadlines have been set.

THE SUPREME JUDGE

RE-CONSTITUTION OF THE UNITED STATES
(THE TURNAROUND VERDICT)

The Re-establishment of The United
States According to Original Intent
| Glory Procession | July 22,
2014 | Faneuil Hall Boston

WE THE PEOPLE of the United States, in order to form a more perfect union, establish justice, secure the blessings of liberty to ourselves and our posterity, etc., do receive the following verdict of the RE-CONSTITUTION of our Nation according to the original intents of our forefathers in Jesus Christ.

"Until the Ancient of Days came, and judgment was passed in favor of the saints of the Highest One, and the time arrived for the saints to possess the Kingdom." This verdict, as recorded in Daniel 7:22, issues from the Highest Court in the Kingdom of God re: the People of God, Plaintiff, to meet with justice their accumulated pleas and petitions for the Nation, and to further establish the verdicts previously granted by this Court, cited below.

1. **IN GOD WE TRUST.** Based upon this Court's review of the Nation's foundational covenants with Jesus Christ, the original intent of the founding principals who made these covenants "in the Presence of God and one another," and the repairing

of these covenants as validated by this Court, it has been decided that the land and government were consecrated to Jesus Christ from inception, and remain in this standing today.

2. **NO KING BUT JESUS.** Covenants establish thrones of governance. The Court therefore rules that the thrones of National governance belong to the Lord Jesus Christ. Therefore at the Plaintiff's request, all previous claims to these thrones through covenants with Death and Sheol are hereby annulled. Further, the Court affirms the separation of power in the three branches of National government as defined by the United States Constitution, and invokes the authority to enforce and defend this covenant at the Court's discretion against all Usurpers.

3. **THE KING'S INHERITANCE.** The Court now rules according to Psalm 125:3 that the scepter of the wicked must no longer remain on the land allotted to the righteous. The scepter, or enforcement of unjust governance, must now be rescinded. Further, the Court grants the wealth of heaven and earth to establish this Covenant sworn to your forefathers by the King. The issuance of the King's land grants and inheritances is now authorized for distribution and stewardship toward this end.

4. **DAWN'S EARLY LIGHT.** The Court notes the promise given by the Plaintiff's Father

that societal awakening and revival shall be granted this nation as the roots of the Nation are dealt with by the Plaintiff, unto the completion of the Divorcement of Baal and Restoration of Covenant with Jesus Christ. As covenant has been repaired, covenant shall now be established, Including the restoration of His Majesty's Glory, Presence and Power in what the Plaintiffs have termed a Third Great Awakening.

The Court notes this verdict, granted at Faneuil Hall Boston July 22, has been twice affirmed by His Majesty during the Glory Procession: by the lightning strike sent upon the Colonial Revival Garden evergreen in New Jersey on July 23, alighting its root even as this verdict was being declared, and by the 'three eagle flyover' July 26 during the ceremony reaffirming covenant with Jesus Christ in Jamestown Virginia.

5. **A MORE PERFECT UNION.** The original intent that Native and Pilgrim—and every tongue, tribe and nation—shall walk as One in Christ in this Covenant Land—is hereby restored. As per request of the Plaintiff, the Hand of the Lord now comes to the far northeastern part of the United States to rend the dark cloud of grief, occult oppression, and free the Native American people of North America to be restored according to their Creator's original intent.

6. **DON'T TREAD ON ME.** The Court notes that Humanism is the cultural expression of Baal worship. Whereas this principality has been pictured as a serpent along roots of the land in the East Coast of the United States, devouring generations, the Court now rules that its claims upon the land, the educational system, the governance of this Nation including its military and intelligence communities, and the generations are hereby rescinded.

7. **HEAVEN RESCUED LAND.** This Court now renders judgment according to Daniel 7:22 in favor of the Saints of the Highest One, and against the Usurper of God's covenant purposes. By order of the Court, the Usurper must hereby be restrained in every realm, dimension, sphere and office in which the saints have been opposed. The saints are granted a Turning Point for National breakthrough—to possess and establish the Kingdom of Jesus Christ according to the original intents of the Nation's founders, and their God (Acts 3:19-21).

Further, the Court grants the Plaintiff's request that Israel, the land and people, be resourced through an enduring covenantal alliance with the repairers of our National Covenant with the Lord. Heaven and earth bear witness to this granting of the Plaintiff's plea that America and Israel remain His Heaven-Rescued Land.

The Gavel has now come down. This being the order of the Court, on and after this date, SO SHALL IT BE.

THE SUPREME JUDGE

Verdicts cited in this hearing include: The Divorce Decree from Baal, Writ of Assistance, Declaration of Covenant, Life Decree, and the Liberty Charter, and others known but to God.

YOM KIPPUR VERDICT—SECURING THE VINEYARD OF PROPHETIC DESTINY

Yom Kippur—September 18, 2018, Washington DC

For Jolene and me, Yom Kippur 2018 began with a special evening tour of the West Wing of the White House. I knew the Lord opened these doors to privately decree this verdict, along with the Revised Divorce Decree and the Capitol Turnaround Decree, from the highest seat of authority in our land. And then to carry His verdict from Rome to Jerusalem. I received this verdict regarding Jezebel from the Lord earlier in the morning. Below are four aspects of God's verdict as of Yom Kippur, as best I understand it. This is for God's work in our government, for Israel and the nations, as well as for many of you personally.

1. **JEZEBEL DOWN.** The Court cites its previous precedent in Jezebel v Naboth. Jezebel sought to take down Naboth to possess his vineyard as her own. The word Naboth means "prophetic words." He was chosen by God to oversee "the vineyard of prophetic destiny" for his land. In the same manner, forces tied to the occult have sought to take over the United States of America and paralyze the people of God from fulfilling the prophetic destiny the Lord has ordained for the nation.

   Jezebel's strategy to overtake the vineyard of prophetic destiny included three facets. First, occult targeting against Naboth.

   Second, false testimony or false accusations in the court of public opinion, especially among the most influential in the land. Third, false testimony or false accusations in the court of law. This same strategy is being employed today.

The sincere Teshuvah, or repentance, and prayers of the saints have been considered in this case as of Yom Kippur 2018. The Court therefore receives the body and blood of Jesus Christ as atonement for the sins of the Nation and has therefore decided the Nation remains in right standing with God's covenant. With the predication that repentance demands a course correction in personal conduct in order to remain valid before this Court.

Just as with Jezebel v Naboth, the Lord has taken into consideration the full scope of false testimony and false accusation through both the media and the justice system of America. He who searches minds and hearts has considered not only the injustice perpetuated by accusations and slander, but the intentionality behind these accusations. The Court rules that the seditious intentions behind these actions ultimately equate to sedition against God Himself.

According to the precedent set in Jezebel v Naboth, God's verdict against Jezebel and Ahab, so the Lord has rendered judgement against Jezebel and those who remain aligned with this expression of the Baal principality through covenant, word and action. The vineyard therefore must remain in the stewardship of those whom He appointed to rule under

God. And the window must remain open for the turnaround initiated by this Court to be completed in all facets of the three constitutionally-ordained branches of government. Judgement in favor of the saints, restraining the enemy and releasing the saints to possess the kingdom. Daniel 7:22.

2. **MID-TERM VISITATION.** With the caveat again that these appointees must continue to align through Teshuvah, as required by Heaven's Court. In its decision to uphold the stewards God appointed over the Nation to secure its turnaround, the Court cites the precedent of Joshua the High Priest as recorded in Zechariah 3. Joshua was set in place by God as the High Priest long before he was fully cleansed from his sins or the sins of his forefathers. When accusations destabilized Joshua's capacities to rule, Heaven's Court was convened. A midterm visitation was decreed. It was decided then, and is decided now, that the Accuser be rebuked and restrained. And that the filthy garments of iniquity tied to these accusations be removed from Joshua, his iniquity taken atoned for, cleansed, and removed, with a new mantle of rulership granted. Finally it was decided that Joshua be recommissioned into the high office in which he was already serving.

According to this precedent, a mid-term visitation has thus been decreed.

3. **TESHUVAH HAS BEEN MANDATED** by the Court for all parties involved in accusation and defilement across the nation. In rendering this judgement the Court cites as precedent Isaiah 6. Isaiah did not perceive that he was a man of unclean lips, and that he dwelt in the midst of a people of unclean lips, until the unveiling of the King of glory. Therefore a move of Holy Spirit bringing the restoration of holy conviction has been decreed. A response of teshuvah is mandated, and fresh grace for cleansing will be released as this becomes the cry of your heart.

4. **ROME TO JERUSALEM.** As conveyed in the Revised Divorce Decree from Baal and the Capitol Turnaround Decree, disengagement from the roots of Roman paganism, and restoration to covenant with Jesus Christ alone has been decreed. As of Yom Kippur 2018, this verdict has been released. LET MY PEOPLE GO!

5. **ONE MORE THING.** The voice of the true victims prevail. A reformational, freedom movement has been birthed by the One who both renders judgement and makes war to uphold His verdict in the earth. The horses have been released. NO KING BUT JESUS...

CAPITOL TURNAROUND DECREE

National and Global Prayer Project

September 27, 2018 (Feast of Tabernacles)

Jon Hamill with Ed Watts

Having received the verdict granting the divorcement from Baal regarding all facets of Roman paganism, aligned and connected with other cumulative verdicts received through the years, we now ask the Court to validate and enforce the following decrees to manifest the legal status obtained through these verdicts in our respective spheres.

1. **Covenants establish thrones of governance.** Father, in Jesus' Name we renounce and repudiate all covenants with Roman paganism and satanism, perceived and hidden, including the Queen of Heaven and all other principalities and powers invoked through the dedication of buildings, positions, and thrones of authority in governance, in every realm and dimension of life and the spirit. We receive the divorcement from Baal on behalf of our Capitol and all seats therein. We hereby request that you annul all covenants with death and hell by which the enemy has claimed these thrones (Isaiah 28), and restrain all these forces from further

influencing these thrones. We come into agreement with Heaven's Court that these seats of authority now belong to Jesus Christ alone by covenant. Let the scepters of wickedness now be rescinded from the land allotted to the righteous (Psalm 125:3).

2. **Sever Ungodly Connections.** Father in Jesus' Name, please sever completely all spiritual ties and ley lines connecting Washington DC and my Capitol to Roman paganism and satanism. We declare the disempowering of these occult power lines and the shutting of all gates of access, in Jesus' Name and by His finished work of the cross. We declare the Blood of Jesus rebukes and silences every voice other than the voice of the Lord.

3. **Moral Clarity Restored.** Father, whereas the Vatican was built on top of the altar of Cybele, who demanded trauma-inducing sexual abuse as part of her worship, we renounce and repudiate all sexual immorality and abuse tied to the religious-political spirit which have been imposed upon our state and government. Now sever all ungodly ties which have formed. Bring redemptive exposure of all sexual abuse tied to this religious-political cabal. Bring perpetrators to justice. May holy conviction and moral clarity now be restored across the spectrum of government in Jesus' Name!

4. **Covenant with Death Annulled.** Lord we renounce and repudiate all governmental decisions to empower abortion. We remind this Court of the precedent set through the 2013 Life Decree. Whereas Rome, the prototype of capitols, sealed covenants with Saturn and other demonic principalities through child sacrifice, we ask that You review and annul all covenants with death and hell directly related to abortion or child sacrifice in my state, and connecting Rome and my Capitol (Isaiah 28). We further agree with Heaven's Court for the abolition of government-funded abortion in our state and nation, in Jesus Name.

5. **Occult Covering Removed.** As these covenants with death and hell are annulled, we ask the Court to enforce its decision cited in Isaiah 28 that the occult covering empowered by these blood sacrifices now be removed. Lord bring redemptive exposure of evil and corruption. We declare the demonic dome of spiritual oppression is cracking and being broken, in Jesus' Name, and His covering is forming. We declare the LORD's crowning of His sons (male and female) in each gate to prevail against the enemy, and turn the battle at the gate! (Isaiah 28:5-6).

6. **Deliverance from Religious-Political Cabal.** Lord we renounce and repudiate all alignments between the religious and political realms through demonic

rulership to control and subjugate those governed, as represented by Herod and Constantine. May this wicked cabal now be exposed and judged by You, Lord, the Righteous Judge. May the royal priesthood of believers be freed from deception, intimidation, and all muzzles from the religious-political spirit. May Jezebel now be deposed from our gates!

7. **Redeem the Time**. Lord we renounce and repudiate all unholy alignments with Constantine's imposition upon genuine apostolic Christianity. Lord we renounce and repudiate all occult-empowered timing imposed upon us by this structure. Please now sever all ties to Roman paganism which have disrupted the flow of Your covenant timing. We declare now You shift us out of occult-influenced timing and into Biblically-defined times and seasons, synergized with Your heart and with the real-time movement of Your throne. May the 7 Feasts of the Lord be restored, and the false feasts of Rome be exposed for what they are. We declare, covenantally and governmentally, the redeeming of time!

8. **Menorah Restored from Rome to Jerusalem**. Lord we declare the restoration of Your menorah from Rome to Jerusalem, disconnected from the roots of Roman paganism and restored to the covenant roots of our faith. Lord we say the fire of Your menorah bears witness to the restoration

of your covenant with us, and the restoration of Your glory in our midst as
a bridal canopy. Now replace the occult
covering over my Capitol with Your tabernacle of glory! May Holy Spirit be the
spiritual undercurrent and overarching
influence of my Capitol. LET THERE BE
LIGHT!

9. **Divorce from Roman Paganism.** In accordance
with the following pleas and decrees, now
grant Washington DC this divorce from
Roman paganism. Grant Jerusalem and all
Israel this divorce from Roman paganism.
Sever all ungodly ties which have connected these cities and regions to Rome.
Sever all ungodly ties between our state
capitol and Washington DC. Realign our
state capitol with Washington DC according to Your covenant alone. SEPARATE
LIGHT FROM DARKNESS!

10. **Restoration of Covenant Wealth, Influence.**
Lord we declare the restoration of covenant wealth which was confiscated or
stolen (Deut. 8:18). Further, we declare
the apostolic mantles of authority that
were imprisoned and stolen in Rome are
being recovered, cleansed and restored
back to the Body of Messiah—in Jerusalem,
in Israel, in my state, our nation,
in Rome, Italy, in Europe, and in the
nations. We declare the apostolic-pro-
phetic-prayer movement now shifts from
the deliberate confinement imposed by
this structure into the full stature and

authority You have ordained, the full provision You have ordained, as well as the full influence You have ordained within our governments.

11. **Martyrs Harvest for Martyrs Seed.** Lord we remember the cries of Your martyrs, those abused or slain for Your Name's sake, which are still resounding before Your throne. Now release a martyrs' harvest for a martyrs' seed! We declare the birthing and commissioning of a new Apostolic messenger movement—burning and shining lamps releasing freedom to the nations. And we covenant with you that, as empowered by Your Spirit and in synergy with the angelic hosts, we will complete the work which was begun in former seasons. We receive Your commission. Not by might nor by power but by My Spirit says the Lord!

12. **Turnaround—Saints Possess Kingdom.** Father God, in accordance with the Divorcement from Baal and these decrees sealed by Heaven's Court, we now ask that you grant the fullness of Your governmental turnaround effective immediately, restraining all occult forces tied to Roman paganism and satanism, and releasing the saints to now possess the kingdom (Daniel 7:22). Turn the tide! Realign our government according to Your covenant alone. May statewide and national breakthroughs even be manifested now, so that the turnaround

You initiated may now be completed. NO KING BUT JESUS!

Father God, just as Jesus Christ, Your ultimate Verdict for all mankind, was vaved to a Roman Cross and resurrected; and just as Luther's decree of Reformation was vaved to the door of the church; and just as Jael vaved the headship of the enemy; so we vav Your verdict, as a witness before Heaven and Earth, into Capitoline Hill, Capitol Hill, Zion's Hill, and capitols across America and the world. "Strike the capitals, and let the thresholds shake" with Your Freedom Movement. LET MY PEOPLE GO!

VERDICT ON THE BRIDE'S VINDICATION IN AMERICA

August 8, 2019—Washington DC

08-08-2019 marks the date I saw in a dream last December, confirming the east coast Glory Train journey. In my dream we were standing at the base of the Washington Monument, looking back at 7-22 as the northeast portion of the Glory Train journey culminated.

Can I just say—on this amazing journey the Lord has put the "Glory" in the "Glory Train!" Words cannot express the honor and gratitude Jolene and I feel as the manifest presence of God moves in our midst at a level we only imagined just a few years ago. THANK YOU JESUS!

From the dream our commission was clear—Jesus was sending us on this Glory Train journey to bear witness that, by verdict from Heaven's Court, grace has been granted to complete the turnaround He has offered us. Shifting us from a covenant with death and hell empowering a culture of death, to a covenant of LIFE and awakening, empowering a culture of life. This is the decree of Heaven's Court—and His verdict shall prevail!

At the forefront of my heart was very simply that America realign with the covenantal bond that our forefathers forged with the Lord some 400 years ago. America married to Jesus. It's what brought us from Zion's gate to Plymouth England to Provincetown and Plymouth MA, where the Pilgrims wrote the Mayflower Compact then established this covenant as a beacon to direct the entire course of American history. God's covenant shall prevail!

All this said, as of 08-08-08 the seal of the Bride is establishing the verdict from Heaven's Court for this hour. Here are eight aspects of the verdict for our time.

1. It has been decided that God's marriage covenant with the land and people, initiated on 11-11-1620 and upheld through many generations, repaired and validated in 2011 through the National Divorcement of Baal and Declaration of Covenant as required by Heaven's Court, remains in right standing before the Throne. The restraining order originally issued shall also continue to be enforced. As of 7-22, 2019, grace and authority has hereby been granted to complete the turnaround initiated by this Court on 7-22, 2014.

2. According to the promise of this Court, and the ceaseless pleas of a faithful remnant of believers in this nation, the governmental Glory of God is hereby

restored. A Third Great Awakening is hereby covenantally and governmentally released (ref: John 11:11).

3. All Covenants with death and hell, intended to hold the Bride of Christ in spiritual slumber, confinement, subjugation and disrespect, have been rendered annulled by verdict of Heaven's Court. By decree of Heaven's Court, the spiritual and natural boundaries established by the enemy shall no longer restrict or restrain the people of God from the LIFE and influence ordained for them by their Father in this land. The Bride is hereby ushered across the threshold into her promised season of "intimacy with God, abundance from His hand, and the best wine saved for last."

4. Both the Bride and her offspring are entitled to a full reconstitution of life, liberty, influence, prosperity, and of covenant destiny, now and generationally, joined to the Bridegroom. You shall no longer be termed forsaken, nor shall your land any more be termed desolate. But you shall be called Hephzibah, and your land Beulah, for the Lord delights in you, and to Him your land shall be married (ref: Isaiah 62).

5. The Court of Heaven has decided in favor of the Bride of Christ in America and against the judges and elders who have relentlessly accused her. Upon reviewing the Bride's petition, the Court cites as

precedent its verdict in favor of Susanna or Shoshana as recorded in Daniel 13 from the Apocrypha version of the Bible. The Court finds that the judges and elders who sought to discredit her faithfulness to the Bridegroom were themselves seeking to violate both her and her offspring, leveraging their accusations against her to force her to comply with their abuse and acquiesce to the plunder of her life and property. The exposure of these corrupt judges and elders across the spectrum of American life, government and culture has thus been decreed. Justice, including punishment for the guilty and restitution to the Bride regarding her life, offspring, property, reputation, destiny and inheritance, has thus been decreed.

6. This Court notes that since its inception, the nation of America has borne a striking resemblance to the Biblical forefather Jacob, son of Isaac, son of Abraham. As with Jacob at Phanuel, both discipline and blessing have served as training for the nation to recover its promised stature before God and man, and perpetuate generationally the promised covenant with God. The Court notes that the people of God responded wholeheartedly to the Father's invitation to cross this threshold at Faneuil Hall on 7-22 as a final step to become transformed as a new Israel, a Nation in covenant with God. Verdict granted!

7. Judgement is thus rendered in favor of the covenant people of God, restraining the enemy, the saints to possess the Kingdom (Daniel 7:22). The Angelic hosts of the Lord Jesus Christ stand ready to partner with the people of God for the enforcement of the completion of His turnaround verdict.

8. As with Esther, to perpetuate this verdict to complete the turnaround, as of 08-08-2019 a new level governmental authority has hereby been bestowed upon the Bride of Christ in America, granting the King's authority against the "Haman-like" accusers who have sought to defraud her of her inheritance, sabotage her influence, and eradicate her posterity. From Esther 8:8—Now you write the decree as you see fit, in the king's name, and seal it with the king's signet ring; for a decree which is written in the name of the king and sealed with the king's signet ring may not be revoked. NO KING BUT JESUS.

THE SUPREME JUDGE

ENDNOTES

1. "U.S. economy shakes free of recession fears in striking turnaround since August," *Washington Post,* December 15, 2019, https://www .washingtonpost.com/business/2019/12/15/us-economy-shakes-free -recession-fears-striking-turnaround-since-august/.

2. "Mayflower and Mayflower Compact," Plimoth Plantation, https:// www.plimoth.org/learn/just-kids/homework-help/mayflower-and -mayflower-compact/.

3. Nancy Eldredge, "Who are the Wampanoag?" Plimoth Plantation, https:// www.plimoth.org/learn/ just-kids/homework-help/who-are-wampanoag/. We consider Plimoth Plantation to be the best source of documentation on both the Pilgrims and Wampanaogs that we know. They strive for accuracy in their presentations and publications and have incorporated Wampanaog leaders into their research teams and leadership.

4. Most of what I am sharing here came from years of research while serving as a photojournalist for the *Cape Cod Times.* I interviewed many Wampanoag leaders, gleaned from books such as *When New England Prays* by Jeff Marks, read the stories of Native revivals in the chronicles of John Eliot and David Brainerd, and learned from scholarship of Plimoth Plantation. I also interviewed Plymouth pastor Paul Jehle, a renowned historian on the Pilgrims and the early foundations of US government. That said, the following article posted by UMass provides insight, though not using the terminology of a "move of God": "Mashpee Wampanoag Nation," Native American Trails Project, https://www.umass.edu/ nativetrails/nations/Wampanoag/ MashpeeWampanoag.html/.

5. The vision of a White House turnaround was part of our prophetic overview for 2016. Jon & Jolene Hamill, "Prophetic Overview for 2016—Jon & Jolene," Lamplighter Ministries, LAMPostings, November 18, 2015, https://jonandjolene.us/prophetic-overview-for-2016-jon-jolene/.

6. "Pneumonia of unknown cause—China," January 5, 2020, World Health Organization, https://www.who.int/csr/don/05-january-2020-pneumonia-of-unkown-cause-china/en/. Laurie Garrett, "Just in Time for Lunar New Year, Another SARS-like Epidemic Is Brewing in China," Foreign Policy, January 8, 2020, 12:56 p.m., https://foreignpolicy.com/2020/01/08/lunar-new-year-hong-kong-pnuemonia-sars-epidemic-wuhan/.

7. Jack Shafer, "Behind Trump's Strange 'Invisible Enemy' Rhetoric," Politico, April 9, 2020, 4:24 p.m., https://www.politico.com/news/magazine/2020/04/09/trump-coronavirus-invisible-enemy-177894.

8. Jon & Jolene Hamill, *Midnight Cry* (Haymarket, VA: Burning Lamp Media & Publishing, 2017).

9. Jon & Jolene Hamill, *Midnight Cry*, 13.

10. Jon & Jolene Hamill, "Breaking—Trump Calls National Day of Prayer for Sunday!" Lamplighter Ministries, LAMPostings, March 13, 2020, https://jonandjolene.us/breaking-trump-calls-national-day-of-prayer-for-sunday/.

11. Donald J. Trump, "Proclamation on the National Day of Prayer for all Americans Affected by the Coronavirus Pandemic and for our National Response Efforts," White House, March 14, 2020, https://www.whitehouse.gov/presidential-actions/proclamation-national-day-prayer-americans-affected-coronavirus-pandemic-national-response-efforts/.

12. "The Killing of Gen. Qassim Suleimani: What We Know Since the U.S. Airstrike," *The New York Times*, January 4, 2020, https://www.nytimes.com/2020/01/03/world/middleeast/iranian-general-qassem-soleimani-killed.html/. Also see Tim Black, "On the assassination of Soleimani," Spiked, January 3, 2020, https://www.spiked-online.com/2020/01/03/on-the-assassination-of-soleimani/.

13. TOI Staff, "Israeli lawmakers praise US for killing Iranian 'arch-terrorist' Soleimani," The Times of Israel, January 3, 2020, 10:32 a.m., https://www.timesofisrael.com/israeli-lawmakers-praise-us-for-killing-iranian-arch-terrorist-soleimani/.

14. Arie Egozi and Colin Clark, "Israelis: Soleimani Intercept Sparked Drone Strike; US Reinforces Region," Breaking Defense, January

3, 2020, 2:29 p.m., https://breakingdefense.com/2020/01/
israelis-soleimani-intercept-sparked-drone-strike-us-reinforces-region/.

15. Mark Porubcansky, "The many reasons a conflict with Iran could spin out of control," MinnPost, January 6, 2020, https://www.minnpost.com/ foreign-concept/2020/01/the-many-reasons-a-conflict-with-iran-could -spin-out-of-control/. Also see Tim Black, "On the assassination," Spiked.

16. "Iran believed to have deliberately missed U.S. forces in Iraq strikes: sources," Reuters, January 8, 2020, 10:33 a.m., https://www.reuters.com/ article/us-iraq-security-targets/iran-believed-to-have-deliberately-missed -u-s-forces-in-iraq-strikes-sources-idUSKBN1Z7283/. Also see Kylie Atwood, Pamela Brown, Kaitlan Collins, et al., "Top US general says Iran tried to kill US troops as some administration officials believe they purposely missed," CNN politics, January 8, 2020, https://edition .cnn.com/2020/01/08/politics/trump-iran-retaliation-missile-attacks/index .html/.

17. Interview with Stephen Strang, "Chuck Pierce: Playing the Trump Card," Strang Report, https://www.mixcloud.com/strangreport/chuck -pierce-playing-the-trump-card/.

18. Dr. Lance Wallnau, *God's Chaos Candidate: Donald J. Trump and the American Unraveling* (Keller, TX: Killer Sheep Media, Inc., 2016).

19. Jason Chaffetz, *The Deep State: How an Army of Bureaucrats Protected Barack Obama and Is Working to Destroy the Trump Agenda* (New York: HarperCollins Publishers, 2018), xiv.

20. Mark Thiessen, "Obama's offensive against Netanyahu backfires," The *Washington Post*, February 2, 2015, https://www.washingtonpost.com/ opinions/marc-thiessen-obamas-offensive-against-netanyahu-backfires/ 2015/02/02/5f800ab2-aae1-11e4-ad71-7b9eba0f87d6_story.html/. See also Mark Thiessen, "Bipartisan report finds Obama campaign advisor used federal money to build anti-Netanyahu campaign organization," American Enterprise Institute, July 13, 2016, https://www.aei.org/foreign -and-defense-policy/middle-east/bipartisan-report-finds-obama-advisor -used-fed-money-anti-netanyahu-campaign/.

21. Kevin Rector and Christine Condon, "Trump points to Opportunity Zones to argue he's helped cities like Baltimore. Are they making a difference?" Baltimore Sun, August 7, 2019, 2:08 p.m., https:// www .baltimoresun.com/business/bs-bz-opportunity-zones-20190730 -3b3koim5wfcovhnp6t32ja2h4m-story.html/.

22. Jacqueline Bueno, "Trump's Palm Beach Club Roils the Old Social Order," The Wall Street Journal, April 30, 1997, 12:01 a.m., https://www .wsj.com/articles/SB862335923489989500/.

23. Chandelis Duster, "Carson says 'reserve judgment' on Trump's remarks in aftermath of George Floyd's death until President speaks again," CNN politics, June 7, 2020, 12:33 p.m., https://www.cnn.com/2020/06/07/ politics/ben-carson-george-floyd-cnntv/index.html/.

24. Heather Long, "U.S. economy shakes free of recession fears in striking turnaround since August," MSN, December 16, 2019, https:// www.msn.com/en-us/news/us/us-economy-shakes-free-of-recession -fears-in-striking-turnaround-since-august/ar-AAK9ByW/.

25. "2019 Ministerial To Advance Religious Freedom," U.S. Department of State, https://www.state.gov/2019-ministerial-to-advance-religious -freedom/.

26. Franco Ordoñez, "Trump Defends School Prayer. Critics Say He's Got It All Wrong," NPR, January 16, 2020, 6:32 a.m., https://www.npr.org/ 2020/01/16/796864399/exclusive-trump-to-reinforce-protections-for -prayer-in-schools. See also Bianca Quilantan and Juan Perez Jr., "Trump to underline his support for school prayer as he courts evangelicals," Politico, January 16, 2020, 4:48 p.m., https://www.politico.com/news/ 2020/01/16/trump-to-underline-his-support-for-school-prayer-religious -freedom-099711/.

27. Lee Smith, "Obama Said to Break With Decades of U.S. Policy to Declare Western Wall 'Occupied Territory' at the UN," Hudson Institute, December 23, 2016, https://www.hudson.org/ research/13183-obama-said-to-break-with-decades-of-u-s-policy-to -declare-western-wall-occupied-territory-at-the-un/. See also TOI Staff, "After vote defeat, Netanyahu lashes out at Obama and UN," The Times of Israel, December 23, 2016, 11:26 p.m., https://www.timesofisrael.com/ after-vote-defeat-netanyahu-lashes-out-at-obama-and-un/.

28. Jon & Jolene Hamill, "Dream Come True—Two Years Ago Today Trump Honored Jerusalem as Capital of Israel," Lamplighter Ministries, LAMPostings, December 6, 2019, https://jonandjolene.us/dream-come -true-two-years-ago-today-trump-honored-jerusalem-as-capital-of-israel/.

29. Caleb Parke, "Iran has world's 'fastest-growing church,' despite no buildings - and it's mostly led by women: documentary," Fox

News, September 27, 2019, https://www.foxnews.com/faith-values/worlds-fastest-growing-church-women-documentary-film/.

30. Joshua H. Stulman, "How 'Iran' and 'Aryan' Are Connected," Haaretz, May 30, 2010, https://www.haaretz.com/jewish/ 1.5127018/. See also Edwin Black, "Exposing Iran's links to the Nazis," Jewish Telegraphic Agency, December 19, 2005, 10:00 a.m., https://www.jta.org/2005/12/19/lifestyle/exposing-irans-links-to-the-nazis/.

31. Benjamin Weinthal, "Germany condemns Iran's 'spread of antisemitism' in a policy reversal," The Jerusalem Post, June 13, 2020, https://www.jpost.com/diaspora/antisemitism/germany-condemns-irans-spread-of-antisemitism-in-a-policy-reversal-631192/. See also Bradford Betz, "Iran's top general says wiping Israel off map is an 'achievable goal,'" Fox News, September 30, 2019, https://www.foxnews.com/world/irans-top-general-says-wiping-israel-off-map-is-an-achievable-goal/.

32. Heather Timmons, "A National Day of Prayer guest drove the demons out of the White House," Quartz, May 2, 2019, https://qz.com/1610930/a-national-day-of-prayer-guest-drove-the-demons-out-of-trumps-white-house/.

33. Ian Simpson, "Cyrus Cylinder, ancient decree of religious freedom, starts U.S. tour," Reuters, March 7, 2013, 12:10 p.m., https://www.reuters.com/article/us-usa-cyrus/cyrus-cylinder-ancient-decree-of-religious-freedom-starts-u-s-tour-idUSBRE9260Y820130307/. See also Gary Endelman and Cyrus D. Mehta, "How Cyrus' View of Religious Toleration May Have Inspired the American Constitution," The Insightful Immigration Blog, July 12, 2013, http://blog.cyrusmehta.com/2013/07/how-cyrus-view-of-religious-toleration-may-have-inspired-the-american-constitution.html/. See also e-course, "The Background of Human Rights," Youth for Human Rights, https://www.youthforhumanrights.org/course/lesson/background-of-human-rights/the-background-of-human-rights.html/.

34. "Remarks by President Trump at the United Nations Event on Religious Freedom, New York, NY," White House, September 23, 2019, https://www.whitehouse.gov/briefings-statements/remarks-president-trump-united-nations-event-religious-freedom-new-york-ny/.

35. "Remarks by President Trump at the United Nations," White House, September 23, 2019.

36. "Trump Vows To Release Ukraine Transcript Amid Impeachment Crescendo," NPR, September 24, 2019, 2:29 p.m., https://www.npr

.org/2019/09/24/763872059/trump-vows-to-release-ukraine-transcript-amid-impeachment-crescendo-in-d-c/. See also Erin Schaff, "Nancy Pelosi Announces Formal Impeachment Inquiry of Trump," September 24, 2019, *The New York Times,* https://www.nytimes.com/2019/09/24/us/politics/democrats-impeachment-trump.html/.

37. "Remarks by President Trump to the 74th Session of the United Nations General Assembly," White House, September 24, 2019, https://www.whitehouse.gov/briefings-statements/remarks-president-trump-74th-session-united-nations-general-assembly/.

38. "Before Trump was even sworn into office the deep state went into overdrive to thwart his presidency," observed former representative Jason Chaffetz in his book, *The Deep State.*

39. Jon & Jolene Hamill, "Deep State Deliverance! Plus Call Tonight with Martin Frankena," Lamplighter Ministries, LAMPostings, June 28, 2017, https://jonandjolene.us/deep-state-deliverance-plus-call-tonight-with-martin-frankena/.

40. Rebecca Morin, "Poll: Majority believe 'deep state' manipulates U.S. policies," Politico, March 19, 2018, 8:49 a.m., https://www.politico.com/story/2018/03/19/poll-deep-state-470282/.

41. Reid J. Epstein, "Franklin Graham: IRS targeted us, too," Politico, April 14, 2013, 5:08 p.m., https://www.politico.com/story/2013/05/franklin-graham-irs-targeting-091362/. See also Peter Overby, "IRS Apologizes For Aggressive Scrutiny Of Conservative Groups," NPR, October 27, 2017, 3:08 p.m., https://www.npr.org/2017/10/27/560308997/irs-apologizes-for-aggressive-scrutiny-of-conservative-groups/.

42. Jon & Jolene Hamill, "American Pharaoh and freedom to worship," Lamplighter Ministries, LAMPostings, July 1, 2015, https://jonandjolene.us/american-pharaoh-and-freedom-to-worship-2/.

43. Ben Caspit, "Kerry to Abbas confidante: 'Stay strong and do not give in to Trump,'" Jerusalem Post, January 24, 2018, https://www.jpost.com/Arab-Israeli-Conflict/Kerry-to-Abbas-confidante-Stay-strong-and-do-not-give-in-to-Trump-539643/.

44. Katia Porzecanski, "George Soros Says Trump Administration Is 'Danger to the World,'" Bloomberg, January 25, 2018, https://www.bloomberg.com/news/articles/2018-01-25/george-soros-says-trump-administration-is-danger-to-the-world/.

45. Mallory Shelbourne, "Schumer: Trump 'really dumb' for attacking intelligence agencies," The Hill, January 4, 2017, https://thehill.com/homenews/administration/312605-schumer-trump-being-really-dumb-by-going-after-intelligence-community/.

46. J. Edward Moreno, "Schumer warns Kavanaugh and Gorsuch they will 'pay the price,'" The Hill, March 4, 2020, https://thehill.com/homenews/senate/486007-schumer-warns-kavanaugh-and-gorsuch-they-will-pay-the-price/.

47. Jon & Jolene Hamill, "I Will Overcome the Deficit of Justice," Lamplighter Ministries, LAMPostings, June 15, 2018, https://jonandjolene.us/i-will-overcome-the-deficit-of-justice-prophetic-word/.

48. Emily Jacobs, "Intel chief declassifying papers showing Brennan had info on Russian influence," *New York Post,* May 13, 2020, 11:06 a.m., https://nypost.com/2020/05/13/grenell-declassifying-other-documents-interviews-linked-to-flynn/. See also Rowan Scarborough, "New intel chief pivotal in releasing classified dossier bombshell," *Washington Times*, April 19, 2020, https://www .washingtontimes.com/news/2020/apr/19/richard-grenell-reveals-russia -fed-christopher-ste/. See also Zachary Cohen, Alex Marquardt, Even Perez and Chandelis Duster, "Acting intelligence chief has declassified names of Obama officials who 'unmasked' Flynn," CNN politics, May 15, 2020, 7:13 p.m., https://www .cnn.com/2020/05/12/politics/dni -declassify-names-flynn/index.html/.

49. Tim Hains, "FLASHBACK, 2018: Joe Biden Brags At CFR Meeting About Withholding Aid To Ukraine To Force Firing Of Prosecutor," RealClear Politics, September 27, 2019, https://www.realclearpolitics.com/video/2019/09/27/flashback_2018_joe_biden_brags_at_cfr_meeting _about_withholding_aid_to_ukraine_to_force_firing_of_prosecutor .html/.

50. Jeffrey Cimmino, "Witch hunt: Occult Trump opponents plan Halloween spell to bind him," *Washington Examiner*, October 18, 2019, https://www.washingtonexaminer.com/news/witch-hunt -occult-trump-opponents-plan-halloween-spell-to-bind-him/.

51. Jon & Jolene Hamill, "Impeaching America's Cyrus—What's God Saying? Call Tonight!" Lamplighter Ministries, LAMPostings, September 25, 2019, https://jonandjolene.us/impeaching-americas -cyrus-whats-god-saying-call-tonight/.

52. Hamill, "Impeaching America's Cyrus," LAMPostings, September 25, 2019.

53. Drudge Report for April 3, 2020, 10:45 p.m., Drudge Report archives, https://www.drudgereportarchives.com/data/2020/04/03/20200403_123403.htm/.

54. William Petersen and Randy Petersen, *100 Amazing Answers to Prayer* (Grand Rapids: Revell, Baker Publishing Group, 2003), 90. See also "The Legend of George Washington's Baptism," Mount Vernon, https://www.mountvernon.org/library/digitalhistory/digital-encyclopedia/article/the-legend-of-george-washingtons-baptism/.

55. Adam Shaw, Gillian Turner, and John Roberts, "Leaked 'Five Eyes' dossier on alleged Chinese coronavirus coverup consistent with US findings, officials say," Fox News, May 2, 2020, https://www.foxnews.com/politics/five-eyes-dossier-chinese-coronavirus-coverup-u-s-findings/.

56. Adam Shaw, Gillian Turner, and John Roberts, "Leaked 'Five Eyes' dossier," Fox News, May 2, 2020.

57. Dutch Sheets, "Conversation With Chuck Pierce About the Coronavirus — Part 4," Give Him 15, March 31, 2020, http://givehim15.com/2020/03/march-31-2020/.

58. "State Department report: China among worst offenders of religious freedom," Catholic San Francisco, June 11, 2020, https://catholic-sf.org/news/state-department-report-china-among-worst-offenders-of-religious-freedom/.

59. "Inaugural address as CA governor, January 5, 1967," Ronald Reagan Presidential Library & Museum, https://www.reaganlibrary.gov/research/speeches/01051967a/.

60. Mahita Gajanan, "Ben Carson Said Saul Alinsky Was Hillary Clinton's Hero. Who Was He?" Time, July 20, 2016, 4:18 p.m., https://time.com/4415300/ben-carson-saul-alinsky-hillary-clinton/. See also Aaron Blake and Frances Stead Sellers, "Hillary Clinton, Saul Alinsky and Lucifer, explained," *Washington Post*, July 20, 2016, 2:15 p.m., https://www.washingtonpost.com/news/the-fix/wp/2016/07/20/hillary-clinton-saul-alinsky-and-lucifer-explained/.

61. Jon & Jolene Hamill, "Rome to Jerusalem—Presenting the Covenant Lampstand!" Lamplighter Ministries, LAMPostings,

August 8, 2018, https://jonandjolene.us/rome-to-jerusalem-presenting
-the-covenant-lampstand/.

62. Jon & Jolene Hamill, "From Abortion to Awakening—Crossing the
Threshold! Call Tonight," Lamplighter Ministries, LAMPostings,
April 17, 2019, https://jonandjolene.us/from-abortion-to-awakening
-crossing-the-threshold-call-tonight/.

63. Hamill, "From Abortion to Awakening," LAMPostings, April 17, 2019.

64. "Remarks by the Vice President at the National Catholic Prayer
Breakfast," White House, June 6, 2017, https://www.whitehouse
.gov/briefings-statements/remarks-vice-president-national-catholic
-prayer-breakfast/.

65. James W. Goll, "Launching the ONE VOICE Prayer Movement," God
Encounters Ministries, October 31, 2019, https://godencounters.com/
launching-the-one-voice-prayer-movement/.

66. Erin Duffin, "U.S. government - budget by agency for 2021," Statista,
March 3, 2020, https://www.statista.com/statistics/200386/budget-of-the
-us-government-for-fiscal-year-2012-by-agencies/.

67. Dara Bitler and Rob Low, "'If I do get Coronavirus I'm attending every
MAGA rally I can'; Denver councilwoman quotes 'solidarity' to tweet,"
Fox 31 News Denver, March 3, 2020, 9:29 a.m., https://kdvr.com/news/
local/if-i-do-get-coronavirus-im-attending-every-maga-rally-i-can-denver
-councilwoman-quotes-solidarity-to-tweet/.

68. Dutch Sheets, *Intercessory Prayer* (Ventura, CA: Regal Books, 1996),
73–74.

69. "America's Covenant with God," 1607 Covenant, http://1607covenant
.com/americas-covenant-with-god/. See also Craig von Buseck, D.Min.,
"Cape Henry: Spiritual Roots of a Nation," CBN, https://www1.cbn.com/
cape-henry-spiritual-roots-of-a-nation/.

70. Jon & Jolene Hamill, "'This Day We Choose to Forgive! Laying Tracks
to Your Future—Nine Covenantal Shifts," Lamplighter Ministries,
LAMPostings, August 29, 2019, https://jonandjolene.us/this-day-we
-choose-to-forgive-laying-tracks-to-your-future-nine-covenantal-shifts/.

71. Jason Daly, "What Caused the 2011 D.C. Earthquake?" *Smithsonian
Magazine,* May 9, 2016, https://www.smithsonianmag.com/smart-news/
what-caused-dc-earthquake-2011-180959019/. See also Joel Achenbach,
"5.8 Virginia earthquake shakes east coast, rattles residents," The
Washington Post, August 23, 2011, https://www.washingtonpost.com/

earthquake-rattles-washington-area/2011/08/23/gIQATMOGZJ_story
.html

72. Dr. John Benefiel, *Binding the Strongman Over America and the Nations: Healing the Land, Transferring Wealth, and Advancing the Kingdom of God* (Shippensburg: Destiny Image, 2020).

73. Olivia Enos and Sarah Roberts, "U.S. Pastor's House Arrest in Turkey Puts Religious Freedom in the Spotlight," Heritage Foundation, July 30, 2018, https://www.heritage.org/middle-east/commentary/us-pastors -house-arrest-turkey-puts-religious-freedom-the-spotlight/.

74. David G. Hansen, "Megiddo, The Place of Battles," *Bible Archeology*, November 5, 2014, https://biblearchaeology.org/research/conquest -of-canaan/3084-megiddo-the-place-of-battles/.

75. David G. Hansen, "Megiddo," *Bible Archeology*, November 5, 2014.

76. Jon and Jolene Hamil3l, *Crown & Throne* (Haymarket, VA: Burning Lamp Media & Publishing, 2013), 59.

77. Edmund DeMarche, Samuel Chamberlain, and Chad Pergram, "Kavanaugh buffeted by more uncorroborated charges as Dems seek to derail nomination," Fox News, September 24, 2018, https://www.foxnews .com/politics/kavanaugh-buffeted-by-more-uncorroborated-charges-as -dems-seek-to-derail-nomination/.

78. "Capitoline Hill," Wikipedia, June 2, 2020, https://en.wikipedia.org/ wiki/Capitoline_Hill/. See also Paola Favaro, "Ancient Rome inspired Washington but its legacy of being open to all has fallen into oblivion," The Conversation, May 9, 2019, 4:07 p.m., https://theconversation.com/ ancient-rome-inspired-washington-but-its-legacy-of-being-open-to-all-has -fallen-into-oblivion-113924/.

79. Judge Jeanine Pirro, "Judge Jeanine: Feinstein's handling of Kavanaugh letter shows complete disregard for truth and justice," Fox News, September 16, 2018, https://www.foxnews.com/opinion/judge-jeanine -feinsteins-handling-of-kavanaugh-letter-shows-complete-disregard-for -truth-and-justice/.

80. Jon Hamill, "America, It Is Time to Turn the Tables!" Elijah List, December 9, 2019, https://www.elijahlist.com/words/display_word.html ?ID=22925/.

81. Clay Trumball, *The Threshold Covenant* (Patianos Classics, 2017), 170, Kindle.

ABOUT THE AUTHORS

Jon and Jolene Hamill are the directors of Lamplighter Ministries, a Washington DC-based ministry that equips the body of Christ through teaching and prophetic ministry. They are popular speakers and serve in many leadership capacities. Their online blog reaches thousands weekly. And they have authored three books, including *Crown and Throne,* the *Midnight Cry,* and the recently published *White House Watchmen.*

Let's stay connected! Please take a moment to visit our website, where you can read postings, receive updates, join conference calls, and sign up for our newsletters. www.jonandjolene.us

To connect with Lamplighter Ministries on Facebook:
https://www.facebook.com/jonandjolene

To follow us on Twitter:
@JonJoleneHamill